The Theatre of Howard Barker

Through his powerful stage poetry, Howard Barker creates a world peopled by characters who live at the extreme edges of experience – characters who challenge the very limits of actors' imaginations. In this acclaimed study of Barker's work, Charles Lamb sets out to make emotional sense of these characters and of their interactions leading to a detailed exploration of the 'scene of seduction' – the challenge, the secret, the abject and the catastrophic processes which dominate Barker's work.

This second, fully revised edition includes:

- a new interview with Barker
- a revised introduction
- an updated bibliography
- a full production chronology.

For students of Barker and for actors and directors working with this unique material, Lamb's book is a vital and illuminating text.

Charles Lamb is Director of Drama at Bournemouth and Poole College and is a director of contemporary theatre. He is an Associate of the Wrestling School, the company formed to produce and perform Barker's texts.

The Theatre of Howard Barker

Charles Lamb

LONDON AND NEW YORK

First published 1997 as *Howard Barker's Theatre of Seduction*
by Harwood
This revised edition published 2005
by Routledge
2 Park Square, Milton Park, Abingdon, Oxon, OX14 4RN

Simultaneously published in the USA and Canada
by Routledge
270 Madison Ave, New York, NY 10016

Routledge is an imprint of the Taylor & Francis Group

Typeset in Goudy by Steven Gardiner Ltd, Cambridge
Printed and bound in Great Britain by TJ International Ltd,
Padstow, Cornwall

British Library Cataloguing in Publication Data
A catalogue record for this book is available from the British Library

Library of Congress Cataloging in Publication Data
Lamb, Charles, 1947–
The theatre of Howard Barker/Charles Lamb.
p. cm.
'First published 1997 as Howard Barker's Theatre of Seduction
by Harwood. This revised edition published 2004 by Routledge'
– T.p. verso.
Includes bibliographical references and index.
1. Barker, Howard – Criticism and interpretation. 2. Dramatists, English – 20th century – Interviews. 3. Postmodernism (Literature) – Great Britain. 4. Barker, Howard – Interviews. 5. Playwriting.
I. Lamb, Charles, 1947– Howard Barker's theatre of seduction.
II. Title.
PR6052.A6485Z85 2004
822'.914 – dc22
2004009905

ISBN 0–415–31530–1 (hbk)
ISBN 0–415–31531–X (pbk)

Viewing the shape of darkness, and delight
Takes in that sad hue, which with th' inward night
Of his mazed powers keeps perfit harmony.

(Philip Sidney: *Sonnets of Astrophel* xvi)

The art of theatre is a darkness, because it speaks to a darkness. How does it protect the wealth of its darkness from the enlighteners?

(Howard Barker: *Death, The One and the Art of Theatre*)

Contents

Illustrations

Acknowledgements

I would like to acknowledge the assistance of Danny Boyle and the RSC Company of *The Bite of the Night*, Kenny Ireland and the Wrestling School company of *Victory*, David Thomas, David Ian Rabey and Roland Cotterill for reading and commenting on my work. More recently, I have benefited from the insights and scholarship of Rhonda Blair, Erik Weissengruber, Elisabeth Sakellaridou, Heiner Zimmermann, Michel Morel, Safaa Fathy, Christine Kiehl, and many other Barker scholars and enthusiasts. For photographs, I am indebted to Donald Cooper. Particular thanks are due to Howard Barker for being most generous with advice and assistance.

Introduction

My original point of departure for this study took the form of a practical problem: none of the contemporary performance theory that I knew was of any real use when it came to staging Howard Barker's plays. This conclusion was based on my own experience of directing and acting in Barker plays as well as a wide acquaintance with major professional productions of his work. I felt somehow that the full dramatic potential, especially of the later texts, was not being realised in performance. On the other hand, there was throughout the 1960s, 1970s and 1980s an unprecedented interest in and awareness of theatre as theatre: theatrical performance was no longer seen as a sort of 'celebration' of a piece of literature but as a craft in its own right quite separate from literature or film. This period witnessed the widespread dissemination of Theatre Studies and Performing Arts in Universities and Colleges, while in schools drama was established as an independent subject within the curriculum. There was, consequently, considerable new interest in theoretical approaches to performance.

Barker, however, seemed to be increasingly at odds with the current theatrical climate of the 1970s and 1980s. He appeared to be pursuing a more classical and, perhaps, more conservative aesthetic – though his plays did not demonstrate the accessibility that such an approach might imply; on the contrary, they became increasingly 'difficult'. There was a sense that directors had very little idea of how to cope with these texts. At the time, I thought this was in no small measure owing to the lack of any kind of theoretical basis on which to proceed with them and their impenetrability to current methodologies. My starting point for this exploration was the problem – the challenge – that Barker's plays posed to contemporary performance theory.

While working on the original part of this study, I was fortunate in being permitted to observe rehearsals of a number of productions of Barker plays. It was at one of these – during the Royal Shakespeare

Company's work on *The Bite of the Night* – that I hit upon the strategy that informs the central argument of this book. The director was having difficulty working on some scenes in the third act and I became aware that a consistent pattern was emerging. A scene would be built up logically, with a pattern of clear and consistent motivations. At a certain point, however, an action would occur which violently broke with the foregoing 'rationale'. Discussion between actors and director yielded no more than that this was an 'irrational' moment. Whereupon the action was proceeded with along the same lines as before, i.e. every effort was made to put the previous logic back together again. I didn't think anyone found this particularly satisfactory – the resultant dramatic structure providing a basic pattern of rationality spotted with isolated and inchoate irruptions of the 'irrational'.

This gave me the idea of reversing the procedure: instead of working through the scene and elucidating it with a set of a priori 'rational' assumptions, what would happen if one started with the irrational moment? If, instead of treating it as a wholly inscrutable aberration, one posited it as the key to everything else? What if – as Heidegger might have put it – one chose to 'dwell' in the irrational moment, making that one's theoretical 'ground'? How does one theorise the irrational? It was this line of thought that led me to seduction. Clearly, it would be paradoxical to hope to discover a coherent logic in seduction but it might nevertheless exhibit characteristic processes which could be described or at least adumbrated. In Chapter 3, I advance certain theoretical postulates relevant to seduction – for which I am particularly indebted to the writings of Jean Baudrillard. Baudrillard provided, in his reflections on seduction, a way of describing the world that focuses on elements which 'rational' social discourses marginalise or suppress. The world of Barker's plays effectively removes or restrains the socio-historical dimension so what we are left with are the unsupported interactions of the characters – unsupported, that is, by reference to rational discourse. In fact it could be argued that Barker does not provide a world at all, and certainly he creates no Tolkien-like Middle Earth kingdom for us to make ourselves comfortable in. In another sense, however, the plays *do* present a world in that certain patterns of behaviour recur, as do particular character types, particular situations and particular thematic preoccupations. This was where I found that Baudrillard made many of the links, and his ideas seemed especially useful for actors and directors attempting to discover the emotional trajectories of the characters – even if only insofar as they provide a way out of the dead ends of Stanislavskian or Brechtian theory.

Over the past ten years, Barker has taken the important step of directing his own work with his own company – The Wrestling School. As such, he has become a theatre practitioner and able to bring the whole creative process under the control of one imagination. I believe that this has led to a greatly enhanced and more consistent level of achievement in the standard of performances of the plays. What remains disappointing however is the complete neglect of his work by the major national producing institutions and – with one or two honourable exceptions – the subsidised theatre in general. In particular, this means that none of the works written for large-scale production has ever been performed as such – an especially unfortunate circumstance because texts like *Rome*, *The Bite of the Night* and *The Castle* demonstrate that Barker's theatrical imagination possesses an extravagance and spectacular lavishness that demands to be matched by the large forces available to a big house.

It is interesting that this continues to be the case in England, while abroad interest in Barker and his plays has grown steadily – particularly in France, which sees regular productions of his work. Part of the problem continues to be a dearth of serious drama criticism in the 'quality' press, where reviewers are not prepared to extend their conception of theatre to include the challenge of having to 'wrestle' with the work. Not that this is anything other than a long and undistinguished tradition in our theatre, as a glance at some of the 'criticism' heaped on early productions of Ibsen illustrates all too clearly.

The first chapter of this book briefly considers Barker's work in the context of the British theatre and the reasons why, after a promising start, his plays were neglected. In Chapter 2, I consider some aspects of postmodernist theory and their relevance to the stage. These reflections were originally prompted by an awareness that radical theorising about theatre at that time still tended to be dominated by a post-Brechtian, Marxist-inclined analysis. I felt that many elements of postmodern thought challenged this consensus and opened up possibilities of different kinds of radicalism in the theatre. Readers familiar with these arguments should skip to Chapter 3, where seduction theory is considered in outline with a number of specific references to Barker plays. In Chapter 4 I analyse a single play, *Judith*, and seek to demonstrate the relevance of seductive thinking to the unfolding of its action. The following chapter – Chapter 5 – is by far the longest of the book and considers in detail one of Barker's most important plays, *The Castle*, while the final chapter attempts to take an overview of a number of plays written in the last decade, concluding with *He Stumbled* (2000):

this survey tries to pick out certain recurring themes and situations. One thing that seems obvious is an increasing focus by Barker on the subject of tragedy and a sharpened definition of what for him constitutes this genre. Particularly important is the appearance of his text *Death, The One and the Art of Theatre*, which sets out more clearly than anything hitherto his thoughts on the relationship between death, desire and what he terms 'the art of theatre'. In this provocative treatise, Barker challenges some of our culture's most unquestioned assumptions, in particular our view of death as an unmitigated evil to be resisted at all costs. The counterpart of this – that life and pleasure represent supreme values – also finds itself open to a critical battering. Barker's journey, like that of Everyman in the medieval morality play, involves a *via negativa*: a process of discarding much of what we prize and discovering in the resultant desolation fresh sources of sustenance and new grounds – not for hope, because that too is jettisoned, but for an exultation of the spirit inconceivable in terms of our current collectivist ideologies and aspirations.

1 Barker and the British theatre

In spite of being widely recognised as 'a major voice', Howard Barker's relationship with British theatre has not developed as one might have expected. In the 1970s, his career evolved initially along lines similar to a number of other 'political' dramatists, such as Brenton, Hare and Churchill. Having achieved a degree of success and recognition at The Royal Court with *Stripwell* (1975) and *Fair Slaughter* (1977), his work was taken up by The Royal Shakespeare (Warehouse) Company, which staged *That Good Between Us* (1977), *The Hang of the Gaol* (1978) and *The Loud Boy's Life* (1980). These plays were received as part of the Warehouse's programme of politically committed work. Howard Davies, then the artistic director of the Warehouse, said of *That Good Between Us*:

> I was keen to do a play by one of the writers who were linguistically orientated and belonged to the tradition of, if you like, intellectual socialists – Howard Brenton, David Edgar, Howard Barker.[1]

The overt and consciously political slant of this company tended to obscure for many critics other less immediately categorisable facets of Barker's plays. So Ronald Hayman could write of *The Hang of the Gaol*:

> What is ultimately stultifying for the audience is the inescapable feeling that each confrontation is being rigged to serve as an illustration for a thesis about class-war, that the dialogue is being written not to penetrate more searchingly into the theatrical reality which the fiction is generating, but to vent a spleen that existed in toto before Howard Barker began to concern himself with these characters or this situation. His interest in people and behaviour is secondary.[2]

Slightly more perceptive leftist critics, however, voiced the suspicion that Barker's work was not essentially informed by conscious political commitment. W. Stephen Gilbert, in a review of *Fair Slaughter*, compared the play unfavourably with the Brechtian style of Bond:

> The trick in Bond's plays is that the analysis percolates the theatricality, that the latter is a precise manifestation of the former. *Fair Slaughter* is not as clear and eloquent. It's a nicely judged pageant history of British Communism, but I'm not sure that Barker's unprecedented engagement with his characters doesn't finally fudge his conclusion.[3]

At the same time there was a growing complaint about a perceived lack of 'authenticity' and realism (see Hayman above) which led James Fenton to dismiss *The Loud Boy's Life* in contemptuous terms:

> The play . . . knows nothing of Britain and nothing of politics. It doesn't want to know. It merely caters sycophantically to the prejudices of a pseudo-political milieu.[4]

Blinkered and at times violent critical responses such as this, reflecting more the political and ideological prejudices of the reviewer, actively served to obfuscate the plays' principally unique and artistically radical qualities. As I have already indicated, Barker's work in the 1970s generally recommended itself to directors on a 'political' level: this was because the plays were overtly concerned with political figures and political questions. Besides, it was clear that Barker's political sympathies lay on the left.

This political overview served for some time to mask a shift in Barker's interest away from the political to the personal, from stereotype to the individual. The political vogue had, however, facilitated a general formal and stylistic diversification, with satiric caricature being particularly favoured. Indeed, Barker himself admits that, for a time early in his career, he allowed the satiric impulse to dominate – as in *Edward, The Final Days* (1972):

> I placed the characters in *Edward, The Final Days* squarely in their social context, but only as subjects of lampoon, because I hated them and was offended by them. I am still deeply offended by society, and still hate as much, but the habit is no longer iconoclastic, as it was automatically then. . . . In that period I was further from any feeling of involvement with my characters than at any

> time before or since. I began to feel that being involved with my characters at all was a weakness.[5]

Claw (1975) marked the end of this tendency and constitutes a landmark in Barker's artistic development. The action begins in familiar 'knockabout' style, tracing the rise of an ambitious working-class youth from a background of deprivation. Noel Biledew is born, the illegitimate son of Mrs Biledew, a munitions worker, while her husband languishes in a German POW camp. When Biledew returns home his anger and resentment at this unanticipated 'son' is compounded by the fact that he has meanwhile been rendered sexually impotent through a violent encounter with the boot of a camp guard. Biledew, a brooding idealist, is presented as intensely and inflexibly 'moral' in the cause of communism. His wife, on the contrary, is thoroughly pragmatic and prepared to brush aside moral scruples when these might conflict with her own material comfort or social advancement. Accordingly, when the infant Noel returns home from school with thirty coronation mugs that have been traded for 'a look at Joan Preston behind the lavatories', maternal disgust rapidly gives way to approbation and his enterprise is compared favourably to his unemployed father's torpor. To an extent, Noel's subsequent career can be viewed as his attempt to reconcile the conflicting imperatives of this genealogy – on the one hand Biledew's moralised class loyalty/hatred and on the other Mrs Biledew's amoral selfish pragmatism.

Apart from this, Noel's poor eyesight has made him an object of hatred and derision:

NOEL. I'm used to being hated. From the first day I went to the infants' school they had it in for me. Because of these. [*He touches his glasses*][6]

NOEL. Serve who? The sods who hid my glasses so I wandered round the playground with my hands outstretched, calling out 'Boss eyes' and 'Blind git' and making me fall on my face?[7]

Noel's personal response to a cruel world is hatred and a desire for vengeance. Although he is the central character in the play, he is not thereby accorded any privileged moral status.

He follows up his coronation mug success by embarking on a career as a pimp, with his first employee being a fellow comrade in the Young Communist League. The way he secures Nora's services is typical of a series of crucial moments in which Noel re-creates himself in his new self-styled identity of 'Claw'. He persuades her – appealing to her desire for a better life while simultaneously inverting the moral taboo by presenting prostitution as a form of class war:

NOEL. This is political action! [*She stops, her back to him*] This isn't theory. This isn't arguing the toss for the millionth time in the Battersea cell of the World Revolutionary Party. This is action, this is carrying anthrax into their woolly nests. [*Pause. She turns, looks at him for some seconds*]
NORA. And what's my share?
NOEL. Halves.
NORA. No.
[*Pause*]
NOEL. All right. 60–40.
[*She grins*]
NORA. Rip their soiled knickers down!
NOEL. Hero of Labour!
NORA. How do we start?
NOEL. Right here. Tonight. Start small and local, then spread our wings.
NORA. There aren't any bourgeois in this street.
NOEL. Of course not. This is just for the experience.
[*She takes a deep breath*]
NORA. All right.
NOEL. First geezer comes along, I proposition him.[8]

What happens here is typical of a process which, I will argue later, lies at the heart of Barker's dramatic method. Noel's proposal, contravening as it does the moral taboo, provokes, initially, simple outrage. Persuasion, however, arouses curiosity and the proposal becomes a challenge. When Nora takes up Noel's suggestion, both are exhilarated through accepting the notion of transgression and proceed to escalate theory into action. In the event, Noel has to deal with the challenge of importuning a policeman (the 'first geezer') and though in strictly material terms he comes out a net loser, he is both rich in experience and launched in his career. It becomes clear, however, as the play progresses that Noel's success in selling Nora the idea of prostitution as class war was no mere cynical casuistry deployed solely for immediate material gain: in convincing Nora, he has, simultaneously, convinced himself. He rejects his communist father's posture of a fruitless but 'moral' political defiance and attempts to achieve the private satisfaction of undermining the hated establishment from within; eventually he rises to the intoxicating heights of supplying prostitutes to the Home Secretary. This provides the ideal opportunity in Act II for the bulk of the play's savagely humorous political satire.

Noel's career is complicated, however, when he falls in love with his distinguished client's wife, a turn of events that leads him into confrontation. The moment he is perceived as a real threat to the political establishment, he is detained in a mental hospital and liquidated; his murder comprises the third act of the play. Of this scene, Barker has said:

> I knew when I'd written *Claw* . . . that I'd made a definite advance, largely because of the third act, which I regarded as a triumph. It was almost a new form for me: in prose with very long speeches – even longer to begin with than they are in the final text.
>
> There was withdrawal from the action on my part, too: it is less insistent. Nothing in the act relies on the shared assumptions that I have expected audiences to respond to in other acts. It was the beginning of a confidence to remove myself from a common ground. I dislike a play in which the dramatist overstates his intentions, making matters easy for his audience. It produces this rather unhealthy expectation that we should all know what it's about by the interval. To continually undermine the expected is the only way to alter people's perceptions.[9]

Act II ends confrontationally as Noel wrestles psychologically and physically with Clapcott, the Home Secretary, as a Special Branch officer armed with a machine-gun bursts in through the window. Act III is set in 'an institution', where breakfast is about to be served to a single diner. Lily and Lusby, attired as waiters in white jackets with napkins, address the audience in turn with lengthy monologues of reminiscence, which gradually reveal that one is an ex-terrorist, the other a redundant hangman. Both men are phlegmatically psychopathic, and the leisurely and reflective pace of these speeches serves transitionally to wean the audience from expectations of hectic comic action and to substitute a deepening sense of insecurity.

Noel enters in 'a battered grey suit' and they serve him breakfast. Apart from its sacramental implications, the eating of food onstage can be a very significant theatrical action – here fruit juice, bacon, eggs, and tea. This consumption is physical – and, in itself, real. By extension it serves to emphasise the reality of the character and further the situation, acting as a device to alter our focus on Noel rapidly and economically; cartoon characters are not substantial in this way. There is no 'human' contact between the waiters and their client. As Noel eats

Figure 1 *Claw* (dir. Chris Parr). Left to right: Peter Adair (Lily), Billy Hamon (Noel). Open Space Theatre, 1975. Photo: Donald Cooper.

the reflective monologues carry on, with occasional lengthy pauses specified by Barker as lasting up to ten seconds; these serve to increase the tension already created by the lack of onstage communication.

When Noel first speaks, he is 'tense and desperate', a startling contrast to his two gaolers, and his speech is a plea, an expression of his feelings of impotence and terror. Here Barker makes use of a device he frequently employs to create a powerful emotional effect swiftly – the cry:

> [*Long pause. Then with a cry of despair*] My home! My ordinary nothingness! I would fall down on the grass and kiss it no matter how many dogs had shit on it . . .[10]

After another pause, Lusby resumes his monologue and the audience are finally given to understand how both men were recruited to form 'a handpicked team to deal with a special category of criminals'. Their impassivity and casual conversation about the sexual proclivities of various pop singers contrast with Noel's desperate desire to live. In this extremity he summons up the hitherto despised figure of his father now dying in the geriatric ward of a hospital 'in the stench of urine and terminal flesh'. After a moving colloquy in which father and son show tenderness for the first and only time, Old Biledew advises Noel to –

> Win them with your common suffering. Find the eloquence of Lenin, lick their cruelty away. . . . Don't despise them, win them Noel! . . . Be cogent, earn their love –[11]

then leaves him alone with his gaolers. After a pause, the son follows this advice in a speech of some sixty lines, an appeal to their humanity and sense of class loyalty which accumulates an enormous emotional charge. Barker's stage directions read:

> [*This speech must begin clumsily and brokenly. By the end it is eloquent and delivered with conviction. It is the significant transformation of the play.*][12]

For the audience, who know Lily and Lusby, Noel's task appears hopeless but the quality of this speech is such that by the end there should be real suspense as to its effect. Noel transforms himself and has, possibly, transformed his situation. After a long expressionless pause, their decision is signalled by Lily's switching on his transistor radio (which happens to be playing 'Hungry for Love') and a bath is lowered in. The horror of the execution is emphasised in the detail of the stage directions:

> [*Lily and Lusby rise to their feet and roll up their sleeves. After some time, Noel begins slowly to undress, removing first his jacket, then his shirt, then trousers, shoes, socks, and finally pants, he goes to the bath and climbs in. With a single thrust, Lily and Lusby force his head beneath the water.*][13]

The theatrical impact of Noel's stripping, apart from its symbolic aptness, serves to reinforce the tragic intensity of this moment; we are a million miles from the cartoon style of Act I, yet Barker has managed successfully to link these two apparently incompatible extremes and forge an artistic whole with a unique integrity of its own. Such was the 'definite advance' that he felt he had made in this scene:

> When I wrote *Claw*, I was vaguely aware I was getting on a helter-skelter of satire and I wasn't being at all engaged with my characters. It was only with *Claw* that I managed to drag myself back from what might have been a fatal precipice. The last act, which I still think is rather a fine piece of writing, surmounts and overcomes the satirical emphasis of the previous two acts. So I was led off and recovered. [*Laughs*][14]

Retrospectively it is possible to see how the satirical impulse leading to the development of a style employing rhetoric, hyperbole and the grotesque ultimately helped Barker to forge his own non-realistic style of fantasy in which the satirical element *per se* has now all but disappeared. By the mid-1980s (*Claw* was staged in 1975), he was stating:

> The time for satire is ended. Nothing can be satirised in the authoritarian state. It is culture reduced to playing the spoons. The stockbroker laughs and the satirist plays the spoons.[15]

> The sense of caricature has been increasingly marginal, has been located in minor characters. In the centre of the plays complexity and contradiction have replaced it. Partly this reflects moves away from class stereotypes.[16]

The action of Noel Biledew attempting persuasion in an apparently hopeless situation both exemplifies and symbolises a shift in Barker's interest; it manifests several preoccupations to which he was to return repeatedly in later plays. First, there is the catastrophic scenario:

> Under ordinary circumstances character remains unexplored, unexposed; the nerves are quite concealed. But in order to force that exposure on the characters, I always set them within catastrophic situations. The characters on stage are not simply in unlikely situations but usually disastrous ones . . . I'm attracted to those circumstances because at times like that people are disorderly. They cease to be the predictable product of social forces – not simply workers or bourgeois or rentiers; they are dislocated from those classic roles by the social struggle.[17]

Second, there is the individual attempt to produce an alteration in the apparently inevitable – solely through the magic of speech. Noel's effort is mirrored in the climactic confrontation of *Stripwell* (Royal Court 1975): in *Claw*, a working-class rebel pleads for his life with establishment assassins; Stripwell, high-court judge and pillar of the establishment, begs for his life at the hands of an anarchic criminal who is about to shoot him. In *Fair Slaughter* (Royal Court 1977), the plot of the play turns upon the prisoner, Old Gocher, succeeding in persuading the gaoler, Leary, to help him escape. In *Crimes in Hot Countries* (Theatre Underground 1983), the magician and rabble-rouser, Toplis, recounts how he persuaded guards to let him escape from custody the night before he was due to be executed for desertion: two successful permutations of Claw's dilemma. In *The Power of the Dog* (Joint Stock 1984), Ilona tries desperately to persuade Stalin to spare her lover, the corrupt Sorge. There are numerous similar instances of attempts at persuasive speech in extremis.

At a more profound level, Barker seems fascinated by the power of language to affect the social event and the individual. This exploratory impulse tends to supersede the simple polemic consistent with satire, and *Stripwell*, premiered in the same year as *Claw*, left some critics who had found the latter play 'legible' as political satire confused as to where Barker's political sympathies lay.[18]

Just as the predominantly conventional forms, albeit disrupted, in *Claw* and *Stripwell* maintained the accessibility of the plays – in the eyes of theatre managements at least – so the political/satirical elements of the Warehouse plays and Barker's very considerable comic gifts ensured their appeal to a contemporary appetite for political drama. It was becoming increasingly evident, however, that his writing was growing in complexity, with far fewer concessions being made to conventional expectations. The Royal Shakespeare Company's commitment to staging Barker (though this had only ever extended as far as studio spaces) faltered when they rejected *Crimes in Hot Countries* – a script they had themselves commissioned. At that time, this was, arguably, the most densely written Barker text to date. The drama was not really satire, nor clear political allegory – and it certainly was not realism.

The 1980s evidenced a growing rejection of Barker's work by the major theatrical institutions. The National Theatre had never shown any interest. The RSC staged a 'season' of Barker plays in the Barbican Pit but the productions were notoriously meagre, while the company channelled all its institutional energies and resources into launching *Les Misérables*. *The Bite of the Night* was staged in similar circumstances. *The Europeans*, again written for the RSC, was rejected by them. There have been productions of Barker plays at the Royal Court but these have generally been promoted as collaborations by actor-led companies such as Joint Stock and, latterly, The Wrestling School. *The Bite of the Night* was originally submitted to the Court but eventually rejected by them. Outside London, Barker did have occasional commissions from more adventurous regional theatres such as Sheffield Crucible, with *The Love of a Good Man* (1978) and *A Passion in Six Days* (1983).

As Robert Shaughnessy indicated in an essay that purported to analyse 'the Barker phenomenon',[19] Barker's main supporters within theatre have been actors – a state of affairs that culminated in the formation of The Wrestling School, a company devoted exclusively to the production of Barker's plays. This association grew out of earlier Joint Stock productions (*Victory* in 1983, followed by *The Power of the Dog* in 1984) and it is interesting that this particular company, officially dedicated to democratic self-organisation, should have abandoned its characteristic process of company-evolved drama in favour of a text-based approach. In the essay cited above, Shaughnessy develops his argument by claiming that the actor Ian McDiarmid is 'a sort of spokesman for the author' and by drawing on a limited selection of McDiarmid's perceptions of the plays' potential. His conclusion is:

> Actors, then, enjoy performing Barker's work because it presents them with the opportunity consciously and ostentatiously to display their skills as performers.[20]

Although he admits later that Barker's dialogue does contain 'a radical disruptive potential', Shaughnessy continues this theme by suggesting that Barker's poetic 'style' is essentially an attempt to promote himself in the role of 'unique authorial figure', a project in which he is abetted by actors who want to 'show off'. This somewhat threadbare but not untypical formulation of 'leftist' criticism makes no real attempt to address what one might perhaps be forgiven for regarding as the key issue – the quality of the plays themselves. Regarding this, however, Shaughnessy's analysis of 'the Barker phenomenon' extends only to a single speech from the first page of *The Castle*.

The fact that it was left to actors to champion Barker was no accident. It reflected and still does reflect the inadequacy of current theoretical orthodoxies relating to the production of plays. The key figure in this respect is the director, who carries final responsibility for transferring text to stage and establishes the philosophical/theoretical approach of the company. Actors, through the nature of their work, tend to function more instinctively. The emergence of the director as a pivotal figure has been well documented in modern theatre studies and this canon (Stanislavsky, Brecht, Meyerhold, Artaud, Grotowski, Brook, etc.) has become a significant element in the educational mythology of the contemporary director. A concomitant movement has been the down-grading of dramatist and text. In the words of Jean Mounet-Sully, 'Chaque texte n'est qu'un prétexte'. The extreme instance of this tendency towards creative control by director is to be found in the case of the film *auteur* who will instruct a writer to produce dialogue for predetermined scenarios. This has tended to be seen as a model for and by theatre directors, particularly those involved in the staging of new work, who expect to have a considerable role in the shaping of the final performance text. While it is now the norm for theatrical practice to make demands of text, there seems to be little expectation or indeed tolerance for text that makes demands on practice – other than in the case of purely technical ('special') effects. Barker's texts, moreover, are not only very intellectually demanding but run completely counter to most of the orthodoxies of received directorial wisdom.

For a considerable period during the 1970s and 1980s, progressive theatre in Britain was dominated by the influence of Brecht. Though this eventually receded somewhat with the collapse of the East European regimes, it remains a powerful element in that very little has appeared to challenge or replace it. While it is true that there were other countervailing forces, such as Artaud and indeed a wide range of theatrical experiment, no particular element of this sustained and developed itself as consistently and pervasively as the Brechtian thematic. There were many reasons for this, but by no means the least significant must be that his theatrical ideals were closely linked to the wider social project of the Marxism he espoused. He left not only a significant corpus of plays and records of his own theatrical practice but also a body of theoretical work that sets a framework of praxis and a relatively coherent programme dedicated to a new ideal – the Theatre for a Scientific Age. As stated, his influence on all aspects of the British theatre has been widespread but nowhere is this more evident than in the cases of the director, William Gaskill, and the dramatist, Edward Bond.

As Artistic Director of the Royal Court Theatre for many years, Gaskill occupied a key position in the world of the British stage in that his company was pre-eminent – certainly from the mid-1950s to the 1970s – in developing new dramatic writing and innovative approaches to performance. Gaskill built on the realist, socially concerned, 'kitchen sink' style of the early Osborne/Arden/Wesker plays a growing awareness of Brechtian stagecraft and theatrical praxis that informed decisively the dramaturgy of Edward Bond and a whole generation of 'Court-trained' directors. In fact, he established a house style at the Court that still prevailed into the 1990s under the aegis of one of his successors as Artistic Director, Max Stafford-Clark. The actor's focus of attention was directed away from the individual psychology of the character and towards the socio-economic significance of their behaviour. This process is well exemplified in the 'lesson' of the cadged cigarette with which Gaskill commenced rehearsals of *Mother Courage* at the Royal Shakespeare Company (1962):

> I decided to begin with a simple Socratic dialogue. I cadged a cigarette from one of the actresses . . . and then asked the group why she had given me the cigarette. The first answers were all psychological – her generosity, her sycophancy, my meanness. Very gradually I led them to understand that the action was a social action and a habitual one, in which the economic value of the cigarette was a factor. This led to very simple improvisations, which were always followed by an analysis of the actions in the scene. In a two-handed scene each actor would narrate the actions as objectively as possible, sometimes in the third person, and this narration was analysed over and over again till both actors would agree on the exact sequence of events; that is, they would tell the same story.[21]

Clearly, the cigarette here is part of a pattern of interpersonal relationships, but Gaskill insists on elevating the object to a dominant role and, furthermore, the identity of the object is no longer dependent upon the particular interpersonal context. It has become a 'thing-in-itself' because it has 'economic value' – a reference to an external value-structure. This approach is carried through into staging, with the tendency to foreground solid, selected objects as properties. The characters then have the possibility of relating not only to each other, but directly to objects that have ceased to be merely instrumental. Bond, who absorbed much of Gaskill's Brechtian theory, exemplifies this dramatic interest in the object. Even in a play as early as *Saved* (1965), for instance, not only is the cigarette, like the copy of the *Radio Times*, an issue in interpersonal relations, but the pram and the chair, in terms of their economic significance, their weight and behavioural characteristics, play important roles in the development of the action.

Gaskill's dramaturgy, of which the cigarette 'dialogue' provides a paradigm, reflects an analysis of human interaction based on exchange value, an extension and analogue of the operations of capitalist society. As a system, it is logical, coherent and clear. This latter quality, clarity, was one of the hallmarks of Gaskill's direction, which is, again, thoroughly Brechtian. The insistence that the actors should arrive at the same story removes the possibility of ambiguity and ensures that in conflict situations the audience will nevertheless be presented with a single view. For a didactic theatre, this is a logical process. It amounts to interpreting the actions presented. As used to be said of Brecht, we are presented not with 'life' but with an 'analysis of life'. Brecht himself was particularly concerned that audiences should come away from his plays with the correct 'message'; to this end, in his work with the Berliner Ensemble he was continually fine-tuning performances in order to manipulate audience sympathies more effectively – *Mother Courage* and *The Life of Galileo* being notable examples.

Whereas at one time it was widely considered that Brecht and Stanislavsky represented opposite polarities with regard to theatrical production, this view has been challenged and it has become clear that both practically and theoretically the two have much in common.[22] Both focus upon a concept of reality: Stanislavsky as the supreme engineer of stage realism, making 'truth' the Holy Grail of acting; Brecht being so reality-conscious that he insists on theatre continually alerting the audience to its status as a mere second-order phenomenon – a re-presentation. Both insist upon the supreme importance of what Stanislavsky referred to as the 'ruling idea', that is, a pre-determined principle, thematic or 'message' that would act as a selection criterion to which every aspect of the *mise en scène* must be subordinated. Both approaches were rigorously analytic and rationalistic, Stanislavsky insisting that his actors should devise personal throughlines, unbroken chains of objectives that had to be both logical and coherent. For every moment they were on stage, the actor had to have formulated a motivation for their character. These were to be expressed in the form of 'I want to . . .' followed by a verb. When performing, the actor could engage with the character's psychology through identifying with the objective and projecting in the imagination its fulfilment. Needless to say this makes a number of assumptions about human behaviour: that it is pre-eminently logical and always clearly motivated, with these stimuli being unmixed and conscious. In practice, this technique works best when characters are 'single-minded' or businesslike. It does not account for the whole range of human behaviour. What it does do, however, is facilitate the clear presentation of radically simplified interpretations of it. This is why the formulation of objectives became integral to the Brechtianism of Gaskill and his successors.

The general ubiquity today of Stanislavsky-based teaching in drama schools reflects the extent of the widespread influence of this reductive rationalism in the theatre. The original aims of the Moscow Art Theatre were identical to those of the enlightenment: according to Stanislavsky,

> We are trying to create the first rational, moral, public theatre and it is to this lofty aim we dedicate our lives.[23]

In this respect, Stanislavsky's attitude was consonant with the traditional progressive ideals of the Russian intelligentsia of his day. Jean Benedetti argues further for the particular influence of Tolstoy:

> Tolstoy is the final great influence on Stanislavski's views on aesthetics. In 1898, he published his essay *What Is Art?*, in which he advanced the notion that a work of art must be immediately intelligible and of moral use to simple, unsophisticated minds, without the need for commentary or explanation. It must be 'transparent' . . . the idea of 'transparent action' became central to Stanislavski's thinking. . . .[24]

The 'transparent' dramatic action is an action that exposes its 'truth', and 'truth' equals the 'rational' equals the 'moral'. Regarding this, one of the most useful aspects of the Stanislavsky system is the emphasis he laid on the quality of 'naivety' and on the actor cultivating a 'natural' stage presence, the naïve persona being essentially 'transparent'.

In *A Short Organum for the Theatre* (1948), Brecht clearly accepts the Marxist elevation of Science as the touchstone of ultimate truth:

> The bourgeois class, which owes to science an advancement that it was able, by ensuring that it alone enjoyed the fruits, to convert into domination, knows very well that its rule would come to an end if the scientific eye were turned on its own undertakings.[25]

For Brecht, this provided the progressive theatre with its proper mission, which was to sweep away the mystificatory and reactionary culture of the bourgeoisie and to encourage a scientific consideration of social relations and human behaviour. Although his 'representations' should never directly create the illusion of reality, thereby risking mere escapist trance, the real world, as opposed to the illusory fantasies of 'false consciousness', is nevertheless very much what Brechtian theatre is all about:

> The theatre has to become geared into reality if it is to be in a position to turn out effective representations of reality, and to be allowed to do so.
>
> 24. But this makes it simpler for the theatre to edge as close as possible to the apparatus of education and mass communication. For although we cannot bother it with the raw material of knowledge in all its variety, which would stop it from being enjoyable, it is still free to find enjoyment in teaching and enquiring. It constructs its workable representations of society, which are then in a position to influence society, wholly and entirely as a game: for those who are constructing society it sets out society's experiences, past and present alike in such a manner that the audience can 'appreciate' the feelings, insights and impulses which are distilled by the wisest, most active and most passionate among us from the events of the day or the century.[26]

I have quoted this passage in full because it seems to me to illustrate a number of significant points about Brechtian theatre. First, the importance of the 'reality' principle is clearly indicated and the mechanistic ('geared into', 'workable') and economistic ('turned out', 'apparatus', 'raw material', 'distilled') metaphors emphasise the nature of this reality. Second, there is a clear endorsement of an academicism (in the pejorative sense of this word): audiences are not to be troubled with the 'raw material' of knowledge, as they are not capable of 'appreciating' this. Instead they are to be the recipients of the suitably processed ('distilled') 'feelings, insights and impulses' of an élite ('the most passionate, etc.') Third, the hitherto implicit authoritarianism is rendered explicit: theatre must conform to this prescription if it is 'to be allowed'. Here, Brecht's comment concerning 'the apparatus of education and mass communication' is interestingly prophetic of the increasing subordination of 'educational' processes to closed structures of objectives, ruling ideas and of 'experiments' that, while offering the semblance of open enquiry, are rigged to produce the 'correct' knowledge.

Edward Bond, above all other British dramatists, demonstrates both in his plays and in his theoretical writings a most profound Brechtian influence. With Bond, the ideal of Science becomes Reason or Rationality, which in turn is equated with reality:

> There's a specialism in art just as there is in technology and politics. It only becomes embarrassing when the artist suggests he's a specialist in another, finer world. He's a specialist in describing this world, and all art is realism. We're the product of material circumstances and there's no place in art for mysticism or obscurantism. Art is the illustration, illumination, expression of rationality – not something primitive, dark, the primal urge or anything like that.[27]

After his initial *succès de scandale* with *Saved*, Bond went on with *The Narrow Road to the Deep North* (1968) to forge a literary/poetic style leading to a series of plays – *Lear* (1971), *The Sea* (1973), *Bingo* (1973), *The Fool* (1975) – which met with a degree of critical success that established his status as a contemporary classic. It was also significant that those involved in producing these plays, especially the directors, understood clearly the Royal Court/Brechtian principles of their stagecraft.

The 'house style' of the Royal Court has been influential well beyond the confines of Sloane Square. Not only has this theatre been a significant training ground for young directors but it has also proved itself a force to be reckoned with by all those concerned with 'progressive' theatre. Howard Davies, discussing the beginnings of a career that has since brought him to the National Theatre, describes how, as director of the New Vic Studio in the early 1970s, he sought to engage Royal Court actors:

> The only way I could implement the new play policy I was hoping to initiate was to rely upon actors who had worked with Gaskill or Stafford-Clark and who understood the language of those plays, those writers and those fringe groups with whom they'd been associated.[28]

Davies moved on to the RSC, where he firmly established his Brechtian credentials by directing Brecht's *Man Is Man*, *Schweik in the Second World War*, Bond's *Bingo* and *The Bundle*. He was in overall control of the RSC Warehouse in London, which during its brief existence staged a remarkable series of new plays. Of the three by Barker, one, *The Loud Boy's Life*, was directed by Davies. *The Hang of the Gaol* was directed by an associate, Bill Alexander, who had worked with Davies at the New Vic Studio in Bristol – 'we talk the same language'[29] – and had come to the Warehouse via The Royal Court and RSC Stratford. He subsequently went on to direct two more Barker plays in The Pit studio at the Barbican – *Crimes in Hot Countries* and *Downchild*. At the Royal Court itself, eight Barker plays have been staged, two directed by Gaskill – *Cheek* (1970) and *Women Beware Women* (1986); also *No One Was Saved* (1970), *Stripwell* (1975), *Fair Slaughter* (1977), *No End of Blame* (1981), *Victory* (1983), and *The Last Supper* (1988). Danny Boyle, who directed *Victory* and later *The Bite of the Night* at the RSC Pit (1988), described himself as 'Court-trained' with a Brechtian/Marxist approach to production.[30] Unfortunately, Barker's dramatic texts do not accord with the very clear notions which directors such as Gaskill, Stafford-Clark, Davies, and Alexander have concerning what a play should be, and the Gaskill/Stafford-Clark directorial tradition, strongly rooted in Brecht, Stanislavsky and social realism, finds itself at a loss when it attempts to 'analyse' a Barker text.

I have used the example of the third act of *Claw* to suggest how, even at this early stage of his artistic development, Barker was headed in an altogether different direction from the prevailing realist/Brechtian school. Rather than demonstrate character conforming to social type, he was drawn to the exploration of character dislocated from the social by means of catastrophe. Because the social is increasingly being accepted as all reality, such dislocations are often described as 'unreal'. Evidence for this is available in the cases of the small number of people in our society who do experience catastrophe – war, major accidents, terrorist incidents, etc. – and subsequently have great difficulty in re-integrating back into 'social reality'. In taking this course, Barker was, as he states, removing his work from the common ground of shared assumptions and reverting in a very radical sense to the characteristic ambiguities and sheer suspense of drama. It will be recalled that the Brechtian epic method tends to negate the suspense element by presenting the action in historicised form so that audiences may focus on the 'how?' rather than the 'what?'

Such was the blanket degree of critical incomprehension – as exampled by the reviews quoted at the beginning of this chapter – that

Barker eventually felt compelled to defend and create a space for his own work. This began with an article entitled 'Fortynine Asides for a Tragic Theatre', printed in the *Guardian* in 1986 and eventually led to the publication of *Arguments for a Theatre* in 1989, which collected all his critical writings up to that date. Fortunately, the previous year saw the first production by the actor-led Wrestling School, which took up the challenge the 'progressive' theatrical establishment was intent on sloughing off. Since the late 1980s, beginning with *The Last Supper* (1988), The Wrestling School has been at the forefront and more or less alone in the staging of new Barker plays in the UK. Latterly, these productions have been directed by Barker himself. If one compares the following extract from Barker's *Arguments* with the quotations from Brecht and Bond cited above, then the full extent of his apostasy becomes apparent:

> The Theatre of Catastrophe addresses itself to those who suffer the maiming of the imagination. All mechanical art, all ideological art (the entertaining, the informative), intensifies the pain but simultaneously heightens the unarticulated desire for the restitution of moral speculation, which is the business of theatre.
>
> The Theatre of Catastrophe is therefore a theatre for the offended. It has no dialogue with
>
> Those who make poles of narrative and character
>
> Those who proclaim clarity and responsibility[31]
>
> The real end of drama in this period must be not the reproduction of reality, critical or otherwise (the traditional model of the Royal Court play, socialistic, voyeuristic), but speculation – not what is (now unbearably decadent) but what might be, what is imaginable. The subject then becomes not man-in-society, but knowledge itself, and the protagonist not the man of action (rebel or capitalist as source of pure energy) but the struggler with self. So in an era when sexuality is simultaneously cheap, domestic and soon-to-be-forbidden, desire becomes the field of enquiry most likely to stimulate a creative disorder.[32]

Perhaps the central irony of the whole 'rational' rhetoric focuses on Brecht's contention – also propounded by Bond – that the field of culture lags behind the development of the physical sciences, that the new scientific thinking has not been brought to bear on human relations, and that this, above all, should be the project of a genuinely progressive theatre. In fact both Brecht's and Bond's supposedly 'scientific' thinking belongs essentially to the nineteenth century, their 'reason' being grounded in a Newtonian universe of absolute space and absolute time regulated by absolute mechanical 'laws' of cause and effect. 'Rational Theatre' is a stranger not only to contemporary chaos theory but also to quantum theory and even to Einstein's theory of relativity evolved almost a century ago. It is to the intellectual upheavals concomitant with and consequent upon such scientific revolutions and how these reflect on the demand for reality in drama – Brechtian or Stanislavskian – that I wish to turn in the next chapter.

2 Postmodernism and the theatre

Edward Bond has stated that 'History is the struggle for reason'.[1] And it has frequently and with some justification been claimed that reason constitutes the foundation of the technological world we live in today. Likewise, it is commonplace to trace the origins of the technological world and the formation of the great intellectual disciplines that have 'informed' it back to the seventeenth and eighteenth centuries – 'The Age of Reason' and 'The Enlightenment'. As one first encounters them today, the discourses of the physical and social sciences such as biology, physics, economics, psychology, or linguistics manifest themselves as repositories of abstract, truth-based structures that underlie and *in-form* the world of superficial appearances. They fall from the sky upon the young mind with a perfection and absence of origin like the new Citroën in Barthes' eponymous essay.[2] If the internal coherence and rationality of these discourses was not sufficient of itself to extinguish incredulity, one is still confronted everywhere with the overwhelming evidence of their works; in a similar way the ubiquity of Christianity in medieval times must have served to confirm the faith in all but the most sophisticated of sceptics.

Each of these discourses has defined its field, set up its boundaries, and established procedures and validation processes for determining its truths and for those authorised to disseminate them. Interlocking with the discourses are political and social power networks. Furthermore, the discourses themselves are concerned directly with power in that (and here the physical sciences tend to serve as a paradigm for the others) they aim to provide the possessor of knowledge with the capacity to manipulate and control – this being the ultimate touchstone of validity for 'scientific truth'.

In the introductory essay to his classic text, *The Age of Enlightenment*, Isaiah Berlin characterises the social project of the eighteenth-century rationalists thus:

> [T]hey also believed, if anything even more strongly than their empiricist adversaries, that the truth was one single, harmonious body of knowledge . . . that all the sciences and all the faiths, the most fanatical superstitions and the most savage customs, when 'cleansed' of their irrational elements by the advance of civilisation, can be harmonised in the final true philosophy which could solve all theoretical and practical problems for all men everywhere and for all time.[3]

In practice, however, the project is not unproblematical: one person's reason can be another's irrationality. In particular, it is reason's urge to validate what it has already constituted as rational that should inspire a level of caution. Hegel was aware of this in his description of 'rational' ontology:

> Reason is the certainty of consciousness that it is all reality . . .
> It demonstrates itself to be this along the path in which first, in the dialectic movement of 'meaning', perceiving and understanding, *otherness as an intrinsic being vanishes*.[4] [My emphasis]

Bond puts it more bluntly:

> Our species can no longer live with the irrational.[5]
> The struggle for rationalism is of course against irrationalism. That's why it may have to be violent.[6]

Not surprisingly, one of the first tasks the devotees of Reason set themselves was the defining, confining and 'curing' of the irrational human mind – madness.

If what is referred to as postmodern thought may be said to share any general features, perhaps the most obvious would appear to be a resistance to this totalising and totalitarian tendency of Reason. In the second half of the last century, a massive work of discursive deconstruction seriously questioned the integrity and truth-based authority of all the 'rational' disciplines. This critique has been levelled at their theoretical bases, with critical distances being established through methods such as *traduction* (critical concepts from one discipline are deployed against another, for instance linguistic concepts in psychology (Lacan) or, most spectacularly, through assisted autocatalysis, where a critical concept is deployed against itself (Derrida), or for that matter, a whole discipline – the history of history, the repressions of psychology, etc. (Baudrillard). Foucault, in particular, demonstrated the possibilities of what might otherwise be dismissed as mere 'theory' by writing alternative discourses, such as *Madness and Civilisation – A History of Insanity in the Age of Reason* as well as all his 'archaeologies' of the human sciences. It is as if the whole apparatus of the truth-producing machine had been turned against itself. To reveal? The elliptical, the aleatory, the arbitrary, political expediency – ultimate evasions that constitute a betrayal of their proper dialectic. In almost all cases, an original act of violence, a founding repression.

Culturally, the shock waves of deconstruction are potentially as devastating as those of the theory of relativity. It takes some effort to realise the extent to which our 'world' is not merely grounded in, but fabricated by these authoritative discourses. What is 'the human' when we discard biology, psychology, sociology, and history? Originally grids for analysing the human but latterly models for fabricating the same, our understanding of ourselves and each other is permeated with assumptions derived from these disciplines. Furthermore, our conception of the human is fleshed out and continually reinforced in the 'realistic' fictions of the mass media. Whether these are satisfying voyeuristic or escapist impulses, providing vicarious sadistic gratifications or the reassurance of the known, the mode of representation seeks almost invariably – within the constraints imposed by its function, its 'formula', to achieve authenticity, i.e. recognition.

Television in particular exhibits two convergent tendencies: the authentication of the fictional and the fictionalising of the authentic. In the latter, the 'real' – such as a fly-on-the-wall documentary or a sporting event – is processed according to rules for dramatic presentation: exposition, build-up of suspense around a central event, resolution, etc. Not only do such fictions explicate human behaviour; they almost invariably moralise it and provide role models. There is a fascinated dialectic between the real and realistic fantasy, whereby each seeks fulfilment through absorption in the other.

One of the principal agents in the appropriation of the real has been advertising. The main strategy of marketing has been to re-define reality in terms of a consumerist ideal: no longer does advertising promote a particular product but, rather, total lifestyles; their targets, longing for the pure happiness these images project, eagerly strive for stereotypical status. Such being the force of this dialectic between the real and realistic fantasy, it is not surprising that hysterical fears are generated around the issue of media control.

Baudrillard has characterised this process as the extinction of reality in *hyperrealism*:

> Reality itself founders in hyperrealism, the meticulous reduplication of the real, preferably through another, reproductive medium, such as photography. . . . A possible definition of the real is: that for which it is possible to provide an equivalent representation. . . . At the conclusion of this process of reproduction, the real becomes not only that which can be reproduced, but that which is always already reproduced: the hyperreal. But this does not mean that reality and art are in some sense extinguished through total absorption in one another. Hyperrealism is something like their mutual fulfilment and overflowing into one another through an exchange at the level of simulation of their respective foundational privileges and prejudices. . . .
>
> In fact we must interpret hyperrealism inversely: today, reality itself is hyperrealistic.[7]

In the face of this level of appropriation, a culture of conventional political opposition is – in any radical sense – redundant.

Within the grid established by the physical sciences, the individual subject is further defined by the economic system in terms of 'needs'. Yet these needs themselves are products of the system; thus Baudrillard:

> Needs are not the actuating (*mouvante*) and original expression of a subject, but the functional reduction of the subject by the system of use value in solidarity with that of exchange value.[8]

This point is particularly important as capitalism's usual justification is that the free market responds to the individual's needs and is thereby the ideal instrument for promoting the happiness of the individual. Yet, in practice, the free market is in the process of being abandoned: according to J.K. Galbraith,

> in addition to deciding what the consumer will want and will pay, the firm must take every feasible step to see that what it decides to produce is wanted by the consumer at a remunerative price. And it must see that the labour, materials and equipment that it needs will be available at a cost consistent with the price it will receive. It must exercise control over what is sold. It must exercise control over what is supplied. It must replace the market with planning.[9]

Many postmodern critiques also part company with Marxist thought in its whole-hearted endorsement of production as such. Marxist political economy's point of contact with the individual, the subject, lies in the concept of 'use value', which is postulated over against 'exchange value'. It is, in fact, the key referent of the entire system. Yet Marx takes it as being self-evident. Baudrillard demonstrates that the concept of use value is an idealisation that provides the alibi for the rest of Marx's political economy:

> Every revolutionary perspective today stands or falls on its ability to reinterrogate radically the repressive, reductive, rationalizing metaphysic of utility.[10]

'Utility' (Baudrillard), 'performativity' (Lyotard), 'functionalism', 'accountability' – all express the essential value systems of our time. The problem hyperrealism poses for the creators of theatrical, filmic or televisual fictions is that audiences have been conditioned to anticipate and accept as credible an increasingly restricted range of human behaviour. The human has shrunk to the typical and the typical has become the rule. The work's status as fiction facilitates its dismissal on the grounds of being simply unbelievable. While it may be conceded that humans are capable of behaving incredibly, it is not felt that such behaviour has any general relevance.

It is in this respect, however, that some have seen a significant role for art – one of whose traditional postures has been to oppose 'life'. Lyotard, for one, lays special stress upon this in a published interview with Brigitte Devismes:

> J.-F.L. I believe it is absolutely obvious today, and has been for quite some time, that, for one thing, the reconstitution of traditional political organisations, even if they present themselves as ultra-leftist organisations, is bound to fail, for these settle precisely into the order of the social surface, they are 'recovered', they perpetuate the type of activity the system has instituted as political, they are necessarily alienated, ineffective. The other thing is that all the deconstructions which could appear as aesthetic formalism, 'avant-garde' research, etc., actually make up the only type of activity that is effective, this is because it is functionally – the word is very bad, ontologically would be better and more straightforward – located outside the system; and by definition, its function is to deconstruct everything that belongs to order, to show that all this 'order' conceals something else, that it represses.

B.D. To show that this order is based on no justifiable authority?
J.-F.L. Yes.[11]

Lyotard's dissatisfaction with the term 'function' betrays an unease about appearing to prescribe a specific role for the aesthetic, whereas it is the very absence of a function that can enable the aesthetic to evade appropriation. In his examination of the aesthetic in the works of Foucault, Derrida and Lyotard, David Carroll coins the term 'paraesthetics' for this movement:

> Paraesthetic critical strategies posit no end to art and no end to theory, because their ends are intricately intertwined and, thus, constantly in question within and outside each. The task of paraesthetic theory is not to resolve all questions concerning the relations of theory with art and literature, but, rather, to rethink those relations and, through the transformation and displacement of art and literature, to recast the philosophical, historical, and political 'fields' – 'fields' with which art and literature are inextricably linked.[12]

For any art – and we are considering here the question of theatre – the issue of form is crucial. The principal mode of almost all popular television, film or theatre fiction is realism: the simulation of prima facie authenticity. In the light of the theoretical position outlined above, it is useless as a vehicle for radical, critical art. It is, however, not only the dominant popular form in 'democracies', but also the only genre totalitarian states feel comfortable with. It lends itself easily to academicism – the purveying of 'messages', ideology, role models, etc. – but one of its chief functions is reassurance. Thus Lyotard:

> Industrial photography and cinema will be superior to painting and the novel whenever the objective is to stabilise the referent, to arrange it according to a point of view which endows it with a recognisable meaning, to reproduce the syntax and the vocabulary which will enable the addressee to decipher images and sequences quickly, and so to arrive easily at the consciousness of his own identity as well as the approval which he thereby receives from others – since such structures of images and sequences constitute a communication code among all of them. This is the way the effects of reality, or if one prefers, the fantasies of realism, multiply.[13]

To 'decipher . . . quickly', and to 'arrive easily at the consciousness' of one's own 'identity', is, as I will show later, the exact opposite of Seduction, which defies interpretation and puts into question the sense of identity. Elsewhere, Lyotard argues that a central distinguishing feature of realism is that it seeks to avoid the question of reality. Key features are immediate accessibility and essential conformity with existent values and codes. A good example of this is the way new writers for theatre or television have their work 'shaped' to the requirements of the medium:

> Under the common name of painting and literature, an unprecedented split is taking place. Those who refuse to re-examine the rules of art pursue successful careers in mass conformism by communicating, by means of the 'correct rules', the endemic desire for reality with objects and situations capable of gratifying it. Pornography is the use of photography and film to such an end. It is becoming a general model for the visual or narrative arts which have not met the challenge of the mass media.
>
> As for writers who question the rules of plastic and narrative arts and possibly share their suspicions by circulating their work, they are destined to have little credibility in the eyes of those concerned with 'reality' and 'identity'; they have no guarantee of an audience.[14]

Some leftist theatre practitioners have tended to argue for a distinction between 'naturalism' and 'realism' on the basis that the former is imbued with reactionary bourgeois and individualist values while the latter represents a progressive socialist alternative. David Edgar, among others, has advocated, as well as attempted to practise, this form of 'realism':

> the dominant form of television drama is naturalism, which shows people's behaviour as conditioned, primarily or exclusively, by individual and psychological factors. The socialist, on the other hand, requires a form which demonstrates the social and political character of human behaviour.[15]

Edgar envisages drama here as a vehicle for ideology and advances the somewhat simplistic notion that whereas the individual and psychological are appropriated, the social and political are *per se* oppositional. Edgar's posture, like Bond's (the ideological artist), is essentially academicist: Edgar (the Marxist) knows the truth and Edgar (the dramatist) will undertake to convey this truth to the unknowing via a demonstration (the drama).

This position raises a number of questions. Why cannot the truth be conveyed directly? Why this detour via the demonstration? As a purveyor of truth, there is always the problem that this kind of drama will find itself in the permanent position of being a pale substitute for documentary where the possibilities for 'reality' are so much more impressive. There is always a difference between film of the event itself and the 'reconstruction with actors'; such a drama can never be more than 'representation'. When drama becomes instrumental in this way, it must tend to lose its experiential integrity and a certain degradation is inevitable. There is also a whole complex of moral dilemmas that pivot around the relationship of those who claim to possess knowledge (and thereby power – such as Edgar, an ideologist and dramatist with access to communicative media) to those who do not ('the masses' – see the quotation below). It is no longer a matter of conveying 'the truth, the whole truth and nothing but the truth', but rather 'the truths they are capable of absorbing', 'the truths they need to know'. The so-called 'élitist' artist, the artist who refuses to deliberately cater for an audience, does not face this set of problems in that s/he tends to communicate 'irresponsibly' only on his/her own terms; the responsibility for responding is left with the audience.

Ironically, Edgar was forced to admit that this stylistic shift (socio-political realism versus 'psychological' naturalism) was, in practice, ineffective:

> However, in the television age, the masses are so swamped by naturalism and, therefore, by its individualist assumptions, that the superficially similar techniques of realism are incapable of countering individualist ideology. The realist picture of life, with its accurate representations of observable behaviour, is open to constant misinterpretation, however 'typical' the characters, and however total the underlying social context may be.[16]

This somewhat comical agonising was very typical of many proponents of political theatre. It highlights the difficulties that face an ideological art that aspires to anything other than reinforcing the status quo. This particular realism/naturalism distinction is, at the level of the work itself, meaningless, i.e. 'realist' and 'naturalist' productions appear identical. Style is about appearances. As Edgar indicates, the realism/naturalism distinction occurs at the level of interpretation. 'Typical characters' in socialist dramaturgy become 'stereotypes' when socialists wish to criticise bourgeois drama. Edgar, however, seems to be in the grip of the 'realist' delusion ('accurate representations of observable behaviour') that realism truly 'reflects' reality – when it is arguably as much a system of signs and conventions as any other art form. For as I have indicated above, realism is characterised by its forms being so 'conventional', decoding being so rapid and easy, that its signs appear transparent.

Brecht was well aware of realism's problems as a radical artistic genre and indeed, with his alienation theory, he seems to have gone to considerable lengths in constructing an alternative: audiences are to be continually alerted to the fact that the representation they are witnessing is *not* real. Brecht's well-known objections to realism were that audiences used it as a vehicle for escapism, or simply marvelled at the virtuosity of its authenticity. Where his critique intersects with Lyotard's lies in his awareness of the reassuring, anodyne effect of realism – it does not encourage a critical state of mind – and he claimed to avoid the simplistic totalitarian audience relation of Social(ist) Realism by forcing a critical attitude upon the audience through the use of alienatory devices.

Brecht's rationalism, however, performs the same controlling function as Bond's or Edgar's Marxism – it is, theoretically, the organising principle of his artistic method. When Brecht succeeds in adhering to his ideological purpose, his 'representational' experiments are rigged so that open critical response from his audience is circumvented. All Brecht's fuss with anti-realist, anti-illusionist devices suggests nothing so much as the posturings of a conjuror, persistently demonstrating empty hands, showing the inside of the top hat, revealing both sides of the handkerchief. The implication is that we see everything, no concealment, no tricks – we are in touch with 'reality' throughout – all of which facilitates the foisting of an illusion.

Thus in *The Life of Galileo*, Brecht represents the confrontation between Galileo and the Catholic Church as symbolic of the 'historic' struggle between Science and Religion, Progress and Reaction, Truth and Falsehood. I cite this play because it seems to be widely revered as a 'classic' throughout the British theatrical establishment, receiving frequent productions, one of which in 1980 at the National Theatre was numbered among their 'biggest and costliest ventures'.[17] The 'great' scientist is presented in the ideologically acceptable stereotype of 'the genius', but the principle alienation effect of the play lies in portraying him as an anti-hero: he is selfish, greedy, dishonest, arrogant, and cowardly. In short, the audience are invited to criticise everything about Galileo except his science. Brecht, who acclaimed himself 'the Einstein of the new stage form',[18] states in his notes on Scene 14:

> What needs to be altered is the popular conception of heroism, ethical precepts and so on. The one thing that counts is one's contribution to science, and so forth.[19]

Much emphasis, therefore, is laid on Galileo's 'brilliance' and his role as a populariser of science by writing not in elitist Latin but ordinary Italian:

> I am still blamed for once having written an astronomical work in the language of the market place.[20]

Of this particular work, *Dialogo Sopra i Due Massimi Sistemi del Mondo*, Koestler, in his account of the 'historical' Galileo in *The Sleepwalkers* says:

> It is true that Galileo was writing for a lay audience, and in Italian; his account, however, was not a simplification but a distortion of the facts, not popular science, but misleading propaganda.[21]

And Stillman Drake, translator and biographer of Galileo:

> A drastic simplification of Copernicus may have seemed to him an easier didactic device. This is, at least, the charitable hypothesis. But the problem remains how Galileo could commit the capital error, against which he had warned others so many times, of constructing theories in defiance of the best results of observation.[22]

In contradistinction to Brecht's version, the actual 'Dialogue' of Galileo that precipitated his trial attempts to prove the Copernican heliocentric system by an incorrect argument based on tidal movement – which is unscientific in so far as it flies in the face of observable facts (there are two tides a day, not one). He contradicts himself concerning the tilt in the axes of rotating bodies and rejects as superstition Kepler's correct explanation of tidal behaviour. Koestler sums up this 'popular' treatise thus:

> The truth is that after his sensational discoveries in 1610, Galileo neglected both observational research and astronomic theory in favour of his propaganda crusade. By the time he wrote the

> *Dialogue* he had lost touch with new developments in that field, and had forgotten even what Copernicus had said.[23]

In fact, there was no essential reason why the Church needed to be committed to the defence of the geocentric model – other than the fact that Galileo appears to have gone out of his way to provoke offence among the clergy: Catholicism had successfully shifted its position on the sphericity of the Earth. More recent research has suggested that the heliocentric/geocentric controversy was a cover for more serious objections to Galileo that hinged on his espousal of atomism, a theory inconsistent with the belief in transubstantiation; this, of course, hit at the heart of Catholic doctrine.[24] Brecht, however, presents a rigorously empirical, 'doubting' Galileo, who challenges all forms of dogma that conflict with his observation of the facts and his reason. What is therefore idealised and shielded from critical appraisal in Brecht's portrait is Galileo the Scientist and Science itself. He achieves this, like his subject, by ignoring or distorting the evidence available to make it fit his ideological preconceptions, covering up this manoeuvre by distracting the audience with his alienation of Galileo as anti-hero.

One of the most unfortunate aspects of Brecht's rational theatre has been the influence of its theory – especially in Britain. In particular, his schematised generalisations of the 'two-legs-good, four-legs-bad' variety became clichés not only of the liberal/left theatrical consensus but also of Theatre Studies pedagogy in educational establishments. This kind of thing:

Dramatic form of theatre	*Epic form of theatre*
Plot	Narrative
Implicates the spectator in a stage situation and wears down his power of action	Turns the spectator into an observer but arouses his power of action
The human being is taken for granted	The human being is the object of the enquiry
He is unalterable	He is alterable and able to alter
Eyes on the finish	Eyes on the course
One scene makes another	Each scene for itself
Growth	Montage
etc.	etc.[25]

The main distinction between these two forms is the organising principle of the narrator, who overtly structures events for the audience using montage and is therefore in a position to unify and resolve contradictions. In dramatic form, there is no narrator, only participants; the structuring principle can only be immanent development from a given scenario – not necessarily growth; it could be decay. This is what Barker means when he talks, in respect of *Claw*, of withdrawing himself from the action. The drama then relies on the conflict of irreducible opposites and, on the strength of this, would appear to be less of a propaganda medium than epic. And of course propaganda aims to arouse its targets to action. One of the most damaging examples of this tendency of leftist thought to simplistic categorisations has been the individual/collectivity opposition, whereby the former concept has been denigrated in favour of the latter (see David Edgar above). The effect of this has been to allow the forces of political reaction to represent themselves as championing the individual in the mythically enshrined form of the choosing producer/consumer.

While therefore Barker's aesthetic, and – as I intend to show – his practice, have been consonant with the most radical trends in post-modern thinking, the immediate context of the liberal/left British theatrical establishment has been characterised by a phase of extreme artistic conservatism. This is reflected not only in the supposedly 'progressive' Brecht/Bond ideal of a Rational Theatre but is further manifest in the wide currency of mechanically rationalistic performance techniques, such as those advocated by Stanislavsky.

In the light of deconstruction, I have indicated some of the central problems of contemporary theatrical practice through a consideration of the major mode of artistic production – realism and the critical realism of Brecht. Though the term 'deconstruction' is frequently encountered in critical writings about theatre, it is rarely employed in the sense I have implied above: more usually it signifies the substitution of 'truth' in place of 'myth' – socialist truths for capitalist lies. Radical deconstruction, however, rejects the truth/falsehood dialectic. Critical activity is carried on not by positing an alternative ideological 'position'; rather, discourses are turned against themselves in a movement of pure inversion or are employed against each other to effect their mutual disintegration. To 'demythologise' – the declared aim of much political theatre – is not, strictly speaking, to deconstruct because, against the myth it postulates a reality/truth value: 'this is how it really was/is'. If one does not share the ideological perspective of the demythologiser, then one myth has been merely substituted for another – as in *The Life of Galileo*. If reality itself has been appropriated by the exchange-value system, the extent to which this might comprise a valid oppositional strategy is open to doubt. It may be objected that such apparently value-free deconstructive strategies are nihilistic and purely destructive, but deconstruction can be positive in that it constitutes a continuous movement of intellectual liberation. The deconstruction of authoritative discourses opens up a space in which desire can perpetually reinscribe itself. By 'liberation' I mean the process of freeing humans from deterministic notions such as historical or social or biological conditioning – what Blake referred to as 'mind-forged manacles'.

It is perhaps not too fanciful to compare our situation today with that in the Renaissance: in the collapse of the medieval Christian 'world', we can glimpse the current collapse of the 'world' of the Enlightenment and Scientific Reason. In both cases a space opens up in which the nature of the human once more becomes an issue and a possibility. In this regard, Peter Szondi's description of the project of the 'Modern Drama' could offer an appropriate contemporary poetics of the theatre:

> The Drama of modernity came into being in the Renaissance. It was the result of a bold intellectual effort made by a newly self-conscious being who, after the collapse of the medieval worldview, sought to create an artistic reality within which he could fix and mirror himself *on the basis of interpersonal relationships alone*.[26] [My emphasis]

Szondi sees the drama as a device for providing a perspective on the human. Particularly important is the relegation of the world of objects:

> Most radical of all was the exclusion of that which could not express itself – the world of objects – unless it entered into the realm of interpersonal relationships.[27]

In the case of the contemporary world, such an exclusion would extend to objects like the authoritative discourses described above. For Szondi, the dramatic world proper is a world of subjective and intersubjective expression:

> By deciding to disclose himself to this contemporary world, man transformed his internal being into a palpable and dramatic presence.[28]

The term 'dis-closure' focuses effectively the difference between Szondi's Drama (which I would argue is also Barker's) and the dramaturgy of a Brecht, a Bond or an Edgar. The former aims at *disclosure* – an opening, an expression that assumes a continuation of dialogue and likewise a continuation of the process of meaning. The latter aims at *closure*: the purpose of the play is to convey a pre-determined set of fixed ideas – and so the process of meaning is arrested. Szondi's drama is radically heuristic and exploratory. The view that the writer who eschews ideological commitment must, of necessity, be in the grip of an ideology is *per se* an ideological view. Where a dramatist is ideologically committed and feels the need to convey her/his views will generally be the least dramatic part of the work; we are all familiar with those moments when characters obviously become mouthpieces – when there is not an equivalent contradiction in the drama.

> The dramatist is absent from the Drama. He does not speak; he initiates discussion. The Drama is not written, it is set. All the lines spoken in the Drama are dis-closures. The are spoken in context and remain there. They should in no way be perceived as coming from the author.[29]

In short, according to Szondi, nothing is 'authorised'. It may be objected that this overt absence of the author/creator is merely a formal absence, that s/he, by 'pulling the strings' of the characters, consciously or subconsciously is still conveying a view laden with ideological values. The absence of a narrator merely serves to conceal the communication of such 'messages', thereby communicating them all the more effectively. And of course, it is a favoured critical game to find evidence in the text to prove such ideological biases. But these are of course 'readings', and the fact that, in the case of sophisticated texts certainly, such readings can be many and contradictory would tend to counter the assertion that all texts are intrinsically ideological. If it is possible to advance widely different political readings of a text, to what extent can one claim that the text itself is 'value-laden'? On the other hand, where there is a narrator to communicate the authorial view – as, for example, in certain plays by Brecht and Bond – the possibilities for diverse readings are correspondingly discouraged.

For Szondi, the Drama does not seek to 'reflect' or re-present 'reality'; it is itself and happens always in the present. For this reason, audiences should not distinguish performers from roles – as prescribed by Brecht. Lear is not a representation of Lear: he is, uniquely, Lear. Because the 'real' world is admitted only in so far as elements of it are filtered through the characters, then authoritative discourses are perceived only as objects of the characters' consciousness – created, sustained and discarded through them. The individual subject is primary – all the rest is secondary. The relegation of the external enables the Drama to generate its own movement – an element that is identical to Aristotle's recommendation of unity of action. Barker's plays tend to set a group of characters within a scenario that they then proceed to work out. The scenario is invariably distanced both for the audience and the characters themselves: usually the circumstances are either catastrophic or immediately post-catastrophic, because, as I have already suggested, such ruptures dispense with the normalising, reassuring, socially enforced patterns of daily existence that we take for reality.

The dialectical, relational character of this dramatic model must necessarily express itself in the dialogue; language, therefore, is of primary importance and, according to Szondi, takes precedence over all the other elements of production. As such, it must accept the burden of responsibility for the anti-realistic project of the Drama and a stylised, poetic speech is essential. Other aspects, such as the visual, are subordinate to language and their function is to situate and clarify speech. The Brechtian notion of 'gestus', where utterance is merely part of a dramatic totality, occupies a less significant role in such a poetic dramaturgy. In fact the whole notion of 'languages' of the body or of design needs to be treated with considerable circumspection. Language is unique and no other system of signs remotely equates to it. The problem with 'gestus' is that it lends itself to appropriation and belongs essentially to hyperreality. It is possible to play with 'gestus': Handke does so in *The Ride Across Lake Constance*, but the effect of this is merely to expose the *aporia* of realism and the real. If language is the fundamental structuring process of human experience, then any fundamental reorganisation of that experience must occur at the linguistic level. The process of this stylisation works to defamiliarise reality by exposing the medium (language) to consciousness; thus Tony Bennett:

> Literature characteristically works on and subverts those linguistic, perceptual and cognitive forms which conventionally condition our access to reality itself. Literature thus effects a twofold shift of perceptions. For what it makes appear strange is not merely the 'reality' which has been distanced from habitual modes of representation but those habitual modes of representation themselves. Literature offers not only a new insight into 'reality' but also

> reveals the formal operations whereby what is commonly taken for 'reality' is constructed.[30]

Those therefore along with Artaud who have insisted strongly on the separation of theatre from literature, arguing that the former possesses its own 'language', have tended to downgrade what is arguably its most radically subversive aspect – articulate speech. There is in fact a firmly established tradition in the post-war British theatre of an inarticulate or deficient speech that has the general effect of rendering its speakers 'transparent'. Some of the plays of Pinter suggest themselves as, perhaps, the most salient examples of this kind of dialogue and the extent to which it can be exploited for dramatic effect. In plays such as *Abigail's Party* by Mike Leigh, however, the inarticulacy becomes positively garrulous: the characters talk incessantly but say nothing. Their utterance is largely neurotic behaviourism that dramatises their incapacity for any genuine interaction. Bond's *Saved* takes inarticulacy to extreme lengths: Scene 1 of the play is fairly typical: the average length of line comprises 4.2 words; only two words in the entire scene exceed two syllables. The final scene – involving four characters in a domestic interior – contains a single line of four words in three pages of detailed stage directions: language has become altogether redundant. The characters' inarticulacy reflects entrapment in their situation: they are doomed to futile repetitions, with their escape routes blocked by pernicious clichés and dead language that weigh them down unchallenged and have acquired the status of self-evident truths. Martin Esslin said of *Saved*:

> their very speechlessness is made to yield communication, we can look right inside their narrow, confined, limited and pathetic emotional world.[31]

Obviously, this kind of transparency is very much in accordance with the Brechtian aim of demonstrating the socially conditioned nature of human behaviour. What enthralled Esslin, however, Barker found repugnant:

> *Saved* was one of the first plays I ever saw in the theatre – and I myself was not a writer then. So I suppose that seeing the life of my own class and background could be represented on the stage made me want to write a play – and, perhaps, write it better. I do remember feeling that Bond's presentation of the South London working class was abominable and contemptuous. The inarticulacy,

> the grunting and the monosyllabics being accepted as a portrayal of working-class people did offend me and may have inspired me to write *Cheek*, which did lend articulacy to the characters.[32]

The whole focus, however, of the Royal Court 'house style' was to direct attention away from speech towards action. One of the regular actors at the Court during this period was Jack Shepherd:

> During the period when I worked intensively at the Court a defined way of rehearsing the actors was in the process of being evolved. . . . A good actor was someone who could draw attention to the thing that was said, as opposed to the way it was being spoken. Naturalness, not naturalism. Altruism, not egotism. And above all, in rehearsal, there was no substitute for doing. As Bill Gaskill repeatedly said: 'Don't talk about it – do it'. And much more. What made it difficult was that a lot of the theory tended to run right across the grain of an actor's instinct. It was very hard to find a synthesis.[33]

Apart from the fact that the literary element is fundamental to the tradition of European drama and to refuse literature is to refuse engagement with that tradition, the anti-literature lobby tend to confuse matters by advancing the argument that while words are clearly the medium of literature, action is the proper medium of theatre. This ignores the fact that most acts that may be said to carry dramatic significance are speech acts. When Aristotle emphasises that tragedy is essentially 'action', it is for the purpose of defining it over against epic, which involves 'reportage' (narration). Δραν, (*dran*), whence the word 'drama' is derived, Aristotle informs us,[34] is the Doric equivalent of the Attic verb πράττειν (*prattein*); the primary meaning of this ubiquitous word is 'to pass through'.[35] It would appear that Aristotle's distinction is between events that are happening *now* and events that are being reported – the present and the past tense. Both, however, are speech events. His conception of drama as an essentially linguistic phenomenon is made clear in his discussion of the elements of tragedy, where spectacle and music are relegated to the end of the list:

> Of the remaining pleasurable elements, the music is the most important, and the spectacle, however seductive, is the crudest and least germane to the poetry. *For the power of tragedy exists independently of performance and actors. . . .*[36] [My emphasis]

And again later, when he argues the superiority of tragedy to epic:

> Also tragedy can achieve its effect without movement – just as well as epic – since its qualities are apparent from reading it.[37]

Most likely, when Aristotle talks of reading, he would be thinking of reading aloud. The principal argument against tragedy that he is anxious to deflect here is that tragedy depends on the 'vulgar' element of spectacle, because

> Epic is said to appeal to cultivated readers who do not need the help of visible forms. . . .[38]

In fact, Aristotle accepts the argument that the 'realisation' of the text is a debasement but counters the criticism by contending that this element is not essential. The fundamental distinction between the epic and the dramatic lies not in the ascription of performance to the latter but in the figure of the narrator – present in the epic, absent in the dramatic. The epic is the narrative organisation of past events: the principle of organisation is a single viewpoint (the narrator's, a 'worldview'). Drama is organised in a present around irreducible conflict – there is no ultimate reconciliation in a universe that is inexorably chaotic. This is what makes the drama, with its agonistic relativism and unqualified opening up to the other, a more promising postmodern art form than the didactic and totalitarian epic.

Aristotle's contempt for performance strikes us today as somewhat snobbish and could well reflect the inferior standards of theatre in his own time – which was reduced to the depressingly familiar practice of rejuvenating classics with gimmickry. It is unthinkable that Aeschylus, Sophocles or Euripides would have shared his aversion, but it is equally certain that they would have rejected any notion of a theatre that decentred the poetic text. Barker's emphasis on literary style, which contrasts sharply with the 'theatre of inarticulacy' as expressed most notably in Bond's *Saved* and numerous other dramas of working class life, should not therefore be seen as 'untheatrical', but rather as restoring language to its rightful pre-eminence in a theatre that aspires to the status of a radical art form.

I have attempted here to argue that Barker's use of the dramatic form is uniquely appropriate to the anti-ideological, deconstructivist moment in that it presents a decentred, purely relational world that goes beyond the quiescent fantasies of realism without the support of any authorising discourses. What does support Barker's aesthetic discourse? Or is it – as Derrida[39] asserts all literature should be (in every sense of the word) – 'insupportable'? The problem with the outright rejection of realism is that what most people regard as their direct experience is structured by Baudrillard's 'hyperrealism'. This is why much avant-garde art can appear totally alienating; it bears no resemblance to 'lived experience'. Ortga y Gasset complains of this 'dehumanisation':

> By divesting them of their element of 'lived' reality, the artist has blown up the bridges and burnt the ships that could have taken us back to our daily world.[40]

In the case of drama, however, the problem of apparent dehumanisation can be overcome through the actors, who need to 'live' their roles with the same degree of total absorption and conviction as demanded by Stanislavsky – albeit that Barker's characters function according to a significantly different ontology. The alienation occasioned by the anti-realistic style can thereby be overcome, though not negated, by the 'human' interactions between the characters. The actors' total immersion in their roles should serve to *seduce* the audience into the emotional life of the plays. In all of this, the key concept is 'seduction'; seduction is the 'rationale' or 'non-rationale'; it is the play of subjects in which the subject disappears. Seduction is more significant to Barker's dramaturgy than alienation is to Brecht's.

3 Seduction

> From the moment that we place desire on the side of acquisition, we make desire an idealistic (dialectical, nihilistic) conception, which causes us to look upon it as primarily a lack: a lack of an object, a lack of the real object. . . .
>
> Desire does not lack anything; it does not lack its object. It is, rather, the subject that is missing in desire, or desire that lacks a fixed subject; there is no fixed subject unless there is repression. Desire and its object are one and the same thing. . . .
>
> (Deleuze and Guattari: *Anti-Oedipus*)[1]

In so far as it presents a deflection that all forms of truth-based discourse must repress, seduction is a concept frequently encountered in deconstructive readings. In normal parlance it is associated, generally, with calculated attempts to gain sexual favours. In deconstruction, the scope of the term is both wider and more precise. Baudrillard, however, begins his essay 'On Seduction' thus:

> Seduction is that which extracts meaning from discourse and detracts it from its truth.[2]

Under such circumstances, repression or resistance might appear perfectly reasonable or legitimate. However, deconstructive discourse is concerned to interrogate what we mean by 'reason', 'legitimacy' and – above all – 'truth'. Particularly problematical is the question of authority, and Derrida has advanced a critique of the Western philosophical 'logos' – from Plato to Lacan – that demonstrates how the logos – essentially a chain of writings – founds itself in a conception of truth as a self-evident or transparent speech. Derrida traces this tradition back to the Socratic dialogues, where truth is described as a writing in the soul, the revelation of which is imparted via the speech of an authorised teacher to genuine disciples – the original seduction.

This notion of truth is related to Derrida's critique of the much more insidious, ubiquitous illusion of self-presence that haunts Western discourses: the notion that things have an identity in and of themselves – an objective reality. Derrida's critique derives from Heidegger's attempt to reconstitute the 'original' structure of being through an etymological scrutiny of the different verbal forms of the concept (*Sein* – *dasein* – being). However, where Heidegger perceives a semantic plurality that nevertheless combines to form a meaningful 'original' totality (Heidegger aims to retrieve the 'truth' about being), Derrida sees a diverse group of signifiers that have drifted together into an arbitrary concept, which has established the central problematics of Western thought without being interrogated itself.

According to Saussure, language signifies through a system of difference: a lexical item has no meaning in itself, no plenitude; it defines itself only in relation to the system of linguistic difference of which it is a part. In spite of his own argument, Saussure continues to defer to the notion of self-presence, derived from phonetic speech, in the incorporation within his system of the 'signified' and the 'referent', which imply the independent existence of a 'world' separate from language. According to Derrida, this conception of meaningful self-presence derives from the 'moment' of utterance when language can appear transparent in the light of thought (*Cogito ergo sum*). Any form of language, however, consists of signs that refer elsewhere and, although speech can appear transparent, when considered within the frame of a general semiology it loses this privilege. This comprises one of the most significant claims advanced by Derrida: specifically, that the whole of our epistemology consists of a writing that clings to an illusion of an immanent, self-present meaning ultimately derived from speech.

Derrida reverses this hierarchy and treats speech as a form of writing. His most significant concept in characterising the operation of writing is 'differance'. This could be seen as fabricated in antithesis to 'being' (in the sense of self-presence). Such a coinage subsumes the Saussurian concept of 'difference' as constitutive of meaning but also incorporates the semantic range of the word 'defer' – especially in the sense of 'putting off/ delaying' and 'acknowledging authority'. In fact, Derrida's linguistic and philosophical views are analogous to developments in twentieth-century physics with the Newtonian universe framed in an absolute space and an absolute time giving way to a general relativity where phenomena exist solely in relation to an observer or observers (i.e. they exist only 'referentially').

This substitution of differance for self-presence is not the only reversal with regard to deconstructive readings of written texts; there are numerous other discursive practices clustered around this same linguistic nexus of 'truth'/'self-presence' that require critical scrutiny. For example, there is the 'literal'/'metaphorical' antithesis; the former term has been conventionally privileged as a 'proper' or 'true' adequation of a term to its referent, while the latter has been relegated (in the 'reality' stakes) to the status of decorative artifice. Yet, from a diachronic perspective, metaphoricity is fundamental to the development of a language, i.e. historically all words are metaphors – though whether they overtly present themselves as such is another matter. The 'literal' effect, which is closely linked to 'transparency', is invariably the product of a 'superficial' reading – which, for practical purposes, is all that most forms of reading require. It does not, however, 'exhaust' any text – as twentieth-century hermeneutics demonstrates.

I have referred to 'truth' in terms of Derrida's conception of self-present meaning, but I wish to enlarge upon the semantic range of the word, for it figures quite significantly in this discourse by way of antithesis to seduction. For Heidegger, whose whole philosophic enterprise involved recovering and authentic knowledge of 'being' from its fallen contemporary state, truth was not confined to mere *adaequatio* (equivalence of words and things). The ancient Greek word for truth, αλήθεια, he etymologised as α-λήθεια: the α prefix meaning 'not' and λήθεια being derived from the verb λανθάνειν – usually translated into English as 'to lie hidden'. He therefore conceived of truth as essentially associated with 'unconcealment'. Heidegger related this to 'appearances' (φαινόμενα, phenomena); a φαινόμενον, however, was not 'mere appearance' but, according to Heidegger,

> appearance . . . does not mean showing itself; it means rather the announcing-itself by something which does not show itself, but which announces itself through something which does show itself.[3]

The 'truth-based discourse' reads all phenomena in this way and attempts to penetrate to the law or organising principle behind appearances; this is a question of authority, of control. Even psychoanalytic discourse, which can subvert manifest discourse, does so in the interests of apprehending the 'truth' of the former. Thus Baudrillard:

> Interpretation is that which, shattering appearances and the play of manifest discourse, will set meaning free by remaking connections

> with latent discourse. In seduction, conversely, it is somehow the manifest discourse, the most 'superficial' aspect of discourse, which acts upon the underlying prohibition (conscious or unconscious) in order to nullify it and substitute for it the charms and traps of appearances. Appearances, which are not at all frivolous, are the site of play and chance, taking the site of a passion for diversion – to seduce signs here is far more important than the emergence of any truth.[4]

Baudrillard advances the theoretical hypothesis that seduction is the ultimate 'reality' in the sense that it encompasses all 'truth' discourses – the image and paradigm of which he sees in the process of Production. It is to this area that he directs the polemical weight of his discourse.:

> Everything is seduction and nothing but seduction.
>
> They wanted us to believe that everything was production. The leitmotiv of world transformation, the play of productive forces, is to regulate the flow of things. Seduction is merely an immoral, frivolous, superficial, and superfluous process: one within the realm of signs and appearances; one that is devoted to pleasure and the usufruct of useless bodies. . . .
>
> Production merely accumulates and is never diverted from its end. It replaces all illusion with just one: its own, which has become the reality principle. Production, like the revolution, puts an end to the epidemic of appearances. But seduction is inevitable.[5]

The world of production must repress the action of seduction, marginalise it, trivialise it or reduce it; seduction's potency is evidenced in its persistence – in spite of an apparently all-powerful rationality, it will not be exterminated. It is in the light of seduction theory, bearing in mind Derrida's conception of discursive truth as deferring ultimately to a self-present speech, that I wish to consider the theatrical moment.

There is a final issue relating to the fundamental structures of the Western 'logos', and the various truth-based discourses it has spawned, that seems to me to be of particular importance with reference to Barker's plays and to the drama in general – especially according to the theoretical model postulated by Szondi in *The Theory of the Modern Drama*. This particular critique achieves its most articulate expression in the work of Emmanuel Levinas, who argues that the 'logos', from its

Greek origins – especially Plato and Aristotle – has constituted itself on authoritarian lines.[6] It has been concerned with power, comprehension, 'grasping' – above all, the reduction of the Other to the Same. The traditional theoretical polarities of subject and object constitute the essential relationship of this thought. As the project of reason is to eliminate the Other and reduce it to the Same, it finds itself haunted by a curious solitude, with thinkers frequently having to fend off the imputation of solipsism. For Levinas, however, the accusation is apt: 'Solipsism is neither observation nor sophism; it is the very structure of reason.'[7]

The alternative relation proposed by Levinas is of a desire, which is respect and knowledge of the other *as Other*. Derrida expresses the relation thus:

> Neither theoretical intentionality nor affectivity of need exhaust the movement of desire: they have as their meaning and end their own accomplishment, their own fulfilment and satisfaction within the totality and identity of the same. Desire, on the contrary, permits itself to be appealed to by the absolutely irreducible exteriority of the other to which it must remain infinitely inadequate. Desire is equal only to excess. No totality will ever encompass it. Thus the metaphysics of desire is a metaphysics of infinite separation . . . here there is no return. For desire is not unhappy. It is opening and freedom.[8]

This is an ethical relation; an ontology founded not in the subject–object polarisation but in the subject–Other. Nor is this what conventional metaphysics would describe as intersubjectivity which is an essentially solipsistic reason's concession that certain existents that are primarily objects for me are, for themselves, subjects like me. This can be subject to a variety of ethnic, religious, sexual, species qualifications. Such a concession is merely an extension of the process of reification to comprehend and assimilate the Other to the Same. It is to those non-authoritarian modes of relating to and knowing the Other, marginalised and repressed by the power discourses of our social institutions, that Barker's drama returns us and Baudrillard's essay 'On Seduction' points a finger. This is not to say that Barker does not concern himself with authority – obviously power relations are of central importance, particularly where they intersect with the personal. The point is that relations of whatever character are not mediated through 'authorised' discourses, i.e. they are not structured in accordance with these by the dramatist.

This includes social 'morality'; ethics cannot be reduced to a system of abstract and universal 'dos and don'ts'. Thus Levinas:

> The fixed point cannot be some incontestable 'truth', a 'certain' statement that would always be subject to psychoanalysis; it can only be the absolute status of an interlocutor, a being, and not a truth about beings. An interlocutor is not affirmed like a truth, but believed. This faith or trust does not designate here a second source of cognition, but is presupposed by every theoretical statement. Faith is not the knowledge of a truth open to doubt or capable of being certain; it is something outside of these modalities, it is the face-to-face encounter with a hard and substantial interlocutor who is the origin of himself, already dominating the forces which constitute him and sway him, a you, arising inevitably, solid and noumenal, behind the man known in that bit of absolutely decent skin which is the face, which closes over the nocturnal chaos and opens upon what it can take up and for which it can answer.[9]

In the world of a Barker play, which Barker himself now describes as 'a-moral', the ethical finds its focus in the relation with the Other. In *That Good Between Us*, the action of the drama shows a Britain descending into the nightmare of a police state. The key aspect of this decline lies not with this or that political agenda or ideology, but the readiness of individuals to sacrifice affective ties and bonds of interpersonal relations in the interests of ideological commitment or preserving/advancing their own status as defined by power and ideology. 'That Good between us' is the 'faith or trust' that Levinas refers to above, which is, according to him, the foundation of morality. Similarly, in *The Unforeseen Consequences of a Political Act*, one of *The Possibilities*, Judith insists that her killing of Holofernes was a 'crime' because she spoke desire to him.[10] The fact that she has saved her race, that Holofernes was a military butcher about to massacre them all, is neither here nor there and cannot mitigate or abate her personal guilt. When Barker talks of restoring to the theatre the task of moral speculation, it would appear that his concern is to investigate what happens to individuals who commit themselves to particular courses of action or strategies – very often conventional transgressions or violations. In this sense his characters are usually explorers who are not content to live their lives within the parameters of received social wisdom and morality. Their dilemmas are resolved not by reference to social norms but instinctively.

I have tried to suggest, very briefly, some of the ways in which truth-based discourses have been problematised. As I hope to demonstrate, *on the one hand*, Barker's texts in their divergence from 'truth/reality/authenticity' principles actively call these into question; *on the other*, the major acting and production discourses employed in contemporary theatre actively pursue these very principles – Stanislavsky, Brecht, Grotowski *et al.* deploy the 'jargon of authenticity' to an extent, it could be argued, that they depend on it. I believe that this has led to problems in staging Barker's plays.

Baudrillard essays to describe some of the processes of seduction and I shall outline these here because it will be necessary to refer to them when I consider Barker's texts. It will be appreciated that the irrational nature of these elements means that they may not, at first sight, easily cohere in an orderly and summarisable form. The first, and perhaps the most important concept is the secret:

> The secret: the seductive and initiatory quality of that which cannot be said because it is meaningless, and of that which is not said even though it gets around. Hence I know the other's secret but do not reveal it, and he knows I know it but does not let it be acknowledged: the intensity between the two is simply the secret of the secret.[11]

Common-sense thinking tends to equate the secret with the 'thing concealed' and that is that. In focusing on the thing, it fails to acknowledge the process; for when the secret is known, it is, by definition, no longer secret. Baudrillard's point is that the secret exercises a fascination, a power that both manifest discourse and psychological discourse tend to invest only in palpable objects. The secret can operate in many ways. Baudrillard asserts, for instance, that the Pope, the Grand Inquisitor and the great Jesuits or theologians knew that God did not exist and that this secret was their secret strength, the foundation of their power. Similarly, in discussing how *trompe-l'œil* exposes 'reality' through an apparent excess of reality, he cites the *trompe-l'œil* studiolos of the Duke of Urbino, Frederigo da Montefeltre, in the ducal palaces of Urbino and Gubbio. Baudrillard argues that these spaces are a 'reverse microcosm' where space is actualised in simulation; this exposes the secret of the ducal power:

> A complete reversal of the rules of the game is in effect here, one which would ironically lead us to think that, through the allegory

> of the *trompe-l'œil*, the external space of the palace and beyond it to the city, as well as the political space, the actual locus of power, would perhaps be nothing more than a perspective effect. Such a dangerous secret, such a radical hypothesis, the Prince must keep to himself, within himself, in strict secrecy: for it is in fact the secret of his power.
>
> Since Machiavelli politicians have always known that the mastery of simulated space is the source of power, that the political is not a real activity or space but a simulation model, whose manifestations are simply achieved effects.[12]

A further example of the seductive power of the secret cited by Baudrillard is to be found in Kierkegaard's *Diary of a Seducer*. A young girl is perceived as an enigma; to seduce her, the seducer must in turn become an enigma to her. The seduction resolves the affair without disclosing the secret. It could be that the true meaning was sexuality, yet there was nothing in the place where others might have deduced sex. Thus Baudrillard:

> And this nothing of the secret, this unsignified of seduction circulates, flows beneath words and meaning, faster than meaning: it is what affects you before utterances reach you, in the time it takes for them to vanish. Seduction beneath discourse is invisible; from sign to sign, it remains a secret circulation.[13]

Baudrillard insists that there is no active and passive in seduction – no subject and object. Within the framework of rationalist causality, seduction evidences itself as the irruption of the irrational, operating instantaneously in a single movement that is its own end. In order to seduce, it is necessary that one be seduced oneself; being seduced is very seductive. The challenge is illuminating in this respect:

> To challenge or seduce is always to drive the other mad, but in a mutual vertigo: madness from the vertiginous absence that unites them, and from their mutual involvement. Such is the inevitability of the challenge, and consequently the reason why we cannot help but respond to it: for it inaugurates a kind of mad relation, quite different from communication and exchange; a dual relation transacted by meaningless signs, but connected by a fundamental rule and its secret observance. The challenge terminates all contracts, all exchanges regulated by law (the law of nature and the law of value) and substitutes for it a highly conventional and

> ritualised pact. An unremitting obligation to respond and outdo, governed by a fundamental rule of the game, and proceeding according to its own rhythm. Contrary to the law which is always written in stone, in the heart or in the sky, this fundamental rule never needs to be stated; it must never be stated. It is immediate, immanent, and inevitable (whereas the law is transcendental and explicit).[14]

I have quoted this paragraph in full because it describes several important aspects of seduction: challenge, the duel/dual relation, vertigo, madness, the suspension of normal constraints and the substitution of a pact, the obligation to exceed. All of these are of particular importance in 'reading' Barker's plays and accounting for the irrational behaviour of his characters. Another significant aspect of the dual relation is the bluff, which often amounts to fooling oneself in order to fool the other. This is implicit in Baudrillard's statement that

> To seduce is to die as reality and reconstitute oneself as illusion. It is to be taken in by one's own illusion and move in a enchanted world.[15]

> The strategy of seduction is one of deception. It lies in wait for all that tends to confuse itself with reality.[16]

These assertions also carry implications for the business of acting.

Seduction goes further than this in its contravention of power/reason. Baudrillard argues that it annihilates power relations not only because to seduce is to weaken but because we seduce *with weakness*:

> We seduce with our death, with our vulnerability, and with the void that haunts us.[17]

Seduction is never a matter of using conventional strength. Once initiated seduction offers the permanent possibility of total reversal; this is part of its charm and its risk. Indeed, reversal is fundamental to seductive strategy in that it comprises an essential energy source: the challenge is the catalyst for turning the 'dead weight' of prohibition, custom, the law, the proper, etc. through a reversal into weightless energy. Aristotle, of course, sets 'reversal' (περιπέτεια) at the very heart of dramatic structure and perhaps it was the seduction of this that created the sense of 'catharsis'.

One of the most obvious convergences of Baudrillard with Barker is in respect of the dead. Baudrillard:

> They are only dead when echoes no longer reach them from this world to seduce them, and rituals no longer defy them to exist.
>
> To us, only those who no longer produce are dead. In reality, only those who do not wish to seduce, nor be seduced, are dead.[18]

The dead abound in Barker's plays. Barker:

> An ugly struggle goes on over the dead. They beckon to the living because their 'sacrifice' (which it never is) is employed to justify further 'sacrifice'. They are forever calling more people 'over'.[19]

In the world of seduction, the dead can be very much alive. The etymology of the Ancient Greek word for seduction – ψυχαγωγεῖν (*psychagogein*) – is interesting in this respect, since the primary meanings cited in the lexicon (Liddell and Scott) are 'to be a conductor of the dead', 'to evoke or conjure up the dead'.

One of the most insistent assertions Barker makes is that the individual is not finally and necessarily determined:

> The individual as the product of deterministic historical and economic forces leaves serious art with nothing but stereotype and ideology, all dead rhetoric. The individual remains the only source of imaginative recreation of society. . . . We need to see self as a potential ground for renewal and not as something stale and socially made.[20]

However, freedom and the capacity to change do not arise through the workings of a solipsistic and determined rationality, but through the seductive duel/dual relation with the irreducibly Other. Rationalists may object that the world of seduction is unpredictable, hazardous and morally irresponsible. Seduction would reply that this may be the case but that the 'security' reason appears to offer is a delusion (in itself dangerous), which nevertheless exacts a high price in terms of desiccation and banality.

I have suggested that the processes of seduction are generalised throughout Barker's work. This is not to argue that seduction is somehow the 'essence' of Barker or indeed that seduction is recommended as some sort of alternative ideology. My point is that our responses to drama – as to the rest of life – are never purely empirical; we bring to it a host of preconceptions and expectations that determine our 'reading'. I have suggested that authoritative rationalist discourses influence these preconceptions to an extent of which we are not always fully aware; further, that there are affective processes that I have generally designated under the name of seduction, the operations of which rational discourse marginalises or represses in the interests of maintaining the closure of its own structures. The affective impulse behind this movement locates itself in the appetite for reassurance that develops with mass interdependency. The seductive processes, however, are experienced as intrinsically dramatic because in any such encounter, the sense of challenge, the sense of a vast opening up of possibilities, energises the participants. One way of suggesting the Barker universe presented in the plays is to imagine a night sky where the moon and stars have been switched off so that we can see instead the black holes; only, we have to adjust the way we look.

Barker has described his theatre as a 'theatre of catastrophe'.[21] Most of his plays are set in catastrophic circumstances, either immediately before or immediately after fairly massive social breakdowns. As I have already suggested, this enables him to detach his characters from the normalising structures of social and economic interdependency thereby opening up the range of possible behaviours. Catastrophe, however, according to Baudrillard, goes much further than this: it abolishes causality:

> It submerges cause beneath effect. It hurls causal connections into the abyss, restoring for things their pure appearance or disappearance (as in the apparition of the purely social and its simultaneous disappearance in panic). This is not, however, a matter of chance or indeterminacy; rather, it is a kind of spontaneous connection of appearances, or of the spontaneous escalation of wills, as in the challenge.[22]

Alternatively, in the world of causality there is no catastrophe but only crisis. Similarly, the idea of chance belongs essentially to rationality. The concept presumes that no other form of connection apart from causality can exist; it is equivalent to the 'accidental'. This is a way of dismissing the wider significance of an event: accidents can happen to anyone. In the world of seduction, however, there are no accidents and there is no chance: everything is destiny. This is what, in the rational world, gives the accidental its peculiar seductive charm.

Direct seduction of the audience

In some of his plays during the late 1980s and early 1990s, Barker 'set the tone' by addressing the audience directly in a prologue. The earliest example of this style of direct address is the dramatic monologue *Don't Exaggerate*, where a dead soldier talks to the living; this is not an exegesis, nor a narration (though it contains elements of both) but a torrent of fluctuating and alternating emotional impulses that appear to interact with the audience's impassivity. This interaction – active performer/passive audience – is, in fact, quite often mirrored within the frame of Barker's drama, whereby a highly vocal character confronts another character who remains silent (e.g. Stucley and Ann in Scene 1 of *The Castle* – see Chapter 5). In the prologues to *The Last Supper* and *The Bite of the Night*, the intention to seduce is obvious and, in the latter case, quite explicit:

> I charm you
> Like the Viennese professor in the desert
> Of America
> My smile is a crack of pain
> Like the exiled pianist in the tart's embrace
> My worn fingers reach for your place
> Efficiently.[23]

In his first stage play, *Cheek*, Barker presents the audience with a working-class youth whose main asset is a talent for seductive utterance, and the title of the piece indicates this. In the prologues, Barker deploys a variety of manoeuvres to 'engage' the listener. In the example cited above, seductive strategy is reflected in the 'use' of weakness (pain).

> I bring you an invitation
> Oh, no, she says, not an invitation
> Yes
> We are all so afraid
> Yes
> An invitation to hang up the
> **Suffocating overcoat of communication**
> Hang it up.[24]

Here, the prologue comically interjects objections to his speech on behalf of an apprehensive audience – the second line, in particular, is reminiscent of the comedian Frankie Howerd. The prologue persists, however, with mock severity ('Yes . . . Yes . . .'). The bold type in the seventh line signals a forceful delivery, which is softened by a more cajoling tone in the following line. This manoeuvre frequently occurs in *Don't Exaggerate* and in the prologue to *The Bite of the Night*: the speaker gets carried away into a display of excessive rage or becomes stentorian, whereupon, realising this is untoward, he attempts to mollify with a more wheedling tone – a process of persistently abolishing his own performance.

The next statement is immediately followed by an example of another ingratiating tactic:

And those with biros write upon your wrist
The play contains no information
Aren't you tired of journalists?
Oh, aren't you tired of journalists?[25]

Sometimes Barker attempts to establish a conspiratorial relation with his audience but the repeated question here, the tone of which parodies the blatant, gossipy populism of its target, seeks to draw listener and speaker into a mutual empathy. This particular prologue ends with the speaker breaking off in mock horror:

When the poem became easy it also became poor
When the art became mechanized it became an addiction
I lecture!
Oh, I lecture you! (A terrible storm of laughter)
Forgive!
Forgive![26]

The laughter here is, of course, the 'canned' laughter of much popular entertainment and its use is ironic. The ending of the prologue, nevertheless, demonstrates a final undercutting of the speaker's own performance, which involves a renunciation of authoritarian communication – lecturing. Through all the pantomime, however, Barker makes it possible for the actor to induce a complicity through this seductive fluctuating uncertainty. Baudrillard points to this quality of 'fluctuation' or 'flicker' as a typical seductive strategy:

> Seduction does not consist of a simple appearance, nor a pure absence, but the eclipse of a presence. Its sole strategy is to be there/not-there, and thereby produce a sort of flickering, a

> hypnotic mechanism that crystallizes attention outside all concern with meaning. Absence here seduces presence.[27]

The essential seductive mode of these prologues is the challenge:

> Should we not
> **I know it's impossible but you still try**
> Not reach down beyond the known for once.[28]

As he implies later in the same prologue, Barker views much contemporary drama as the theatrical equivalent of pre-cooked, pre-digested food; everything must be instantly meaningful:

> **Clarity**
> **Meaning**
> **Logic**
> **And consistency**
> None of it
> None
> I honour you too much
> To paste you with what you already know. . . .[29]

As I indicated above, the seductive relation is a mutual one – subject/Other rather than subject/object. The use of the word 'honour' here indicates the respect for radical alterity that this form of engagement implies. Seduction is an alternative to the manipulative, controlling relation that characterises communication in our society, and it is with this in view that one must consider Barker's frequent denunciations of 'authoritarianism', both in the theatre and in society at large.[30] This rejection does not merely concern the crude manipulations of the commercial stage but, perhaps more particularly, the Brechtian aim of presenting an analysis of 'the world' along the theoretical lines of – let us say – 'The Street Scene'.[31] For Barker, such approaches invariably entail the degradation of language itself:

> If language is restored to the actor he ruptures the imaginative blockade of the culture. If he speaks banality he piles up servitude.[32]

The importance of speech is also highlighted by Levinas:

> Speech is a relationship between freedoms which neither limit nor negate, but affirm one another.[33]

Seduction within the action of the plays

This is ubiquitous, continuous and often quite explicit, forming through various different permutations a central dramatic focus. More often than not, the action of seduction is indirect: we seduce the one in order to seduce the other. In this way, character A's seduction of character B can indirectly seduce the audience. This is by far the most common situation in drama: it comprises the actor's strategy. Barker's very first stage play, *Cheek* (1970), focuses upon an idle and cynical working-class youth's attempts to fulfil his sexual ambitions through his rhetorical skills (hence the title). 'Cheek' – defined in the *Concise Oxford Dictionary* as 'effrontery' or 'shameless audacity' – is calculated to challenge without alienating the other to the extent that they simply break off the encounter; the tactic of refusing shame is often adopted by Barker's characters. In essence, it challenges by transgressing the limits of the (socially defined) self and attempting to lure the other into a complicity, a pact. Laurie's schemes end in failure because, like all effective seducers, he is seduced himself – to a considerable extent by his own articulacy.

In *Claw* (1975) and *Stripwell* (1975), speech seductions or attempted speech seductions in particularly extreme circumstances make up the crucial dramatic episodes of the plays. These attempts at an extreme reversal all have in common the aim of deflecting or diverting another from their established truth, from their identity. The same is the case in *Fair Slaughter* (1977), where the central figure, Old Gocher, is incarcerated in a prison hospital. Seventy-five years of age, he has been transferred from an old folks' home, where he murdered a fellow inmate on account of a dispute that arose out of their mutually antipathetic political loyalties: Gocher is a dedicated communist. The action turns around his success in persuading one of the warders, Leary, to help him escape. The rigidly ideological Biledew in *Claw* is clearly the theatrical prototype for Old Gocher, whose biography is traced through a series of flashbacks beginning in Siberia in 1920 where he made his first contact with communism via the Franco-British Expeditionary Force. Young Gocher's initial insight into the nature of capitalism occurs when the Allies' entire military machine grinds to a halt because their 'capitalist oil' has frozen. His life-long commitment to communism is forged when he shares a prison cell with Trotsky's engine driver. This man, known only as Tovarish (comrade), is killed by the Whites and Gocher is given the task of burying the body of his new-found friend in the frozen Arctic ground. As a symbol of his commitment, he severs the Russian's hand and retains it.

Figure 2 *Fair Slaughter* (dir. Stuart Burge). Nick Edmett (Young Gocher). Royal Court Theatre, 1977. Photo: Donald Cooper.

The present of the play begins with Old Gocher attempting to conceal the bottled hand from his gaoler, Leary, whom he subsequently persuades to assist him escape in order to return the hand to the buried body of its rightful owner in Russia. Other flashbacks present Gocher's struggle to maintain his ideological commitment and survive in England from the 1920s through the Second World War to the present. He sacrifices personal success as a popular entertainer; his wife leaves him because he puts Russia before her, and his relationship with his only child is poisoned owing to his bitterness in the face of consistent political failure. Gocher is typical of a number of Barker characters who commit themselves to a truth – in this case, the truth of communism. His posture puts him in the position of having habitually to resist seduction in order to maintain his class loyalty in the alien environment of England.

Throughout the play, Gocher's antagonist is the capitalist Staveley – his CO in Russia and his theatrical manager; later he appears as the owner of a distillery. Leary helps Gocher to escape and, through a delicately portrayed and highly comical process of sustained mutual deception, the pair arrive on the steppe – actually the South Downs – and prepare to lay the hand to rest. At this point, the geriatric Staveley appears, having wandered off from an old folk's outing; he is subjected to an impromptu trial and found guilty by the now thoroughly anti-capitalist Leary. Gocher, however, feels sorry for the old man and intervenes to save him just before dying himself haloed in a beatific vision of Tovarish in glory. Leary runs off with the hand and Stavely is left alive squalidly gloating over a crumpled reproduction Picasso.

Once a seduction is embarked on, what rules and obligations then operate on the participants? Leary, the gaoler, initially transgresses by offering to turn a blind eye to Gocher's escape. This gesture, in turn, obligates Gocher to persist with the escape – a course of action he had by this time, in his heart, probably relinquished with a degree of relief. He escalates the challenge for Leary by asking him to come with him and help him return the hand. Leary does so and the two become engaged in what is clearly a mad relationship, with the Brighton train becoming the Trans-Europe Express and the South Downs the Siberian steppe. This would no doubt be pure farce were it not for the fact that Gocher is dying (in itself one of the most powerful seductions). Leary initiates the illusion to satisfy the old man but it becomes clear that Gocher is aware of this: in part he feels he owes it to Leary – who has just sacrificed everything – to persist. All the same, he continues to exploit the situation and to challenge:

GOCHER. Don't give in to patriotism, Leary. It's their way of closing yer eyes . . . [*Leary looks at him. Long Pause*] You are sitting on the Trans-Europe Express, and I don't think you know why. You have done an action out of impulse, and it's frightened you. [*Pause*] Pity's not enough. You've got to find an ideology. [*They look at one another. Leary suddenly points out the window.*]

LEARY. Look! It's the USSR!

GOCHER. We never stopped in Poland! What happened to Poland?

LEARY. No one wanted to get off.

GOCHER. [*Grabbing the bottled hand*] Tovarish! Your homeland!

LEARY. Congratulations, Tov!

GOCHER. His long exile, over!

LEARY. [*Breathing deeply*] Soviet air!

GOCHER. Arise, ye starvelings from your slum-bers. Arise, ye criminals of want! [*He breaks down into a fit of deep coughing. Leary watches, helplessly. Pause. Gocher recovers.*] We'll have trouble finding him. [*Leary looks appalled.*] A skeleton with one hand missing. Won't be easy. [*Pause*] Will it? Not easy.[34]

The fundamental rule is not to break off the seductive duel, which either party can do by invoking the reality principle: this would be a betrayal, provided the momentum of challenge and counter-challenge does not slacken. Leary cunningly evades an ideological lecture, resisting Gocher's 'legacy', by announcing the USSR; Gocher, temporarily nonplussed, recovers to pick up the challenge and join in the triumph, using the momentum of this to launch his next challenge – finding the corpse. Another typical feature of seduction very much in evidence here is bluff. Both participants know, and know that the other knows they know, but they cannot acknowledge this and know that the other cannot acknowledge, etc. Here, Barker's stage directions are essential – the pauses, the looking at each other at crucial moments. It has often been said of Barker's writing that everything is articulated – there is no subtext. Arguably this could be true of the passage just cited, in that nothing of substance is communicated. Alternatively, this is a very pregnant 'nothing', an intense and spiralling complicity.

Eventually, as the hand is about to be interred, the geriatric Staveley, Gocher's capitalist oppressor, wanders on. Leary makes an impassioned speech for the prosecution. As with *Claw* and *Stripwell*, this is the speech of his life and he indicts Staveley, the capitalist, as ultimately guilty of all he has had to suffer as a gaoler. When he demands immediate execution, Gocher, who has already murdered one geriatric without compunction, pleads for mercy. As a result of the seduction, a

Figure 3 *Fair Slaughter* (dir. Stuart Burge). Left to right: Max Wall (Old Gocher), John Thaw (Leary). Royal Court Theatre, 1977. Photo: Donald Cooper.

reversal has occurred, with the gaoler becoming the hardline ideologist and the dying man a 'sentimental humanist'. Leary now insists that the hand is rightfully his:

GOCHER. Give me Tov.
LEARY. No.
GOCHER. Give it to me.
LEARY. You are not fit to have Tov.
GOCHER. Christ, do not lose sight of your humanity! You have so much good in you!
LEARY. To be licked up by that specimen. To be sucked on by his class.
GOCHER. Keep an open heart, son. Feed your heart. The angrier you feel, the more you have to feed the heart!
LEARY. I do what Tov says.
GOCHER. Fuck him! He was an ordinary bloke, that's all. Think for yourself. They stuck Lenin under glass, and look what they have done in his name.[35]

One could say that Gocher's return of the hand allows him to bury his ideological commitment and release his pity. But the hinge of his apostasy here, however, is that he does not want to bequeath to Leary the sterile life that he himself has led. As he dies in a heavenly vision of Tovarish in glory (who appears armed with dahlias), it is his disciple, Leary, who goes off with the hand.

In the figure of Toplis in *Crimes in Hot Countries*, Barker explores a character almost directly antithetical to Gocher. Though both, in the context of capitalist society, are subversives and revolutionaries, their personalities function in entirely different ways. Gocher's personal ambition is to achieve an historical status in the Marxist-Leninist pantheon; Toplis, based on the historical Percy Toplis, a ringleader in the First World War Etaples Mutiny, is dedicated purely to the process of seduction. Since escaping the death penalty as a mutineer by seducing his guards, he has lived by seducing women. At the outset of the play he returns to the military life at a desert outpost of the post-war British Empire. Appropriately disguised as a conjuror, he sets about repeating his previous triumph amongst the bored and disaffected soldiers. Eventually, the mutiny breaks out in a bizarre auction scene where Toplis' rhetoric involves him in an increasingly irrational duel with T.E. Pain – Barker's version of Lawrence of Arabia. Toplis' subversion, however, is entirely irresponsible and amoral, with little concern as to the consequences of his action for others. His personal lifestyle is predicated upon temporary imposture and moving on before chickens come home to roost. When Erica, the governor's daughter who has fallen in love with him, commits herself by shooting his would-be executioners, he refuses or is unable to respond to the gesture. Concerning his revolutionary activities, he admits:

> I have to conjure with them, Erica. Like the women on the boulevard. See what I can drive them to. In their madness, I taste something like life. . . .[36]

As Baudrillard states:

> To challenge or seduce is always to drive the other mad, but in a mutual vertigo: madness from the vertiginous absence that unites them, and from their mutual involvement.[37]

Toplis' lack of truth and consequent lack of reality is supported in the play by continual references to his death and suggestions that he is a ghost.

In the plays that followed, Barker demonstrated an increasingly sophisticated and complex awareness of the processes and interactions of seduction. A common scenario involves the 'magisterial' relation – 'teacher' and 'pupil', a classic example of a duel where the participants attempt to drive each other mad. In *Fair Slaughter*, Old Gocher's relation to the warder, Leary, is essentially 'educative'. In *That Good Between Us*, the transformation of the degraded police informer, McPhee, is effected by Major Cadbury, who functions largely as a guru. In *Crimes in Hot Countries*, the subversive, Toplis, supplants Pain as the soldiers' intellectual mentor. In *The Bite of the Night*, the pedagogic relation of Professor Savage and his student, Hogbin, figures prominently.

Perhaps the most spectacular deployment of this relation is in *The Last Supper*. Based on the Christian archetype, it extends the ritual leave-taking from 'disciples' by a guru into ritual murder and anthropophagy. The prophet, Lvov, maintains a seductive relation with each of a very diverse group of 'apostles': he secures their permanent adherence by persuading them to kill him and eat his corpse. What Barker does show, before the denouement, is that each relationship is a vertiginous and unrelenting duel between master and disciple, so that Lvov's final gesture of invoking his own death seems the only escalatory response available to him that is extravagant enough to cope with them all. As Lvov knows full well, his grisly condition, that the Lvovites consume his corpse, is utterly binding according to the unspoken, unwritten 'rule' of their seductive engagement. This is what Baudrillard is referring to when he talks of 'an unremitting obligation to respond and outdo'.[38] In taking this step, Lvov seduces them beyond the transcendental law, beyond the prohibition, and this, of course, becomes the 'secret' that binds them and will be the source of their power. It is therefore appropriate that the act of cannibalism should not be seen by the audience, and the fact that it is literally 'unspeakable' is emphasised in the final scene:

SUSANNAH. He had the flavour of –
ALL. **Don't mention it!**
SUSANNAH. He had the texture of –
ALL. **Don't dare describe it!** [*Pause. The knot of disciples drifts, first one way, then another. The cloud passes overhead.*][39]

These are the final lines and images of the play. There is clearly a convergence here with Baudrillard's discussion of the secret reversibility at the heart of imperium:

> Thus the Pope, the Grand Inquisitor, and the great Jesuits or theologians all knew that God did not exist; this was their secret and their strength.[40]

It is also common practice amongst clandestine social groups who regard themselves as élites to have their members undergo ritual humiliation in order the better to bind them together with unspeakable secrets: the individual concerned is compelled to traduce the boundaries of their identity. In *The Loud Boy's Life*, Barker illustrates this in Act I Scene 4, where the 'loud boy', a right-wing populist politician called Ezra Fricker, is attending a dinner of the Ancient Order of Savages. When the scene begins, he has just been coerced, much to his embarrassment, into performing an impromptu strip-tease.

In the world of reason, motivation is founded always in positive causality and individual behaviour is structured upon biological drives modified according to various social and psychological determinants. In the world of seduction, purely negative forces are capable of intervening decisively, like pools of accumulated anti-matter. The secret is a negative force. So is the meaningless. In *The Bite of the Night*, one of the principal characters, Gay, persistently attempts to impose an intellectual order upon her chaotic life; this order is forcibly maintained in the face of seduction and violence by an authoritarian exclusion of the Other:

Figure 4 *The Last Supper* (dir. Kenny Ireland). Philip Sayer (Lvov). The Wrestling School, 1988. Photo: Donald Cooper.

GAY. You say yes as if I were supposed to feel bereft. You say yes with a hush, as if you know something that I do not –

CREUSA. I don't know either –

GAY. **I am tired of this idea there's something else. It's used to bully me, to hit me on the brow and brain and crush my life –**

CREUSA. I don't know either, I said –

GAY. There's nothing else![41]

Seduction in its orthodox sexual context is frequently encountered in Barker's plays. *The Bite of the Night* is structured around the archetypal seducer, Helen of Troy. Barker's adaptation of *Women Beware Women* focuses directly on the power of a sexual relationship to transform those involved; similar relationships are featured strongly in *Victory* (Bradshaw and Ball), *Crimes in Hot Countries* (Toplis and Erica) and *The Power of the Dog* (Sorge and Ilona). In the latter case, a complicity is established between the two characters, which relates to the mysterious death of Hannela, Sorge's ex-mistress and Ilona's sister – this is the 'secret' of the play. The transformations effected by such complicities do not necessarily 'improve' the individuals concerned.

The Power of the Dog, subtitled *Moments in History and Anti-history*, explores further the truth/seduction antithesis. Barker sees historical narratives as ideological constructions that seek to assimilate and annex the individual. A classic example is Marxism–Leninism, in this play embodied in the character of Stalin, who believes that he has 'emptied the cupboard' of his personal individuality in order to achieve a total identification with his ideology. As such, he exhibits the kind of insanity that generally attends upon absolute power. The anti-history scenes focus on a Hungarian photographer/model, Ilona, who has collaborated freely with both Nazis and Allies in order to pursue her career across the battlefields of Europe. She represents an antithesis to Stalin in that her strategy is founded upon her seductive charm:

ILONA. . . . Shall I tell you what I believe? I believe that every murder is an acquiescence, and every victim possessed the means of her escape. I believe in your eyes and in your mouth you own the means of your salvation, whether you want to be loved, or whether you want to be saved. At the door of the restaurant, or the gate of the camp.[42]

The charmed life she leads is also contingent upon accepting everything and resisting nothing:

> To anyone who thinks it is a mystery, how we cope with so much history, I say the answer lies in pain, what my mother went through I can again. Swallow the monster and don't strain, murders from the Bosphorus to the Hebrides render all complaints absurdities. Don't ask what makes the system, if it is a system, work, cover your indignation with your foot, don't think that black stuff is burned bodies, really it is only soot. . . .[43]

As her words here suggest, Ilona refuses the order of truth/reality by bluffing herself as well as other people. As he becomes conscious of his approaching death, Stalin finds himself increasingly charmed by the thought of the accidental:

> STALIN. I would give up all the authority I possess to meet a beautiful woman on a train. . . . It is a sad fact I cannot meet a woman on a train unless both the woman and the train are commandeered for me. But of course that entirely removes the significance of the occasion. Accident, which is the essence of experience, has been eliminated from my life. . . .[44]

Because he is concerned to bequeath to posterity a 'true' likeness of himself, he orders a photographer to be randomly selected from 'somewhere in the Polish desert'. This engineers the final scene of the play – captioned 'History Encounters its Antithesis' – where Ilona and Stalin meet, providing the former with her most extreme challenge and the latter – possibly – with his 'woman on the train'.

I have already referred to the functioning of the secret in *The Last Supper*. In *Not Him*, the final play of *The Possibilities*, secrets are even more important. A woman greets her husband who returns after seven years of warfare brandishing a bag of severed heads. Both husband and wife have changed, however, and she is undecided whether the man who arrives really is her husband. Initially she counters this uncertainty by making herself an enigma for the man – she wears a veil. The piece ends after she's made love and killed him. It is clear that the third character in the play – the wife's female companion – shares with her a complicity, the substance of which is withheld from the audience. When the friend states, after the killing, 'You have killed your husband . . .', she is promptly hushed by the wife; as with the eating of Lvov, the event is unspeakable. The killing itself occurs offstage and is only communicated to the audience in an indirect and cryptic fashion:

SECOND WOMAN. And did he yell?

WOMAN. He cried out with the awful cry of disbelief that all men make, and his eyes were searching for their focus.[45]

In the first place, the woman's response is ambiguous: she could be referring to sexual climax here. It is only the Second Woman's following line that makes the audience re-interpret these words. Further, her use of the words 'all men' suggests she may have killed others. Earlier, under pressure from the 'husband', her female companion had attempted to deny that soldiers had passed through the village. When he objected that he had seen wheeltracks, the story was amended and he was informed that his 'wife' had hidden – 'Even from her allies'. The women have quite clearly had to deal with the prospect and possibly the actuality of the rape and murder that the 'husband' boasts of inflicting on the enemy. What happened then is their secret; we are aware of its presence and its power.

The salient feature of the piece is its sustaining throughout of the ambiguity concerning the man's identity: 'Him?' or 'Not him?' The 'wife' has two possibilities: the man is her husband, with all the burden of moral and social implications that implies. Alternatively, he is merely 'another' raping, murdering soldier who it is possible to enjoy sexually and then kill without compunction. Her neighbour appears to be prepared to collude with whatever choice she makes and, in fact, actively assists in keeping options open. This is rendered possible because his long absence and the war have clearly changed the man so that he confronts his wife with a different identity. In the world of reason and logic, one of the fundamental axioms is that it is not possible for something simultaneously to both *be the case* and *not be the case*; this is sometimes referred to as the law of non-contradiction. Seduction abolishes this and substitutes the flicker, which we have already described above. In *Not Him*, the man is both 'him' and 'not him'; objectively the issue is never resolved and the piece is all about this paradox. The woman's desire thrives on the ambiguity, as she states in the final lines:

WOMAN. Shh . . . [*Pause. She sits.*] He thrilled me. Oh, his words of violence, how he thrilled me! And his murders, how they flooded me with desire . . .

SECOND WOMAN. It was him . . .

WOMAN. It was him. Did he think I was fooled?[46]

As in a number of these plays, the ending presents us with a final twist: having murdered, the woman decides that she can not merely accept but positively relish the idea that she has killed her husband. Her final sentence indicates the potential for reversal in the seductive duel. For the audience there is a contradiction between the two sentences – 'It was him. Did he think I was fooled?' The man asserts continually that he is the husband, so how is he attempting to 'fool'? Possibly by appearing as 'Other', by assuming the swaggering and boastful identity of the military butcher in order to render himself sexually attractive. (His exaggerated claims and the heads business seem to be a performance calculated to impress.) The woman, however, appears to be ready to fool herself: in the absence of objective proof she will believe what she wants to believe. Baudrillard's dictum applies to them both:

> To seduce is to die as reality and reconstitute oneself as illusion. It is to be taken in by one's own illusion and move in an enchanted world.[47]

The line also suggests that she sees the man as attempting to conceal his identity and attempting to deceive her in order to escape his destiny – seduction is destiny. Such a perspective renders him ethically inferior and serves to validate her action. Now that the event has passed, she imposes its 'truth' like a headstone on a corpse.

In *The Bite of the Night*, the student Hogbin is about to be killed by the thuggish soldiers, Epsom and Gummery; like Claw and Stripwell, he talks for his life – as it happens – with some success. He suggests to them that their lives are unfulfilled:

EPSOM. You 'ave the echoing tones of an advert for a mother's tonic –
HOGBIN. **Well, yes, because great truth shares language with great error**, and luscious sunsets are reflected in slum windows . . . [*Pause. Hogbin waits.*]
GUMMERY. [*At last*] Yes. . . .[48]

For Gummery this is no mere deflection from an immediate task; Hogbin's phrase has shattered the basis of his whole life. He undergoes a complete transformation, akin to religious conversion, and from what he says later, it is clear that he has been seduced, not by rational argument but essentially by the image Hogbin, in his extremity, employs here. This brings us to language.

Seduction of language

The ambiguity of this heading is apposite. Language is obviously the medium of Barker's drama but, though it is perceived as being deployed by the characters, it possesses a peculiar force of its own and often actively resists the attempts of individuals to control it. Language, as is suggested in the example cited above, seduces in its own right. In *The Europeans*, set in the aftermath of the Siege of Vienna by the Turks in 1683, Katrin struggles to describe the experience of being raped and maimed to a priest charged with the duty of recording Turkish atrocities:

> . . . then one of them threw up my skirt – excuse me –
> [*She drinks*]
> Or several of them, from now on I talk of them as plural, as many-headed, as many-legged and a mass of mouths and of course I had no drawers, to be precise – I owned a pair but for special occasions. This was indeed special but in rising in the morning I was not aware of it, and I thought many things, but first I thought – no, I exaggerate, I claim to know the order of my thoughts WHAT A PREPOSTEROUS CLAIM – strike that out, no, among the cascade of impressions – that's better – that's accurate – cascade of impressions – came the idea at least I DID NOT HAVE TO KISS.
> [*Pause*]
> The lips being holy, the lips being sacred, the orifice from which I uttered my most perfect and religious thoughts only the grass would smear them but no.
> [*Pause*]
> Can you keep up? Sometimes I find a flow and then the words go – torrent – cascade – cascade again, I used that word just now I have discovered it, I shall use it, probably *ad nauseam*, cascading! But you –
> [*Pause*]
> And then they turned me over like a side of beef, the way the butcher flings the carcass, not without a certain familiarity, coarse-handling but with the very vaguest element of warmth, oh, no, the words are going, that isn't what I meant at all, precision is so – precision slips even as you reach for it, goes out of grasp and I was flung over and this MANY MOUTHED THING –
> [*She shudders as if taken by a fit, emitting an appalling cry and sending the water flying. The nun supports her. She recovers.*][49]

This speech exemplifies one of the most striking features of Barker's dramaturgy – his ability to forge text that reflects sensitively the fluctuations of a consciousness struggling to cope in extremity. Katrin's discourse appears to strive for objectivity – for accuracy and truth – against the insidious seductions of language. It is arguable, however, that even her apparent successes are in fact seductions, and the reason why the word 'cascade' recommends itself does not lie in its precision but in its ameliorative connotations and its capacity to anaesthetise – albeit only a little – one aspect of an unbearable trauma.

Katrin comments later that she feels she is mad and, certainly, the structure of her discourse here is by no means rational, with its narrative impulse constantly baffled, deflected and seduced. In order to convey this, Barker ruptures the normal patterns of syntactic relations: sentences begin forcefully, then break off without explanation; on other occasions they flow on, one into another, without any punctuation. But, above all, speech persistently doubles back to comment on itself. One is aware of different levels of consciousness – consciousness of the rape itself, of language and of the silent Other who is transcribing all this; in particular, what kind of complicity exists between Katrin and the latter who, because he is invisible, in darkness, merges and is in turn complicit with the audience? We have seen how Baudrillard characterises the action of seduction as a kind of flickering; in this case, what flickers is Katrin's sense of identity – constantly dissolving then re-emerging elsewhere.

This fluctuation is comparable particularly with the celebrated prose style of the French novelist, Louis Ferdinand Céline. In her analysis of Céline's style, Julie Kristeva isolates two typical features:

> . . . segmentation of the sentence, characteristic of the first novels; and the more or less recuperable syntactical ellipses which appear in the late novels.
>
> The peculiar segmentation of the Célinian phrase, which is considered colloquial, is a cutting up of the syntactic unit by the projected or rejected displacement of one of its components.[50]

Kristeva argues that the ejected element is de-syntacticised but is typically charged with the speaker's emotion or moral judgement – an exclamation, an interjection, exaggeration or abuse. Hence the logic of this 'message' dominates the logic of the syntax. Kristeva goes on:

> This 'binary shape' in Céline's first novels has been interpreted as an indication of his uncertainty about self-narration in front of the Other. Awareness of the Other's existence would be what determines the phenomena of recall and excessive clarity, which then produces segmentation. In this type of sentence, then, the

> speaking subject would occupy two places: that of his own identity (when he goes straight to the information, to the theme) and that of objective expression, for the Other (when he goes back, recalls, clarifies).[51]

As in Barker's prologue to *The Last Supper*, Céline often pre-empts the Other's response to his narration in the narration itself. This is facilitated by the de-syntacticising process further developed in the later novels through the use of the famous three dots. This is Céline's own prologue to his final novel, *North*:

> Sure, I tell myself, it'll be all over soon . . . whew! . . . we have seen enough . . . at sixty-five and then some what difference can the worst H . . . Z . . . or Y superbomb make . . . they're zephyrs! . . . nothings! The only terrible thing is this feeling of having wasted all my time and all those myriatons of effort for that hideous satanic horde of alcoholic cocksucking flunkeys . . . lady, lady! have pity! . . . 'Shut up and sell your gripes!' . . . hell, why not? . . . I'm willing but to whom?[52]

Obviously, this technique allows the fluctuating emotion of utterance to dominate the demands for clarity and objectivity made by syntax. Kristeva also points out how this stylistic device allows for long syntactic periods in which the sense of each phrase overflows into the totality: it is rhythmic, reflecting easily current levels of intensity; it refuses the normal subordinations and hierarchical structures of syntax; it allows the invasion of non-meaning and the dominance of intonation. Kristeva sums up the style thus:

> It is as if Céline's stylistic adventure were an aspect of the eternal return to a place which escapes naming and which can be named only if one plays on the whole register of language (syntax, but also message, intonation, etc.). This locus of emotion, of instinctual drive, of non-semanticised hatred, resistant to logico-syntactical naming, appears in Céline's work, as in other great literary texts, as a locus of the ab-ject. The abject, not yet object, is anterior to the distinction between subject and object in normative language. But the abject is also the non-objectality of the archaic mother, the locus of needs, of attraction and repulsion, from which an object of forbidden desire arises. And finally, the abject can be understood in the sense of the horrible and fascinating abomination which is connoted in all cultures by the feminine or, more

> indirectly, by every partial object which is related to the state of abjection (in the sense of the non-separation subject/object). It becomes what culture, the sacred must purge, separate and banish so that it may establish itself as such in the universal logic of catharsis.[53]

I have quoted this passage in full because it seems to me that Kristeva is describing here – within the terms of a feminist/psychological discourse – a locus that shares similarities with Baudrillard's seductive relation – a relation outside the subject/object polarities, where the identity of self and Other is indefinite before the ego has erected its structures of dominance and repression.

Apart from the stylistic connection with Barker's writing, there are two other areas of convergence that come to mind here. First, there is the pre-emptive gesture which Barker describes thus:

> the character gives a performance that he then proceeds to subvert. So that they pre-empt other characters' right to judge them. The character says – 'I know myself, my qualities. So don't think you can accuse me because I already know that.' That's the way a lot of political figures negotiate.
>
> You see the performance attempt and the failure. And the reason the performances are put up is because people need carapaces in order to endure what history has imposed upon them within the play. The girl in *The Europeans* who's been raped, plays complete absorption and a complete understanding of her situation. She continually plays self-knowledge but as the play progresses this is continually demolished.[54]

This insistent movement towards completeness and self-possession is what Kristeva is alluding to in the quotation above from 'Psychoanalysis and the Polis', when she asserts culture's need to purge itself – to resist the abject. For Derrida it manifests the desire of the subject for self-presence, for origin, for an end to differance, for truth. It is a gesture of exclusion and exclusivity aimed at 'the Other'.

Abjection

Excretion, in particular, is 'partial object . . . related to the state of abjection'. Partial in respect of Freud's anal phase, as representing a crucial arena of ego-mastery in the constitution of the 'subject' proper. As Derrida relates in his essay on Artaud, 'La Parole Soufflée':

> Proper is the name of the subject close to himself – who is what he is – and abject the name of the object, the work that has deviated from me. I have a proper name when I am proper. The child does not appropriate his true name in Western society – initially in school – is not well-named until he is proper, clean, toilet-trained.[55]

One of Barker's most scatological works is *The Hang of the Gaol*. Set in the ruins of a burnt-out gaol, the action consists of the progress of an official enquiry into the cause of the fire. In our society, the convicted criminal represents the abject par excellence. Like the insane, the convict does not possess the requisite degree of 'self-control' to be permitted the normal freedoms. Abjection is forced upon him – most notably, as Barker astutely indicates, in the routine of 'slopping out':

STAGG. No. You called them –
JANE. Bucket-shitters [*Pause. He stares.*] I thought everybody called them that.
STAGG. No.
JANE. Well, they do shit in buckets, don't they?[56]

For Jane, who is wife of the governor, Cooper, the prisoners' identity is defined by this process – the essential element of which is that the individual is not permitted to dispose privately of his personal waste. In the opening scene of the play, two prison officers contemplate the ruin:

UDY. The old screws never left a gaol without depositing a turd in it.
WHIP. Burglar's trick.
UDY. Superstition, obviously. One I adhere to. Sort of symbolic clearing out. Shedding of guilt. [*He looks round quickly.*] Anybody coming?
WHIP. I don't think I will.
UDY. [*Removing his coat and jacket*] Help you, Michael. Face the enquiry with an open mind.[57]

Udy then proceeds to deposit his ritual turd on stage; Whip decides to make the attempt but without success. Superstition apart, by sharing the ritual with Whip, Udy is attempting to set the seal on a complicity that will bind them together in the face of the enquiry. However, the central focus of the play and the nexus of the scatological thematic lies in the character of Jardine, the civil servant charged with conducting the official enquiry. This role is one of the most theatrically impressive and subtly drawn of the entire corpus of 1970s' drama. I will limit myself here, though, to the description of Jardine proffered by his colleague, Matheson:

MATHESON. . . . Mr Jardine wants you to take the piss out of it. Do you follow? Shit all over the job. And yet persist in doing it. It's a sort of grand machismo.
JARDINE. Careful, Elizabeth.
MATHESON. He is one of these people psychiatrists believe is partially complete. Only by abusing what he's doing can he extract the slightest satisfaction from it. Like a man who can't enter a woman unless he's poured vitriolic filth all over her. Called her a prostitute and so on.
JARDINE. Elizabeth, you are being very stupid.
MATHESON. He is a first-class civil servant but he will wallow in this self-contempt. . . .[58]

Matheson's comment is cut short by Jardine physically attacking her, a response which would tend to confirm her analysis. In fact, Jardine's sole source of pride lies in his vaunted incorruptible and remorseless professional integrity. As such, he provides an outstanding example of a character in which the sacred/profane opposition alluded to by Kristeva, with its accompanying cathartic rituals, is particularly strong. Céline's attitude (in respect of his medical practice) fits Matheson's analysis just as accurately as Jardine's.

The denouement of the play comes when the Home Secretary, Stagg, requires Jardine to falsify the enquiry's findings for 'political considerations' – to help Labour win the coming election. Jardine, reluctant to forgo his knighthood, gives his assent at the garden party given by the Coopers to mark their departure:

STAGG. . . . George, where does a bloke go for a slash round here?
JARDINE. Where ye're standing, I imagine. Down the leg.
STAGG. Join me, will yer? Piss for socialism. Piddle martyrs we shall be. [*Jardine goes to him, stands at his shoulder. They urinate.*] Well, son? What's it to be?
JANE. He is urinating on my Harry Wheatcrofts . . .
JARDINE. I am laying down my honour. For your honour.[59]

The combination of Jardine's moral collapse with this striking physical gesture is remarkably significant. It is an expression of contempt, a form of abuse directed at the Coopers and the social class the Coopers represent, but it is also conscious self-degradation, a disburdening of guilt (as Udy suggested), a ritual of complicity, a defiant flaunting of the state of abjection – which is ultimately the badge of their subservience. It is the gesture that reduces Jardine to the same level as the Labour Home Secretary, as the prison officers, Udy and Whip, as the 'bucket-shitters'. Because the carceral he has just 'got the hang of' is England. As Matheson remarks in her final line: 'England brings you down at last. . . .'[60]

There are numerous other examples of Barker's interest in the state of abjection. In *The Bite of the Night*, there is the 'public marriage bed rite' of Savage in his reconstituted marriage with Creusa; in *The Europeans*, there is Katrin's insistent publicising of her rape, which culminates in the attempted public exhibition of her childbirth. Through being taken in by their own illusion, fooling others in order to fool themselves, Barker's characters regularly refuse conventional shame, thereby reversing the normal interpersonal dynamics of the situation. This is particularly the case in the play I wish to consider next.

4 *Judith* – a seduction

Judith, published in 1990, is based on the apocryphal story of the eponymous Jewish heroine who conveyed herself secretly to the tent of Holofernes, her country's oppressor, seduced and then murdered him, taking away as trophy his decapitated head. Besides the two central protagonists, Barker includes another woman who accompanies Judith, referred to in the dramatis personae as 'the Servant'. Such is the function initially ascribed to this character by Judith when the two women arrive at Holofernes' tent, but Barker also describes her as 'An Ideologist' – something that becomes more apparent later in the play. In *The Possibilities*, Barker dealt with the aftermath of this episode in a play entitled *The Unforeseen Consequences of a Patriotic Act*, where Judith, having lost the power of speech, has retired to the country to give birth to the murdered Holofernes' child. When a representative of the state comes to urge her back into public life, Judith describes her deed as 'a crime' because murderer and victim had desired each other. When the representative extends her hand to Judith to reassure her, the latter cuts it off with the words:

> I cut the loving gesture! I hack the trusted gesture! I betray! I betray![1]

Barker is focusing again upon the point where personal morality, the intuitive sense of the ethical, is violated in the interests of the political. Where the face-to-face with the Other (*That Good Between Us*), in which Levinas locates the foundation of the ethical, is savagely betrayed.

Judith begins with Holofernes alone in his tent. As emerges in subsequent dialogue, he has completed his plan of battle; with this and his own charismatic presence in the ranks, he is complacent that he will defeat Israel, as he has done before, and put the entire nation to slavery and the sword: the conclusion is foregone. The moment of the play then lies in a strange hiatus between action and event – all the more strange because the event is a slaughter. This is the familiar Barker territory of the catastrophic: a twilight zone where the 'real', regulated world of social ties and obligations fades and desire is free to express itself.

Holofernes begins with what appears to be a soliloquy reflecting on death. The status of the speech – as soliloquy – is undermined when the general interjects an order to others outside his tent to enter. This introduces immediately an area of ambiguity: conventionally audiences trust the soliloquy, assuming that the absence of any other characters on stage disposes of any motive for pretence on the part of the speaker. This is a device Barker uses in other dramas to play upon the ambiguities of the performer/role split. (There is a similar situation in *The Europeans*, Act I Scene 3, which begins with what appears to be a soliloquy from Katrin but auditors subsequently emerge from the darkness.) In spite of seeming to be absorbed in his own thoughts, Holofernes is acutely aware – more so than the audience – of what goes on around him. His words indicate a considerable level of intellectual sophistication:

> For while victory is the object of the battle, death is its subject, and the melancholy of the soldiers is the peculiar silence of a profound love.[2]

Holofernes presents himself as being aware of his own seduction here; victory is the rational justification for battle, its object, but it is not why he desires battle. As I suggested, in seduction the end is seen as a means to a means. This same melancholy love is celebrated in the works of the Great War poets, the rational, socialised object of whose poems is, in complete contradiction, the 'pity' and the condemnation of war. The fact that Holofernes' self-analysis is not befogged by humanist ideology is clear when he talks about his cruelty:

> But cruelty is collaboration in chaos, of which the soldiers are merely the agents.
>
> (p. 49)

His words suggest a self-conscious awareness of his posture as challenging conventional morality – which he mocks:

> Because I walk among the dead they will ascribe to me feelings of shame or compassion. This is not the case. Rather, I am overcome

> with wonder. I am trembling with a terrible infatuation. . . . And some generals talk of necessity. They talk of limited objectives. There are no limitations, nor is there necessity. There is only infatuation.
>
> (p. 49)

When the two women enter, they kneel silently; Judith uncorks a bottle. Holofernes remarks disparagingly that he does not drink and there is a long pause. When the servant appears to offer Judith to the general, her register, in contrast to his, is colloquial, commonplace and obviously ingratiating:

> I heard – futile now, I see – I heard – you liked women.
>
> (p. 49)

Holofernes announces that he wishes only to talk of death. The servant's response – that Judith is similarly pre-occupied with mortality – appears an ingratiating lie and her persistence prompts Holofernes to seize and choke her. Up to this point, Judith has remained silent – leading Holofernes to dismiss her as 'shallow', 'a bitch', 'a thing that giggles'. She lacks any quality of 'otherness' – a vacuous sexual object that has been proffered many times before, the Same. He focuses upon the servant as being responsible for their intrusion. When Judith utters her first line,

> You are killing my property.
>
> (p. 50)

he is startled and engaged. He realises that he has been mistaken concerning the relative status of the women, that he is, in Judith's eyes, dignifying a mere object, a slave, with an interest which should be beneath him. He is also intrigued at the manner of her intervention – not humanitarian – which suggests that she may be as 'cruel' as himself. This latter aspect may have been a successful bluff on her part. Her objection to his behaviour is, anyway, a challenge to his authority to do as he pleases – and she herself begins to take on the status of a challenge. After a pause, he attempts to re-assert his status with the put-down:

> I do not wish to fuck tonight.
>
> (p. 50)

A little later, he makes the admission:

> I do like women, but for all the wrong reasons. And as for them they rapidly see through me. They see I only hide in them, which is not love. They see I shelter in their flesh. Which is not love. Now, go away.
>
> (p. 50)

As is made clear later, nothing that any of the parties to this dialogue says may be taken entirely at face value. Expressions like this, which may appear to be an admission of weakness, can in fact be a tactic to enlist sympathy – or a challenge.

A pause is broken by the cry of a sentry and Holofernes commences the next section of the dialogue by suddenly appearing to question his whole career:

> HOLOFERNES. It is of great importance that the enemy is defeated.
> JUDITH. Oh, yes!
> HOLOFERNES. Or is it? Perhaps it only seems so.
> JUDITH. Seems so?
> HOLOFERNES. Always the night before the soldiers die I think – perhaps this is not important after all. Perhaps it would be better if the enemy defeated us. I mean, from a universal point of view. Perhaps my own view is too narrow.
> JUDITH. [*Thoughtfully*] Yes . . .
>
> (p. 50)

This, in itself, is a very seductive gesture because of its openness; it seems to invite participation on an equal level and Holofernes appears effectively to be putting his very identity – as war hero – into play. Judith's measured and cautious response leads on to Holofernes dismissing serious consideration of the idea and escalating the duel by rapping out another challenge:

> Take your clothes off now.
>
> (p. 51)

He interjects this order almost as an aside in the middle of a speech. I do not think this is so much a calculated tactic as a drop on to a different level of consciousness. He makes clear some lines later exactly what her attraction is:

> I long to be married, but to a cruel woman. And as I lay dying of sickness in a room, I would want her to ignore me. I would want her

> to laugh in the kitchen with a lover as my mouth grew dry. I would want her to count my money as I choked.
>
> (p. 51)

This seems to represent a denial/refusal of any possibility of love and one would think that the invitation he seems to give here would be quite satisfactory for Judith's purpose – a purpose well-known to the audience. She finds, however, in spite of a massive effort of will, that she is unable to comply with his instruction. In her confusion, she turns on and attempts to dismiss the Servant whom Holofernes, now triumphant, detains – probably to increase Judith's embarrassment.

There is another pause, after which Holofernes sums up; he seems to interpret her confusion as meaning that she came not merely with the idea of fornication, but of loving him:

> I am a man who never could be loved. I am a man no woman could find pitiful. Pity is love. Pity is passion. The rest is clamour. The rest is just imperative. . . . When a woman loves a man it is not his manliness she loves, however much she craves it. It is the pity he enables her to feel, by showing, through the slightest aperture, his loneliness. No matter what his brass, no matter what his savagery, it creeps, like blood under a door. . . .
>
> (p. 53)

This again could be perceived as a kind of challenge. If one is seduced by weakness and vulnerability, then the apparent humiliation he forces on Judith can rebound upon the perpetrator: Holofernes puts himself in danger of pitying her. There is a reversal and weakness becomes strength. Perhaps Holofernes realises this and when Judith expresses the desire to dress, he escalates the encounter by removing some of his clothes – exposing himself. Judith's request for confirmation of his bloody intentions for the following day is perhaps an attempt to confirm her own murderous purpose. Her increasing impatience with the servant's interventions shows that she resents this third-party view of the duel. She confesses her own unhappiness to him and there is an important silence:

> [*Long pause. They look at one another.*]
>
> HOLOFERNES. I can't be loved.
>
> (p. 55)

The reiteration of this point suggests again that the possibility or the hope is very much in his mind. Something flows between them in the look.

Holofernes returns to philosophising by contending that the sole purpose of existence is reproduction, that this is absurd, and in view of this, his career as a military butcher is no less moral than any other. Judith suggests an alternative:

> Yes, but if life is so very – is so utterly – fatuous, should we not comfort one another? Or is that silly?
>
> (p. 55)

At this point, the Servant, obviously feeling that the interaction is drifting dangerously, intervenes to cut short this almost tender melancholy and, indirectly, to bring Judith back to her original objective:

> Tomorrow you'll be different! You'll have done the killing of a lifetime! Tomorrow you won't know yourself! 'Did I go on about death?' 'Was I miserable?' Off with yer skirt, darling!
>
> (p. 56)

Judith responds to this:

> All right, let's fuck.
>
> (p. 56)

She tries to dismiss the emotional validity of their previous intensity, to undercut the enchantment of seduction:

> You want me to say how much I, how magnificently you, all right, I will do, I'm far from educated, so I'll stop pretending, and anyway, nothing you say is original, either. Do I insult you? Do I abolish your performance? It needs abolishing. [*Pause. The Servant turns away in despair. Holofernes stares at her, without emotion. The pressure in Judith dissipates. She shrugs.*] I am reckoned to be the most beautiful woman in the district. So I thought I had a chance. [*She goes to pick her clothing off the floor. She stops and lets out a scream. The scream ceases. She remains still.*]
>
> (p. 56)

Judith tries to force an objective view on their encounter – not only of Holofernes who is not 'original', but also of herself – 'reckoned to be the most beautiful woman'. The Servant clearly thinks Judith has gone too far in insulting Holofernes, but he controls any impulse of anger he feels and allows her to exhaust her tension. When he resumes, he does so from where he left off with a challenging admission:

HOLOFERNES. And yet I want to be. [*Pause*] I, the impossible to love, require love. Often, I am made aware of this. [*Pause*]

(p. 56)

When the Servant, seeing an opportunity of salvaging the situation, encourages him to continue with this, he silences her:

HOLOFERNES. Do you think I can't see you? [*The Servant is transfixed.*] Your mask. Your fog. Do you think I can't see you? [*Pause*]

(p. 56)

The moment is highly ambiguous. What does Holofernes mean? The Servant is 'transfixed' presumably at the possibility that Holofernes 'sees through her', i.e. knows why she is pandering to him. Is he bluffing? Or is he merely objecting to her patently false interest in him? What he says immediately after this, although it appears to be – and may actually be – generalisation, takes on a very particular significance: he is referring initially to his need to be loved:

> The way in which it asserts itself is as follows. Frequently I expose myself to the greatest danger. I court my own extinction. Whilst I am exhilarated by the conflict I am also possessed of the most perfect lucidity. So absolute am I in consciousness, yet also so removed from any fear of death, I am at these moments probably a god.
>
> (p. 56)

Is Holofernes suggesting that he knows the women have come to kill him, that in his godlike 'lucidity' he has perceived their intention, that he is deliberately courting death? Whatever may be the case on his part, his words must surely make this impression, however fleeting, on the women. When they arrived, they came concealing a secret; Holofernes sensed this and he is now attempting to turn the seductive power of their secret against them, while maintaining his enigma for them. To return to Baudrillard:

> I know the other's secret but do not reveal it, and he knows I know it but does not let it be acknowledged: the intensity between the two is simply the secret of the secret. . . . Only at the cost of remaining unspoken does it maintain its power, just as seduction functions from never being spoken or desired. . . .[3]

Holofernes, however, goes on to say that after the ecstasy of courting death, he is haunted by the need to know that, if he had indeed died, some other person would have died of grief for him:

> I am not the definition of another's life. That is my absent trophy. I think we live only in the howl of others. The howl is love. [*Pause*]
>
> (p. 57)

This is the reverse of the desire he expressed earlier for a 'cruel woman'. The Servant, again trying to use the opportunity to put matters back on course, gives Holofernes a 'lecture' to the effect that 'strong' men must show a woman a little weakness – as a kind of concession to their inferior dignity. In response to this Holofernes shows a complete collapse – he bursts into tears and clasps the Servant. The tears may be 'real' but it would seem likely, especially in the light of what has just been said, that Holofernes is deploying them tactically. In fact the violence and immediacy of his response suggest he may be mocking the Servant – particularly as the stage directions read that he should release her just as abruptly as he seized her. The effect of this could be quite comic, though there should be no overt hint of a comic intention on Holofernes' part. He then proceeds to tell them what a weak and cowardly child he was:

> There was none weaker than me.
>
> (p. 57)

His confession of abject weakness leads on to a description of how he learned to compensate for this:

> But being weak I discovered cunning. I learned to say one thing knowing it would satisfy the expectation, whilst carrying on a second and more secret conversation with myself. I led people away from my true intention, my speech became a maze, I used speech to trap my enemies, my speech was a pit, I lived in speech, making it a weapon.
>
> (p. 57)

Judith, however, draws the immediately relevant conclusion from all this:

> You mean, nothing you say is true? [*He looks at her.*] I don't mind that. I am perfectly able to lie myself. I am almost certainly lying now in fact.
>
> (p. 57)

Surprisingly, perhaps, Judith says she finds this a great relief:

> Excellent! Forgive my hysteria, it was the pressure, the sheer suffocating pressure of sincerity. And now I am light! I am ventilated! A clean dry wind whirls through my brain! I intend to kill you, how is that for a lie? And that must mean I love you! Or doesn't it! Anything is possible! I think now we have abandoned the search for truth, really, we can love each other!
>
> (p. 58)

Judith's exhilaration is owing to a number of factors: first, she is courting death in the manner Holofernes said he did ('I intend to kill you') – perfectly 'lucid' and 'godlike'; second, she has freed herself of the burden of her original intention – her duty (she may or may not kill Holofernes); third, she is energised by the opening up of possibilities ('Anything is possible'), which is characteristic of seduction:

> The relief of knowing you are simply an element in a fiction! I think before this moment I never was equipped to love.
>
> (p. 58)

Judith has put her own identity into play – Jewess, widow, mother of about-to-be-massacred children; the magnitude of the stakes in this seductive game adds to its intensity. As I indicated in the previous chapter, seduction relieves one of all obligations one is under in respect of the Law. In Barker's earlier treatment of this subject in *The Unforeseen Consequences of a Patriotic Act* (one of *The Possibilities*), Judith says of this moment:

> I could not have cared if he dripped with my father's blood, or had my babies' brains around his boot, or waded through all Israel.[4]

The moment of seduction detaches the individual from both personal and political history.

Interestingly, it is not Holofernes' confession of social inadequacy that engages her (if love is pity), but his admission that he lies:

> When you told me you could not help yourself lying I fell in love with you. That was the moment.
>
> (p. 58)

She ends by encouraging Holofernes to continue lying, thereby maintaining their enchanted, seductive world of pure artifice. The point is, however, not merely to lie – which would be to tell the truth by saying the opposite – but to preserve the dangerous tension of ambiguity:

JUDITH. . . . Lie, do lie! [*Pause*]
HOLOFERNES. I know why you're here. [*Pause. The Servant stares.*]
JUDITH. I know why I came.
HOLOFERNES. I know what you intend.
JUDITH. I know what I intended.
HOLOFERNES. I know it all.
JUDITH. I knew it all. [*Pause*] I knew it all. And now I know nothing. [*He looks into her.*]
HOLOFERNES. We love, then.
JUDITH. Yes.
HOLOFERNES. And I, who is unlovable, I am loved.
JUDITH. My dear, yes. . . . [*Pause*]

(p. 58)

Judith's immediate response to Holofernes' challenge is inspired. While preserving the secret as secret, she acknowledges his challenge in the most direct way but implies that, although she may have come with a particular intention, Holofernes has caused her to abandon it – very flattering to his sense of himself as godlike. Their professions of love are particularly interesting with regard to the lying pact. Baudrillard states:

> Only signs without referents, empty, senseless, absurd, and elliptical signs absorb us.[5]

And:

> Seduction lies with the annulment of the signs, of their meaning, with their pure appearance.[6]

Both parties here have agreed that what they say is strictly 'meaningless' – which serves to intensify their duel. So when Holofernes says 'We love, then' and Judith affirms it, the words are not a communication: they are the thing itself, pure presence.

While they embrace, the Servant intervenes – almost like a chorus. She presents the perspective of 'reality', the world of truth, concerned not with processes but ends, not with the magic of superficial appearances but interpretation:

> One of them is lying. Or both of them. This baffles me, because whilst Judith is clever, so is he. . . .
>
> How brilliant she is! How ecstatic she is! She convinces me! But she must be careful, for with lying, sometimes, the idea, though faked, can discover an appeal, and then we're fucked!
>
> (pp. 58–9)

In the charmed world of seduction, language ceases to be instrumental: we can be seduced by our own words.

When Holofernes appears to be asleep in Judith's arms, the 'Servant' changes:

SERVANT. [*Abandoning her persona*] Judith. . . .

(p. 60)

From this point on, she drops her role of procuress or servant and addresses Judith as an equal. Realising that Judith has been seduced, she puts as much pressure on her as she can to carry out the murder:

SERVANT. Israel commands you. Israel which birthed you. Which nourished you. Israel insists. And your child sleeps. Her last sleep if –

JUDITH. **I am well drilled**. [*She glares at the Servant. The Sentry cries. Pause. Judith goes to the sword.*]

SERVANT. Excellent. [*She unsheathes it*]
Excellent.
My masterful.
My supreme in.
My most terrible.
My half-divine. [*Judith raises the weapon over Holofernes*]

HOLOFERNES. [*Without moving*] I'm not asleep. I'm only pretending. [*Pause. The sword stays.*]

My dear.
My loved one.
I'm not asleep. I'm only pretending. [*Pause. Judith closes her eyes.*]

(p. 60)

It becomes clear here why Barker added the description of 'Ideologist' to the Servant in the dramatis personae. The echoing of her formal, ritual invocations by Holofernes serves to underline the conflict here between power on the one hand ('My masterful', 'My terrible') and desire on the other ('My dear', 'My loved one'). The surprise, however, is Holofernes' final seductive gesture: he puts his life absolutely in Judith's hands; he has reversed their situations:

HOLOFERNES. I can win battles. The winning of battles is, if anything, facile to me, but.
JUDITH. My arm aches!
HOLOFERNES. But you.
JUDITH. Aches!
HOLOFERNES. Love.
JUDITH. My arm aches and I lied!
HOLOFERNES. Of course you lied, and I lied also.
JUDITH. We both lied, so –
HOLOFERNES. But in the lies we. Through the lies we. Underneath the lies we.
SERVANT. **Oh, the barbaric and inferior vile inhuman bestial and bloodsoaked monster of depravity!**

(pp. 60–1)

It is interesting that Barker writes Holofernes' last speech here with a single full stop at the end of each sentence rather than a short line of dots that would have indicated an intention to complete the utterance. These *are* complete because Holofernes is alluding to an unspoken pact that must not be uttered but which is pointed at in the 'we'. His words, coupled with the gesture of complete vulnerability, paralyse Judith. She repeats the Servant's slogan but cannot act:

JUDITH. **Oh, the barbaric and inferior** – [*Seeing Judith is stuck between slogan and action, the Servant swiftly resorts to a stratagem, and leaning over Holofernes, enrages Judith with a lie.*]
SERVANT. He is smiling! He is smiling! [*With a cry, Judith brings down the sword.*]

(p. 61)

The notion that Holofernes is grinning in confident anticipation of another easy victory is enough momentarily to abolish his performance in Judith's eyes; the very intensity of their pact is turned against itself and she has ample power to kill him.

The Servant rushes to complete the job of removing Holofernes' head; she is practical and businesslike but Judith is stunned. Her speech indicates two violently dislocated levels:

> A right bitch cunt, I was, nearly ballocked it, eh nearly – [*She staggers.*] **Oh, my darling how I** – [*She recovers.*] Nearly poxed the job, the silly fucker I can be sometimes, a daft bitch and a cunt-brained fuck-arse – [*She staggers.*] **Oh, my – Oh, my** –
>
> (pp. 61–2)

This parallels the levels of mind and brute body into which the Servant has hacked Holofernes. A constant theme in Barker's work is the struggle between state and individual for possession of the individual's pain, their suffering. In this case, the Servant's seizure of the head forms part of this expropriation:

> We take the head because the head rewards the people. The people are entitled symbolically to show contempt for their oppressor. Obviously the spectacle has barbaric undertones but we. The concentration of emotion in the single object we et cetera. So.
>
> (p. 62)

Barker here is clearly highlighting the double standards of the state 'ideologist' – condemning but endorsing 'barbarism' for her own purposes.

Judith focuses on the headless body and announces her intention of making love to it. I have already indicated that, in the world of seduction, death does not end the engagement; in fact, *The Last Supper* shows how it can be used to prolong it indefinitely. The Servant is utterly horrified and protests:

SERVANT. It demeans your triumph and humiliates our –
JUDITH. How can he be an enemy? His head is off.
SERVANT. **Enemy. Vile enemy.**
JUDITH. You keep saying that . . . ! But now the head is gone I can make him mine, surely? The evil's gone, the evil's in the bag and I can love! Look, I claim him! Lover, lover, respond to my adoring glance,

it's not too late, is it? We could have a child, we could, come, come, adored one, it is only politics kept us apart!

SERVANT. I think I am going to be sick . . .

JUDITH. No, no, count to a hundred . . .

SERVANT. I will be made insane by this!

JUDITH. You weren't insane before. Is it love makes you insane? Hatred you deal admirably with. Come, loved one . . . ! [*She lies over Holofernes' body. The Servant is transfixed with horror.*]

(p. 62)

Judith's comment here is significant: we are presented with two contrasted atrocities: first the killing and severing of the head, then the attempted necrophilia. The first is applauded by the state as an act of heroism, the second abhorred, not least because this behaviour is hardly consistent with being a heroine – which is what the state will now require Judith to be.

After the failure of Judith's attempt to love Holofernes, she is physically unable to move. This hysterical paralysis reflects her own mental state – she cannot adjust to what has happened. Dramatically, this is very convenient because it poses the problem in a very acute way; they have to escape, but the Servant will have to persuade Judith to come to terms with her action before they can do this. First she says she will find Judith a husband and prophecies a vision of idyllic marital bliss and contentment. This is probably totally counterproductive: in the light of what has just taken place, such a dream can never attain any degree of reality for Judith. Thereafter, when Judith says she wants to go but cannot, the Servant asserts she is being punished by God for trying to make love to Holofernes' corpse. Judith asks the Servant to pray for her – she does but to no avail. As the Servant is leaving, Judith gives 'a profound cry of despair' which causes her companion to stop. The Servant suddenly has an idea:

I say God. I mean Judith. [*Pause*] I say Him. But I mean you. [*Pause. The cry of the Sentry is heard. The Servant places the head on the ground, and, leaning on her knuckles, puts her forehead to the ground. Pause. Judith watches.*]

JUDITH. You are worshipping me.

(pp. 64–5)

It is no doubt the extremity of the moment that lends the Servant the persuasive power of her next speech, which articulates a number of Barker themes and deserves to be quoted in full:

SERVANT. Firstly, remember we create ourselves. We do not come made. If we came made, how facile life would be, worm-like, crustacean, invertebrate. Facile and futile. Neither love nor murder would be possible. Secondly, whilst shame was given us to balance will, shame is not a wall. It is not a wall, Judith, but a sheet rather, threadbare and stained. It only appears a wall to those who won't come near it. Come near it and you see how thin it is, you could part it with your fingers. Thirdly, it is a facility of the common human, to recognise no act is reprehensible but only the circumstances make it so, for the reprehensible attaches to the unnecessary, but with the necessary, the same act bears the nature of obligation, honour and esteem. These are the mysteries which govern the weak, but in the strong are staircases to the stars. I kneel to you. I kneel to the Judith who parts the threadbare fabric with her will. Get up now. [*Pause. Judith cannot move. The Servant counts the seconds. She perseveres.*] Judith, who are those we worship? What is it they possess? The ones we wrap in glass and queue half-fainting for a glimpse? The ones whose works are quoted and endorsed? The little red books and the little green books, Judith, who are they? Never the kind, for the kind are terrorized by grief. Get up now, Judith. [*Nothing happens. Pause.*] No, they are the specially human who drained the act of meaning and filled it again from sources fresher and – [*Judith climbs swiftly to her feet.*]

(p. 65)

The entire argument, from the Servant's point of view, is pure hypothesis; as she herself said earlier:

> . . . you can know a thing and still not know it.
>
> (p. 56)

Her words, however, are sufficient to transform Judith from a state of abject powerlessness to one of godlike dominance. Again, this demonstrates another example of the reversal process in seduction: by refusing the overwhelming burden of grief and shame, these negative emotions are replaced by a positive glorying in her action. She must escalate the stakes. Judith experiences again the sense of liberation she experienced when she felt free to lie to Holofernes: she will use the murder to create a powerful new self. She has assumed the absolute character Holofernes displayed at the beginning of the play. The first person she tests her shamelessness on, ironically, is the Servant, whom she humiliates by treating as a slave:

JUDITH. **Who said you could get up.** [*The Servant stops.*] And any version that I tell, endorse it. For that'll be the truth.

(p. 65)

She abolishes any truth apart from that she herself creates; her word is all the reality there is. It is only by escalating the game in this way that Judith can be re-energised through the opening of new possibilities:

> I shall be unbearable, intolerably vile, inflicting my opinions on the young, I shall be the bane of Israel, spouting, spewing, a nine-foot tongue of ignorance will slobber out of my mouth, and drench the populace with the saliva of my prejudice, they will wade through my opinions, they will wring my accents out of their clothes, but they will tolerate it, for am I not their mother?
>
> (p. 66)

Barker has been criticised for a writing which, as fantasy, has no purchase on the 'real' world, yet I have no difficulty in recognising the 'power-crazed' mentality Judith demonstrates here. While humiliating the Servant by forcing her to cut her hair off, Judith reflects on testing further her superhuman status:

> To kill your enemies, how easy that is. To murder the offending, how oddly stale. Real ecstasy must come of liquidating innocence, to punish in the absence of offence. . . .
>
> (p. 66)

Because of her role as ideologist, Judith particularly despises the Servant, who is temporarily discomforted with her companion's new-found character but on the whole approves:

JUDITH. . . . for you nothing is really pain at all.
Nor torture. Death. Or.
Nothing is.
It's drained and mulched, and used to nourish further hate, as dead men's skulls are ground for feeding fields. . . .

(p. 67)

Sewage disposal is a persistent Barker metaphor for the ideological/political scene – most notably in *The Hang of the Gaol*. Because suffering is continually justified, expropriated, used by political ideology, it is also, and in consequence, not experienced fully by the individual. Although the Servant thinks that Judith has been safely secured for the state – which will tolerate her tyranny and corruption – Judith's last words before she leaves the stage:

> Israel
> Is
> My
> Body!
>
> (p. 67)

suggest another reversal. Israel claims Judith, but she claims Israel, a transformation similar to the case of Stalin in *The Power of the Dog*.

If one were to consider this play from the Stanislavskian point of view of a structure of consistent and linked objectives, it is clear that this could be appropriate only for the Servant, the Ideologist, who maintains throughout the play the superobjective of killing Holofernes and maximising the political capital therefrom. In a way, this is an important part of her function – to offset the seductive relation between the other two. It might be objected that I have advanced an interpretation of the play, a practice which I have, on the whole, tended to condemn. I would argue that, given a text, it is the job of those staging it to take the written lines and turn them into actions – mainly speech acts; in considering Barker's text, I have been concerned to describe what is *happening*. My approach has been ontological and subjective, not ideological and objective. I believe that the 'thought' expressed in the text of *Judith* (as well as Barker's other writings) points strongly to the kind of focus I have attempted to outline in this study.

5 *The Castle*

One of the most highly acclaimed of Barker's plays to date has been *The Castle*, which was first performed as part of a 'Barker season' in the RSC Pit at the Barbican in 1985. At the time, the drama was widely perceived as being principally concerned with the Reaganite intensification of the arms race and with 'Greenham Common'-style feminist oppositional values. This connection, while not without substance, does not dominate the play and certainly does not sanction the extrapolation of simple political or social messages. The text comprises one of the richest and most densely written of Barker's entire *oeuvre*, providing an intellectual canvas surpassing in its breadth while simultaneously depending upon a symbolic weave of astonishing economy and tight integration. In this chapter, I wish to examine this major work in some depth, an exercise that will entail a scrutiny of literary/symbolic elements as well as dramatic/theatrical considerations, since both are relevant to the theoretical concepts and processes of seduction I have advanced hitherto.

The plot is relatively straightforward. An English knight, Stucley, returns home to his domain after years spent fighting in the Crusades. His followers have been killed or fallen by the wayside; only a single retainer, the appropriately named Batter and a captive Arab engineer, Krak, accompany him. While he has been away, however, the women have evolved a different lifestyle which is feminist, collective and non-exploitative of human or natural powers. Further, Stucley's wife, Ann, is involved in this on the level of a personal as well as political commitment in so far as she is the lover of Skinner, a ploughman's widow, whose feminism is both militant and profoundly ideological. Stucley is disgusted by what appears to him to be rank neglect of his estate, but his chief concern is to find Ann and to resume a relationship that infatuates him and which he has carried like a grail in his heart through all his military travels. She informs him that she has been unfaithful and that he should leave. In a blind fury, he sets about 'restoring order', and implements the construction of a massive castle designed by Krak. The latter, hating his captors, an alien cut off from any positive emotional ties with the land in which he is held, intends the castle as an engine of destruction aimed as much at its possessors as their potential foes. Stucley also re-establishes his lapsed priest, Nailer, as bishop of his own unique sect of Christianity – the Church of Christ the Lover.

Against this array of male power, spiritual and temporal, the opposition of the women can do little. Skinner, the most resolutely opposed to the castle, realising that Ann's love for her is ebbing, in desperation seduces and murders the builder – Holiday. She is tortured in the dungeons of the castle, tried for the murder and sentenced by Stucley to be turned loose with the rotting corpse of her victim chained to her.

As her husband becomes increasingly paranoid, ordering more and more fortifications and corresponding increments in his police state, Ann seduces Krak, whose awakened emotions introduce confusion into his hitherto single-minded devotion to the castle. Ann, pregnant with his child, pleads with Krak to run away with her: he tells her that there is nowhere to go – the castle is inescapable. She kills herself along with her unborn infant, and that act is followed by an epidemic of suicides amongst pregnant women who throw themselves off the castle walls. Grief-stricken and by now quite mad, Stucley is given the *coup de grâce* by his bailiff, Batter, who in consultation with Nailer asks Skinner to become head of a feminist-type Earth-mother religion. Skinner, transformed by her sufferings, has remained at the castle and has become the focus of a secret and quasi-religious popular veneration. When she refuses to prop up Batter's state, he offers power to her directly. In a surge of desire, she promises vengeance on all who have made her suffer, but almost immediately realises she will be 'too cruel' and declines the offer. Krak steps out of the shadow of the castle wall and insists she accept: the play ends with Skinner struggling to recall a time when 'there was no government', as jets streak overhead.

Considered from the perspective of the basic interrelations of the characters, a clear pattern emerges that focuses on Ann, who seduces or has seduced the other roles. She is worshipped by her husband, Stucley, whose subsequent degeneration can be seen as a consequence of her rejection. If anything, she is even more essential to Skinner's moral universe:

SKINNER. . . . They talk of a love-life, don't they? Do you know the phrase 'love-life', as if somehow this thing ran under or beside, as

> if you stepped from one life to the other, banality to love, love to banality, no, love is in the cooking and the washing and the milking, no matter what, the colour of the love stains everything, I say so anyway, being admittedly of a most peculiar disposition I WOULD RATHER YOU WERE DEAD THAN TOOK A STEP OR SHUFFLE BACK FROM ME. . . .[1]

Skinner herself makes clear later in the action that she is shattered not by the return of male power or even by her torture but by the loss of Ann's love. After Skinner, Ann seduces Krak, simultaneously rocking his cosmos to its very foundations. Her suicide precedes and precipitates the final catastrophe – the mass suicide of the pregnant women, Stucley's assassination and the offer of power to Skinner. All three of her 'victims' commit themselves to various 'truths' – they resist. Ann steadfastly refuses to sacrifice any of her instinctive desires in the interests of ideology or even of sparing others pain. Her power to seduce others lies in her own openness to seduction.

Stucley is, as I have indicated, committed to truths: he has been engaged in an ideological conflict, the Crusade, and his agonisings over religious matters show that his theological concern is not mere hypocrisy:

> I found the church bunged up with cow and bird dung, the place we married in, really, what – [*pause*]. So I prayed in the nettles.
>
> (p. 8)

His 'faith' has been reinforced in so far as he has suffered for it. Returning home to his wife, he extends his religious feeling to her:

> . . . I have seen your face on tent roofs . . .
>
> (p. 7)

> I was saying to the Arab every hundred yards I have this little paradise . . .
>
> (p. 8)

> . . . I who jumped in every pond of murder kept this one thing pure in my head, pictured you half-naked on an English night . . .
>
> (p. 8)

This kind of exaggerated veneration of woman, within the predominantly medieval context of the play, strongly accords with the chivalric 'courtly love' phenomenon, the secular counterpart of the cult of the Virgin Mary. Stucley himself has struggled to remain 'pure'. When Cant, one of the women, proffers sexual intercourse, he reacts violently and is immediately ashamed:

CANT. My man's not come back so you do his business for him – here – [*She goes to lift her skirts. Stucley knocks her aside with a staggering blow.*]

STUCLEY. I won't be fouled by you, mad bitch, what's happened here, what! I slash your artery for you! [*He draws a knife*] Down you, in the muck and nettle! [*She screams*] MY TERRITORY! [*He straddles her.*]

BATTER. HEY! [*Stucley wounds her, she screams.*]

STUCLEY. My shame, you – LOOK WHAT YOU'VE MADE ME DO! I've – I've [*He tosses the knife away, wipes his hand*] To come home and hear vile stuff of that sort is – when I am so clean for my lover is – no homecoming, is it?

(p. 4)

Stucley's violence is directly occasioned by the need to defend his 'purity': he is aroused but simultaneously threatened by Cant's desire. As such, he experiences a momentary loss of self-control that results in the mutilated/mutilating act of wounding Cant's breast – an act of which he is immediately ashamed. It is the first act of violence in the play and provokes wide resonance. It signals an important and ubiquitous theme in the drama – the archetypal equating of the land and the female body: Stucley emphasises this with his cry – 'My territory!' – as he straddles Cant on the ground. A few lines later in the scene, Ann says 'A woman, this country . . .' (p. 5). Stucley's rage at this particular point is because his 'territory' has returned to 'nature' – the result, not of sloth, but of the deliberate policy of the women; as Skinner states later in the scene:

SKINNER. First there was the bailiff, and we broke the bailiff. And then there was God, and we broke God. And lastly there was cock, and we broke that too. Freed the ground, freed religion, freed the body. And went up this hill, standing together naked like the old female pack, growing to eat and not to market, friends to cattle whom we milked but never slaughtered, joining the strips and dancing in the commons, the three days labour that we gave to priests gave instead to the hungry, turned the tithe barn into a hospital and FOUND CUNT BEAUTIFUL that we had hidden and suffered shame for, its lovely shapelessness, its colour all miraculous, what they had made dirty or worshipped out of ignorance. . . .

(p. 6)

Here again this female freedom is linked to the hill where the scene is set (Ann tells Krak to get off her hill). The hill, in fact, becomes the focus of the struggle that develops between male and female forces. Stucley, who has concentrated his energies on resisting seduction, resisting change, preserving his ideal, has vested everything in control and the violence of brute mastery. His action in wounding Cant prefigures his 'wounding' of the hill through the building of the castle; Skinner, conversely, later exerts her witchcraft to activate the natural power of the hill against this imposition:

SKINNER. OLD HILL SAYS NO . . . ROCK WEEPS AND STONE PROTESTS. . . .

(p. 15)

It is left to Krak, however, hitherto practically silent, to step into the confusion of Stucley's encounter with Cant and restore order:

KRAK. So much emotion, I think, is perfectly comprehensible, given the exertion of travelling, and all your exaggerated hopes. Some anti-climax is only to be expected.
STUCLEY. Yes. [*He shrugs*] Yes.
KRAK. The only requirement is the restoration of a little order, the rudiments of organisation established, and so on. The garden is a little overgrown, and minds gone wild through lack of discipline. Chaos is only apparent in my experience, like gravel shaken in water abhors the turbulence, and soon asserts itself in perfect order.

(p. 4)

Krak demonstrates here that he is a rationalist, espousing the scientific perspective of a universe ordered by inexorable laws. The apparent chaos of appearance belies the 'true' underlying reality whose principle is founded upon the highly classical notion of equilibrium – balance, economy, equivalence. Though Stucley embraces Krak – at one point, literally – as architect of his castle, he does not embrace the Arab's rationalism; his own universe remains inexorably fatal and – in spite of his attempts at resistance – seductive.

Stucley, temporarily restored to spirits and all childish enthusiasm, chases off to find his wife:

STUCLEY. . . . I run to my wife's bedroom. Catch her unprepared and all confusion. Oh, my lord, et cetera, half her plaits undone. Oh, my lord and all. . . .

(p. 5)

However, no sooner does he leave the stage and his wife appears. She has apparently been watching them and has emerged to confront Krak:

ANN. My belly's a fist. Went clench on seeing you, went rock. And womb a tumour. All my soft rigid. What are you doing on my hill?
KRAK. [*Turning*] Looking. In so far as the mist permits.
ANN. It always rains like this for strangers. Drapes itself in a fine drench, not liking to be spied on. A woman, this country . . .

(p. 6)

In an interview in *New Theatre Quarterly* 8, Barker said:

> actually no conclusions can be arrived at by expertise, only by instinct. I think that one of the great powers of Greenham, although it has been ignored, and is probably destroyed now. But as a terribly important historic metaphor, it does stand for the power of instinct – which is what the play, 'The Castle', is about.[2]

Ann's immediate hostile reaction to Krak is entirely instinctive and fundamentally irrational. When Skinner appears moments later, she reinforces Ann's feeling and acts instantly to 'stab him'. Both women sense that they may have lost their only chance of averting catastrophe:

ANN. I hope that wasn't – I do hope that wasn't – THE MOMENT AFTER WHICH – the fulcrum of disaster – I hope not.
SKINNER. Miss one moment, twice as hard next time. Miss the next time, ten times as hard the next.
ANN. All right –

(p. 5)

As the play unfolds, their instinct is proved correct. Another element of Krak's reason evident in the quotation above is the gaze: when asked what he is doing, he replies simply: 'Looking'. The stage directions at the head of the scene, the beginning of the play, commence with

A hill. A MAN, wrapped against the rain, stares into a valley . . .

(p. 3)

He continues to stare until, a full page later, he is asked the object of his gaze by Stucley:

KRAK. I am looking at this hill, which is an arc of pure limestone.

(p. 4)

This is clearly a gaze of some considerable penetration and, combined with Krak's enigmatic taciturnity, represents a significant element in the interactive dynamics of the scene. Later, when Stucley is presented with the results of Krak's deliberations – the plan for the castle – the moment is echoed by the theatrical text in a very spectacular fashion:

Stucley's long stare is interrupted by a racket of construction as a massive framework for a spandrel descends slowly to the floor.

(p. 14)

The visual is of course the rational sense *par excellence*: Krak's visual 'rape' of the hill is a far more effective form of violence than Stucley's botched assault on Cant. It penetrates analytically – the limestone, and imposes geometrical form – the arc. It is this that Ann instinctively recognises, and her words again reinforce the affinity of female body and hill.

As Krak makes good his escape, a fissure emerges in the women's unity. Skinner has heard Ann refer to her husband as physically 'beautiful'; she freely admits that outwardly, at least, she finds him more attractive:

SKINNER. You called him beautiful. Your husband. Beautiful, you said.
ANN. He was. The bone has made an appearance. [*Pause*] Well, he is. HE IS.

(p. 5)

This is indicative of how Ann refuses to deny her own instinctive responses in the interests of ideological or, even, personal commitment. She will not pacify the jealous Skinner by retracting or amending what she has said.

The remark is the hairline crack that opens up a gulf that finally overwhelms their love. Skinner's suspicion makes her ugly in Ann's eyes:

ANN. You go so ugly, in a second, at the bid of a thought, so ugly.

(p. 6)

Taken with the line quoted above, this comment of Ann's is further indication of her tendency to surrender to the aesthetic quality of pure appearances. Although the women seem reconciled, their separation has begun. It is interesting that the feelings concerning the lost opportunity to kill Krak, thereby preventing the castle – the 'fulcrum of disaster' – apply in exactly the same moment to their own relationship. Skinner, at any rate, explicitly states later that the castle and her love are one and the same.

In the dialogue that follows, Skinner talks volubly of their female society and their relationship; it is almost a monologue in that Ann only seems to absorb and humour her lover.

SKINNER. I helped your births. And your conceptions. Sat by the bedroom, at the door, while you took the man's thing in you, shuddering with disgust and trying hard to see it only as the mating of dumb cattle –

ANN. It was –

SKINNER. Yes, and I managed. I did manage. And washed you, and parted your hair. I never knew such intimacy, did you? Tell me, all this unity!

ANN. Never –

(pp. 6–7)

It emerges later that Skinner herself is barren – an irony, considering her militant espousal of nature, that nature should have denied her personal fertility. The womb is frequently seen as the uniquely female attribute which links woman to nature. Skinner, perhaps sensing an evasive complaisance in Ann, is determined to confront her:

SKINNER. . . . Europe is a million miles long, isn't it, how did they pick their way back here, AN ANT COULD PASS THROUGH A BONFIRE EASIER! [*Ann laughs. Skinner looks at her.*] How? [*Pause*]

ANN. Why are you looking at me like that?

SKINNER. How, then?

ANN. I suppose because –

SKINNER. You drew him. [*Pause*]

ANN. What?

SKINNER. You drew him. With your underneath. [*Pause*]

ANN. I do think – if we –
SKINNER. DOWN THERE CALLED TO HIM ACROSS THE SPACES!
ANN. Look –
SKINNER. I HATE GOD AND NATURE, THEY MADE US VIOLABLE AS BITCHES!

(p. 7)

Skinner's espousal of feminist attitudes is very much a consciously willed gesture. She stated earlier how she exerted all her witchcraft, her natural magic, to prevent the Crusaders returning. There is a sense, however, that she doubts profoundly what she professes most passionately, and this contradiction emerges in her outburst here. She has little faith in the efficacy of her witchcraft. Her inclination to hate both 'God' and 'Nature', the latter the conventional feminist antithesis to the patriarchal deity, means that there is for her no ideological refuge in an alien universe. This intense feeling of exposure leads her to invest everything in her relationship with Ann. Her contention here, that Ann drew her husband back, is an accusation that is consistent only with the magical world of seduction, implying as it does, action at a distance and the *reversal of causality*: it would be reasonable to say that Stucley was drawn to his wife – she being the passive object; it is entirely irrational to argue that 'DOWN THERE CALLED TO HIM'. Yet seduction does not absolve the passive object from complicity in seductive action.

According to Baudrillard, to become object is the seductive strategy *par excellence*.[3] The subjective 'truth' of this can be evidenced in the 'irrational' guilt that one can experience at the death of close friends or relatives. Because no direct causal link can be established, reason insists that we dismiss such emotions, even though the feelings are nevertheless real enough. A similar, though less dramatic seductive reversal, is claimed by Stucley when he assaults Cant:

STUCLEY. . . . LOOK WHAT YOU'VE MADE ME DO! . . .

(p. 4)

The scene between Ann and Skinner is cut short by the arrival of Stucley. Skinner leaves and there follows a cataclysmic confrontation between husband and wife. The writing here represents an extraordinary achievement on Barker's part in delineating with exquisite precision a mind fighting disintegration in the face of catastrophe. As I have already observed, Stucley feels for his wife a quasi-religious devotion and he has been dreaming of this moment for years. When he enters, carrying 'a white garment' he wishes her to put on, Ann dismisses Skinner with the injunction 'trust me'. Stucley obviously hears this and part of his mind is disturbed:

STUCLEY. Trust you? Why? [*He looks at her*] You look so – [*Pause*] Trust you? Why? [*Pause*] Imagine what I – if you would condescend to – what I – the riot of my feelings when I look at – [*Pause*] Trust you to do what exactly? [*Pause*] In seven years I have aged twenty. And you, if anything, have grown younger, so we who were never boy and girl exactly have now met in some middling maturity, I have seen your face on tent roofs, don't laugh at me, will you? [*Pause*]

ANN. No.

STUCLEY. That is a ploughman's hag and you – what is it, exactly? [*Pause*] I found the church bunged up with cow and bird dung, the place we married in, really, what – [*Pause*] So I prayed in the nettles. [*Pause*] Very devout picture of young English warrior returning to his domain et cetera get your needle out and make a tapestry why don't you? Or don't you do that any more? [*Pause*] Christ knows what goes on here, you must explain to me over the hot milk at bedtime, everything changes and dreams are ballocks but you can't help dreaming, even knowing a dream is – [*Pause*] It is quite amusing coming back to this I was saying to the Arab every hundred yards I have this little paradise and he went mmm and mmm he knew the sardonic bastard, they are not romantic like us are they, muslims, and they're right! Please put this on because I –

ANN. No. [*Pause*]

(pp. 7–8)

The confrontation is a seductive duel – increasingly desperate on Stucley's part – as he struggles to engage Ann on a level that will reassure him that 'everything is as it was'. Her apparent passivity, and I have discussed passivity above, is a strategy on her part that preserves her seductive enigma: she does not immediately present him with 'a position' – as Skinner would desire. She has already stated that she finds his appearance 'beautiful', so there is an attraction on her part – which is presumably what sustains his 'performance' in this 'moment' for so long. A directly comparable scene – to which I have already alluded – is to be found in the final play of *The Possibilities – Not Him*, where a wife confronts a husband returning after years in the war. She remains veiled for much of the time and the central tension, expressed in the title, is the question of identity – in every sense the man is, paradoxically, both 'same' and 'Other', an ambiguous quality which renders him sexually intensely desirable but, simultaneously, morally dispensible. Here the veil is suggested in Ann's silence and ambiguity.

To return to the passage quoted above, it can be seen that most of Stucley's pauses are invitations to Ann to intervene – invitations or perhaps temptations which, for the most part, she refuses. It is important that the confrontation is presented as genuinely dramatic, i.e. that Ann is, initially at least, 'open' to being seduced. The audience should have the feeling that Stucley might win and, in a way, this outcome is heralded by Skinner's irrational accusation. A 'closed' performance from Ann would invalidate the scene. On his part, Stucley can be seen to be suspended between different levels, which demand an extraordinary technical agility from the actor. There is the persistent nagging suspicion expressed in the 'Trust you? Why?'s; this contrasts starkly with the rapture expressed in the other lines, where Stucley assays to seduce Ann by performing his passion. He is well aware that one seduces with weakness and not only parades his vulnerability but draws attention to it: 'don't laugh at me, will you?' This phrase is interesting in its possible resonances and ambiguities. It is in fact an invitation to Ann to do precisely that – laugh at him – though indulgently rather than derisively. The 'will, you?' can be read as a plea. For her to laugh in this way, would be to release the tension and give him the reassurance he craves. Her 'No', though superficially accommodating his plea, positively reinforces the tension. It must be borne in mind that every instance where Ann refuses a gesture of vulnerability leaves Stucley terribly wounded and confused. At the same time it is also highly likely that Ann also feels his pain but she must bluff and conceal any sympathy from him in order to preserve her will.

This particular refusal causes him to recall his suspicion. He attempts pompously to regain the authority of the high moral ground with restrained indignation at the state of the church. When Ann does not respond, he immediately adjusts this with what is intended to be an attractive demonstration of humility and perhaps an element of pathos: 'So I prayed in the nettles.' Her silence again undercuts his performance, leaving his gesture sadly exposed and ridiculous in its self-conscious calculation. Simply by not responding she imposes, yet does not impose, that meaning on him. He tries to retrieve the gesture and cover the wound by burlesquing himself – a frequent strategy of his: 'Very devout picture . . . make a tapestry why don't you?' As Stucley's agony continues, it becomes clear that he would be prepared to concede anything provided Ann still loved him. His comment about her explaining 'over the hot milk at bedtime' amply illustrates this – and his dependency. Her second 'No' is a direct refusal to comply with his wishes.

In the speech that follows he tries to retrieve their relationship by recalling their wedding night, going on to describe how he has carried her image like a shrine in his heart through all the horrors and degradations of war:

> STUCLEY. . . . what we did in Hungary I would not horrify you with – they got more barmy by the hour. Not me, though. I thought she'll take my bleeding feet in her warm place, she'll lay me down in clean sheets and work warm oils into my skin and food, we'll spend whole days at – but everything is contrary, must be, mustn't it, I who jumped in every pond of murder kept this one thing pure in my head, pictured you half-naked on an English night, your skin which was translucent from one angle and deep-furrowed from another, your odour even which I caught once in the middle of a scrap, do you believe that, even smells are stored. I'm sorry I chucked your loom out of the window, amazing strength comes out of temper, it's half a ton that thing if it's – trust me, what does that mean?
>
> (p. 8)

One of the aspects of Stucley's character – his sense of identity – that should be noted concerns social class. He is self-consciously upper class, very much in the 'stiff upper lip' English public school mode, an influence which also finds expression in some of his more childish behaviour. Later in the play, when he begins seriously to regress, this becomes increasingly obvious:

> STUCLEY. . . . Gang meets at sunset by the camp! The password is – [*He whispers in Krak's ear*] DON'T TELL! [*He goes to leave*] Gang meets at sunset and no girls . . .
>
> (p. 30)

> STUCLEY. . . . Play snowballs with me! I did love boyhood more than anything! Play snowballs!
>
> (p. 25)

The latter request is also addressed to Krak and indicates how Stucley, having failed disastrously with women and sexuality, yearns for the simple pre-pubertal male companionship of 'school'. In the context of the Crusades, such references, though strictly 'prochronistic', are entirely consistent with Barker's dramatic method.

Returning to Stucley's confrontation with Ann, this sense of superior identity asserts itself like a tic in the phrase 'Not me, though', which he repeats four times in this scene. This is a superiority, as the context of the phrase invariably implies, founded in a rigorous self-control. Class is also evident in his disparaging reference to Skinner as 'a ploughman's hag' and it even enters his relationship with his wife: earlier, when he rushed off anticipating catching her in confusion, he imagined her saying 'Oh, my lord'. The language of the fantasy he expresses here – 'I thought she'll take my bleeding feet in her warm place, she'll lay me down in clean sheets and work warm oils into my skin . . .' – carries Biblical connotations, specifically of Mary Magdalene and Christ, a theme which returns later. (It is not difficult to understand why Ann does not want to continue the marriage.) The 'pond of murder' image is equally eloquent: the two concepts are not linked in any obvious way – a pond connoting stillness rather than the violence associated with murder. The image reflects Stucley's psychology: what he does not register is that he brings the violence to the pond by jumping in it; as a gesture, it also expresses a Canute-like fatuity. The reference to Ann's skin as 'deep-furrowed' again reinforces the affinity of woman and earth. Stucley's apology for the loom is yet another desperate climb-down that serves to emphasise his abjection.

It is at this point that Ann utters her first sentence of the encounter; it is highly significant and decisive:

> You've not changed. Thinner but the same. For all the marching and the stabbing. Whereas quietly, here I have.
>
> (p. 8)

It is as if she had been coolly assessing him while he spoke and had finally come to her decision. The physical difference had interested her and she was obviously curious to know if his personality had altered. Ann has, presumably, decided in embarking upon her relationship with Skinner to abandon the husband she knew before the war; the only question that might arise would be whether this was the 'same' man. She concludes that he is and that her decision will therefore stand.

She proceeds without delay to tell him that she has not reciprocated his fidelity. Barker's stage directions indicate again his fascination at the moment of catastrophe:

ANN. No. [*Pause. He is suspended between hysteria and disbelief.*]

(p. 9)

The 'suspension', however, does not last long before giving way to full-blown hysteria. Stucley finds in this moment a revelation of truly firmamental proportions. All his experience is suddenly illuminated by a cruel and shattering light:

STUCLEY. I think when God says – CRUSH THIS BASTARD – I wish there was a priest here, but there isn't so I offer you my version, you hark to my theology – he really is the most THOROUGHGOING OF ALL DEITIES, no wonder we all bow down to him his grasp of pain and pressure is so exquisite and all-comprehending . . . And I have just fought the Holy War on his behalf! Oh, Lord and Master of Cruelty, who has no shred of mercy for thy servants, I worship thee!

(p. 9)

As Ann proceeds to confirm his worst fears, his view of the deity is simultaneously confirmed:

STUCLEY. . . . now tell me she has children by the very interlopers who greeted me as I climbed my very own steps.

ANN. Yes.

STUCLEY. Yes! Yes! I know the source of our religion! It is that He in his savagery is both excessive and remorseless and to our shrieks both deaf and blind!

(p. 9)

Stucley's excesses can appear comical to an audience, but it is important that the performer should not play to this particular effect. His words here are not mere rhetoric, hysterical exaggerations; they are borne out in his subsequent behaviour. The actor playing Stucley needs to counterbalance the potentially ludicrous with a strong sense of the man's terrible pain. There is a tendency to dismiss his claims because they are obviously irrational and 'the balance of his mind' is clearly disturbed. Yet the world of *The Castle*, and Barker's plays in general, is not rational: it is seductive and fatal. Baudrillard:

> The power of events that happen to you without your having willed them, without your having anything to do with it. But not by chance. They happen, and this coincidence touches you, it's

> destined for you. Even if you didn't want it, because you didn't want it, you're seduced by it. That's the whole difference between destiny and chance. For pure chance, even supposing that it exists, is entirely indifferent to us; pure occurrence has nothing seductive about it for us – it's objective, period. It is the strategy of chance we adopt to neutralise an event or attenuate its effect: 'It happened by chance' (Not my doing). . . . And here chance is quite helpful: it's enough to think (difficult as that is) that things happen without reason, or for a maximum of objective reasons (technical, material, statistical) that remove the responsibility from us, and which, in fact, absolve us from whatever the event could contain of a profoundly seductive nature, whose cause we might have wanted to be. . . .[4]

It is in this way that the rational world of reality is reassuring. Reassurance, however, comes at a price, because this draining off of the world's symbolic potency reduces what is left to grey banality.

> Thus from a moral point of view, we may want to protect ourselves by all sorts of alibis (including chance), from the fatal interconnections of events, but from a symbolic perspective it is deeply repugnant to have a neutral world, ruled by chance and thus innocuous and meaningless, and similarly for a world ruled by objective causes; neither one, although easier to live, can resist the fascinating imagination of a universe entirely ruled by a divine or diabolical chain of willed coincidences, that is, a universe where we seduce events, where we induce them and make them happen by the omnipotence of thought – a cruel universe where no one is innocent, and especially not us, a universe where our subjectivity has dissolved (and we joyously accept it) because it has been absorbed into the automatism of events, into their objective unfolding. It has in some way become a world.[5]

In a rational world, the world of 'reality', the fact for instance that Stucley had thrown his knife into the bushes during his previous encounter with Cant, thereby rendering it unavailable for stabbing his wife now, would be ascribed to chance. Chance, however, is not possible in seduction, where everything that happens is destiny. Stucley, who believes in power, must make sense of why an all-powerful deity chooses to treat him in this way. His strategy is to 'joyously accept' his pain, a seductive reversal: in gleefully anticipating new horrors, humiliations and frustrations that subsequently come to pass, he

Figure 5 *The Castle* (dir. Nick Hamm). Ian McDiarmid (Stucley), Pennie Downie (Ann). Royal Shakespeare Company, 1985. Photo: Donald Cooper.

experiences the exhilaration of racing ahead of the mind of God; he 'understands' God and has the perverse satisfaction of willing events – as he says later, on the discovery of a rival castle:

STUCLEY. Everything I fear, it comes to pass. Everything I imagine is vindicated. Awful talent I possess. DON'T I HAVE AN AWFUL TALENT? TALENT?

(p. 34)

When, therefore, he has exhausted his hysteria and regained some self-control, he becomes – in a godlike way – cruel. He considers the possibility of cold-bloodedly murdering Ann:

STUCLEY. . . . I could kill you and no one would bat an eyelid.

(p. 9)

She still feels she can influence him and suggests that he goes away. He pretends to give her suggestion reasonable consideration:

ANN. Don't stay.
STUCLEY. Don't stay?
ANN. No. Be welcome and pass through.
STUCLEY. One night and then –
ANN. Yes.
STUCLEY. What – in the stable, kip down and –
ANN. Not in the stable.
STUCLEY. Not in the stable? You mean I might –
ANN. Don't, please, become sarcastic, it –
STUCLEY. Inside the house, perhaps, we might just –
ANN. Useless sarcasm, it –
STUCLEY. Under the stairs and creep away at first light –
ANN. Undermines your honour –
STUCLEY. WHAT HONOUR YOU DISHEVILLED AND IMPERTINENT SLAG. [*Pause*] You see, you make me lose my temper, you make me abusive, why not stay, it is my home.

(pp. 9–10)

Here, Stucley has acquired a sufficient degree of detachment and self-control to be able to play with Ann's seriousness. The moment she realises he is doing this, she attempts to use his sense of 'honour' to subdue him. He rebuts this tactic by highlighting her hypocrisy in attempting to use it: the epithet 'dishevilled' no doubt refers to her appearance, particularly her hair (much reference is made to her 'plaits' in the course of the action). She tries to challenge Stucley with the suggestion that he should simply go away:

ANN. Go on.
STUCLEY. To where?
ANN. The horizon.
STUCLEY. I own the horizon.
ANN. Cross it then. [*Pause*] I'm cruel, but I do it to be simple. To cut off hopes cleanly. No tearing wounds, I'm sorry if your dreams are spoiled but –
STUCLEY. It is perfectly kind of you –
ANN. Not kind –
STUCLEY. Yes, perfectly kind and typically considerate of you, I do appreciate the instinct but –
ANN. Not kind, I say –
STUCLEY. YES! Down on your knees, now.
ANN. What –
STUCLEY. On your knees now –
ANN. Are you going to be –
STUCLEY. Down, now –
ANN. Childish and –
STUCLEY. Yes, I WAS YOUR CHILD, WASN'T I? [*Pause. He suddenly weeps. She watches him, then goes to him. He embraces her, then thrusts her away.*] PENITENCE FOR ADULTERY!

(p. 10)

Ann's suggestion here is an important article of faith with her: she believes that it is always possible 'to pass on', to begin again somewhere else; she has faith in the permanent possibility of 'the Other' – other places, other times, other people – which is integral to her open seductive nature. Later, she gives to the horribly tortured Skinner the same advice as she offers here to her husband. She herself, pregnant with Krak's child, pleads with him to leave the castle and 'go on over the horizon' with her. He tells her that there is nowhere to go to escape the castle and this brings about her suicide. Her final words –

ANN. . . . [*Pause. She looks at Krak.*] There is nowhere except where you are. Correct. Thank you. If it happens somewhere, it will happen everywhere. There is nowhere except where you are. Thank you for truth. [*Pause. She kneels and pulls out a knife.*] Bring it down. All this.

(p. 39)

To return to the confrontation, Stucley deliberately plays with Ann's sincerity, emphasising her kindness. It would seem, however, that he is now concerned with appearances and with power. He insists – against Ann's sincerity – that she **is** being kind – the appearance of kindness. He also tries to insist on the appearance of submission to his will – the kneeling. Her accusation of childishness causes him to confront her – and simultaneously, perhaps, himself – with the truth about their relationship: 'I WAS YOUR CHILD, WASN'T I?' She does not answer his question – tacitly admitting that he was. This confirmation is a further blow and he collapses in tears, first instinctively seeking, then refusing, the maternal comfort she offers.

Barker prefaces the title page of *The Castle* with the question 'What is Politics, but the absence of Desire . . . ?' When Stucley's desire is violently checked in this scene, he reverts abruptly to power and is seduced by the playful quality in power that is cruelty. His failure to enforce submission on Ann is followed immediately by the arrival of Hush – a decrepit octogenarian left behind by the Crusaders, who has been used by the women to father the children of the new commonwealth. He forces Hush to kneel and confess his sins to his lord:

STUCLEY. . . . Kiss my hands and tell me what you did against me. The more extravagant, the more credence I attach to it, I promise you.
HUSH. I did not praise you in your absence.
STUCLEY. Oh, that's nothing, you mean you abused me, surely?
HUSH. Abused you, yes.
STUCLEY. Excellent, go on.
ANN. This is disgusting.
STUCLEY. Disgusting? No, he longs for his confession!

(p. 11)

In Hush, Stucley has found a subordinate who is prepared to be totally obsequious and say whatever he wants to hear. He is satisfied with appearances. Ann is horrified; the women have accorded dignity and respect to every individual, besides, she is concerned that he will confess his sexual intercourse with her. Eventually, at Stucley's direct prompting, Hush admits to precisely this but, ironically, he is not believed:

HUSH. I lay with her and on others naked and did put my seed in them and –

STUCLEY. Oh, rubbish, it's beyond belief. I hate bad lies, lies that fall apart, there's no entertainment in them.

(p. 11)

The truth or falsity of Hush's confessions is not the significant feature to Stucley: what concerns him in his world of appearances is the purely seductive quality of those appearances. It is interesting that Hush claims to find Stucley's mistreatment of him refreshing:

HUSH. Thank you.
STUCLEY. Thank me, why?
HUSH. Because the worst thing in age is the respect. The smile of condescension, and the hush with which the most banal opinion is received. The old know nothing. Fling them down. They made the world and they need punishing.

(p. 11)

Or is this merely bluff on his part, designed to endear him to Stucley? – who does in fact respond with some signs of affection. His exit lines express his new resolution:

STUCLEY. I cherish nothing, cherishing's out, and what was soft in me has liquefied into a poison puddle. Not to be fooled. That's my dream now, THANK YOU, UNIVERSE! [*Pause*] Educated me. Educated me . . . [*He goes out.*]

(p. 12)

His words here indicate the acceptance of the cruel universe indicated earlier in the scene. This confrontation between Stucley and Ann is of crucial importance to the development of the action, leading on directly in the following scene to the building of the castle – an action clearly linked to the former's state of mind.

The scene ends with Ann briefly upbraiding Hush because she feels he will do or say anything in order to continue his existence and is appalled at his lack of moral sense:

ANN. Why do you love your life so much? [*He stops*] So much that even dignity gets spewed, and truth kicked into blubber, and will itself as pliable as a string of gut? You have no appetite but life itself, I mean breathing and continuing. [*He shrugs*] There can't be a man alive with more children and less interest in the world they grow up in.

(p. 12)

She herself has had the courage to face up to Stucley and defy him – which could easily have cost her her life. She is naturally concerned that her husband should not be able simply to re-impose his former authority. Hush's apparent will to self-subordination, however, is inauspicious in this respect. Her words remind one of the notion that the traditional role of women in the nurture of children predisposes them to have a wider moral concern than men. Her parting shot at Hush expresses a strong resentment of injustice, which nevertheless strikes a characteristically 'matronising' note:

> IF YOU ACHIEVE IMMORTALITY I SHALL BE FURIOUS.
>
> (p. 12)

Scene 2 begins with Batter telling another aged sycophant, Sponge, about his relationship with Krak. Batter is a thug who glories in his own violence but is respectfully fascinated by the intellectual engineer. He feels a sense of proprietorship over the Arab whom he personally saved from slaughter:

> BATTER. . . . And he is mine, in all his rareness, mine, as if I'd birthed him, yes, DON'T LOOK AT ME LIKE THAT, I am his second mother!
>
> (p. 12)

He describes how he was engaged in an orgy of violence after entering Jerusalem – sparing no one. Suddenly he encounters Krak:

> BATTER. . . . And he stared into the little lights of what must have been – my kindness – and I stopped, the dagger in my hand tipped this way . . . and that . . . slippery in my fist. I pondered. AFTER EIGHTEEN STAIRCASES OF MURDER . . . and of course, because I pondered, the genius was safe. Funny. Funny that I pondered when this was the very bugger who designed the fort. . . .
>
> (p. 13)

Batter is describing a moment of pure seduction. His action in 'pondering' is a mystery to him. Krak had apparently touched a quality hitherto completely repressed, something he was wholly unaware of within himself – his 'kindness'. This again is the kind of reversal that is typical of seduction. It is interesting that Batter thinks of this moment as a birth – as if the old Krak had died and a new one been reborn in that instant; certainly the moment marked the commencement of a new life for Krak, and symbolically the character presented in the play is the child of death and destruction. Later, Ann tells him that he needs to be reborn again:

> It is you that needs to be born. I will be your midwife. Through the darkness, down the black canal –
>
> (p. 35)

Batter's present infatuation with Krak is based upon his profound respect for the engineer's violence – a violence he recognises as being far in excess of his own.

After Stucley has dragged in and dusted off his lapsed priest, Nailer, sending him finally to clean the church, Krak reveals his plan for the castle. This again is a crucially seductive moment:

STUCLEY. . . . Go on . . . [*Krak holds out a large sheet of paper.*] Has he made a drawing for me? [*He smiles*] He has . . . [*He looks at Krak beamimg*] The Great Amazer! [*He takes it, looks at it*] Which way up is it? [*He turns it round and round.*] I genuflect before the hieroglyphs but what –

KRAK. No place is not watched by another place. [*Stucley nods*] The heights are actually depths.

STUCLEY. Yup.

KRAK. The weak points are actually strong points.

STUCLEY. Yup.

KRAK. The entrances are exits.

STUCLEY. Yes!

KRAK. The doors lead into pits.

STUCLEY. Go on!

KRAK. It resembles a defence but is really an attack.

STUCLEY. Yes –

KRAK. It cannot be destroyed.

STUCLEY. Mmm –

KRAK. Therefore it is a threat –

STUCLEY. Mmm –

KRAK. It will make enemies where there are none –

STUCLEY. You're losing me –

KRAK. It makes war necessary – [*Stucley looks at him.*] It is the best thing that I have ever done.

[*Stucley's long stare is interrupted by a racket of construction as a massive framework for a spandrel descends slowly to the floor.*]

(p. 14)

The significance of this castle is signalled in the title of the play, and during the course of the action it is physically built on stage – a prominence not often given to a physical object in Barker's plays. I have asserted that his drama follows the Szondi model of interpersonal action, which seeks in general to banish the world of objects. *The Castle* is not a serious exception; if anything, it serves to reinforce the essentially interpersonal focus of his work because the castle in question is first and foremost a mental phenomenon. It arises from and constitutes the interrelations of the characters. This is not to suggest that the castle is not a 'thing-in-itself'; it certainly possesses an identity of sorts. In discussing the focus of Barker's dramaturgy, I have advanced the view that the essential reference point of the 'interpersonal' is not the 'personal' but the 'inter'; the castle is such an 'inter' – a complex but nevertheless identifiable force field of negative energies. The sudden appearance of the castle here emphasises simultaneously its insubstantial/magical quality and its substance: an ambiguity that adds to its seductive potency; it is summoned out of nowhere in response to a profound impulse of the human mind.

Stucley, as we have seen, is bent on a cruel dominance and the castle recommends itself to him for this reason. Historically, Barker is suggesting the castle of the Norman barons: not a system of communal defence like the Celtic or Saxon hill forts but an alien imposition, offensive, the property of a private individual, the function of which was to dominate and exploit the land. According to Professor R. Allen Brown:

> there is no doubt that castles stood for lordship in men's minds and were the expression as well as much of the substance of lordly power and control.[6]

The castle enabled this dominance to be achieved by a relatively small élite of armoured cavalry:

> Because of the developing strength of fortification, because throughout the period of the castle's ascendancy defence was in the ascendant over attack, garrisons could be and were comparatively small; yet that small force could and did hold the district in which it was based unless it was locked up by a full-scale and prolonged investment involving a far greater force. . . .[7]

The fact that the castle was also a residence (and in the post-medieval world this became its principal function) has tended to obscure from a modern perspective some of its more brutal aspects, of which the *Anglo-Saxon Chronicle* provides eloquent testimony:

> For every great man built him castles and held them against the king; and they filled the whole land with these castles. They sorely burdened the unhappy people of the country with forced labour on the castles; and when the castles were built they filled them with devils and wicked men. By night and by day they seized those whom they believed to have any wealth, whether they were men or women; and in order to get their gold and silver, they put them into prison and tortured them with unspeakable tortures, for never were martyrs tortured as they were. They hung them up by the feet and smoked them with foul smoke. They strung them up by the thumbs or by the head, and hung coats of mail on their feet. They tied knotted cords round their heads and twisted it till it entered the brain. They put them in dungeons wherein were adders and snakes and toads, and so destroyed them.[8]

Barker's castle draws upon all these conventional historical functions and associations, yet its initial impact on Stucley is manifestly seductive. In the first place, he is in awe of Krak's intellectual power – 'The Great Amazer' – but does not understand the drawing. Krak elucidates, moving from concrete particularities to abstract generalities. Barker expresses the seduction in a kind of stichomythia which, instead of conveying conflict (as is usual in classical drama), draws the characters together in an escalating vertigo of enthusiasm – Krak for his creativity and Stucley for the power it offers. It is significant that the lord does not understand the wider implications of the edifice: 'You're losing me'. All of Krak's comments can be seen to refer directly to particular physical attributes of the medieval castle, but Barker does also intend that the definition should have a wider resonance. Hence 'No place is not watched by another place' suggests the mass surveillance of modern totalitarianism. His comments about 'heights', 'weak points' and 'entrances' are all reversals, with the weakness/strength antitheses particularly associated with seduction. The castle is a labyrinth of deception and bluff. But, perhaps above all else and for Stucley in particular, it holds all the fascination of an enigma.

In this respect (its seductive, deceptive, enigmatic qualities), Barker's castle suggests Kafka's in the novel of the same name. There, the central figure, Joseph K, arrives in a small town that is entirely dominated by a mysterious and sinister bureaucracy lodged in the castle. He becomes enmeshed in an irrational seductive duel with this authority, a game of bluff and counter-bluff, fought out through an endless series of intermediaries. In typical seductive fashion, K's aim, if it ever existed, is lost in the absorption of the duel and the inexorability of the next move. In this sense, Barker's castle, like Kafka's, suggests a model of the more contemporary state, the origins of which literally date back to the castle society of William the Conqueror. It symbolises politics. At the time of the play's first production, the castle was widely seen as a metaphor for the Cold War arms race, which had recently intensified under Reagan; in this respect, the constant need to improve and extend the castle, the way it seemed to draw everything else into its orbit, its growing threat of total Armageddon (as manifested in Skinner's vision at the end of Act I) bore out this particular connection, as do Krak's comments that the castle will serve to make war necessary. Having said this, the castle is nevertheless a symbol that develops with the action of the play in the direction of less conventional associations.

Very shortly after the sudden and dramatic arrival of the beginnings of the castle, Skinner appears, 'draped in flowers'. She attempts to challenge Krak, as author of the castle, urging him to look at the 'superior geometry' of a flower. She is simply ignored both by him and by Holiday; her feminist protest is brushed aside. She reacts with anger:

> . . . – all right, don't look at it, why should I save you, why should I educate you –
>
> (p. 15)

The antithesis between a masculine culture of rationality (Krak's sharp, hard instruments) and a feminine one of nature and instinct is emphasised by Skinner; however, the manifest failure of her protest causes her to harden her attitude and she menacingly threatens Holiday with her witchcraft. Her instinct is to reject the male altogether. With the arrival of brute force in the shape of Batter, she departs with a gesture of contempt – she flings up her skirts and shows her arse.

Batter and Holiday consider her, and their language, again, connects the female body with the land:

HOLIDAY. . . . are these towers really going to be ninety foot above the curtain? I don't complain, every slab is food and drink to me, but ninety foot? Who are you – it's a quiet country what I see of it – no, the woman's touched, surely?

BATTER. [*contemplatively*] Skinner's arse . . .

HOLIDAY. What?

BATTER. He told me how he lay upon that arse, and she kept stiff as a rock, neither moaning nor moving, but rock. So when the bishop asked for soldiers he was first forward, to get shot of her with Christ's permission.

(p. 16)

Krak has seen the hill as 'an arc of pure limestone'; Ann had described her 'soft' as going 'rigid' at the sight of the engineer. Rock, of course, was the ideal site for a castle because of the difficulty in undermining it. The implication here is that the castle is not purely and simply a product of the masculine but that the resistant feminine is also involved. Significantly and ironically, both Skinner and her husband find in the figure of Christ a solution to their sexual problems

Holiday attempts to quiz Krak about the design of the castle but is met with silence and returns to work. Batter has watched this non-exchange and continues to watch Krak, who for the first time, responds by stating his own feelings:

KRAK. Dialogue is not a right, is it? When idiots waylay geniuses, where is the obligation? [*Pause*] And words, like buckets, slop with meanings. [*Pause*] To talk, what is that but the exchange of clumsy approximations, the false endeavour to share knowledge, the false endeavour to disseminate truths arrived at in seclusion? [*Pause*] When the majority are, perceptibly, incapable of the simplest intellectual discipline, what is the virtue of incessant speech? The whole of life serves to remind us we exist among inert banality. [*Pause*] I only state the obvious. The obvious being the starting point of architecture, as of any other science. . . .

(p. 16)

Krak uses silence to preserve his emotional detachment from the world in which he finds himself. His intellectual supremacy and pride in his reason allow him to dismiss others contemptuously as 'idiots'. Reason does not recognise 'the Other' as such since it considers everything in the universe as reducible to its own laws. As a rationalist he finds verbal communication particularly distasteful because words are never merely definitive – they connote and can, at worst, be ambiguous. His world is secluded – even solipsistic ('we exist among inert banality') and this, according to Levinas, is the very world of reason itself, a world that must exclude and repress all forms of seduction and its irrational magic. As we discover later, Krak's rationalism is also an alibi: the life among 'inert banality' may be sterile and grey – as Baudrillard says:

> . . . from a symbolic perspective it is deeply repugnant to have a neutral world, ruled by chance and thus innocuous and meaningless, and similarly for a world ruled by objective causes. . . .[9]

but on the other hand this view does

> . . . absolve us from whatever the event could contain of a profoundly seductive nature, whose cause we might have wanted to be.[10]

We see later that Krak's attitude has helped him to repress, to some extent at least, his emotional responses to the horrific butchery of his entire family. His character is as much in a state of violent reaction as Stucley's or Skinner's. It is necessary to point out, however, that Krak's scientific detachment here is also a performance for the benefit of his admirer, Batter, from whom he is consciously concealing a personal commitment – the wholesale destruction of his captors. Conceivably, this is the enigma that renders him such a fascinating figure to both Stucley and Batter.

The following scene, Scene 3, begins with Skinner physically tackling Cant, whom she has caught having sex with one of the bricklayers. Cant describes her predicament:

> . . . It was easy before the builders come, but there are dozens of these geezers and they – I gaze at their trousers, honestly I do, whilst thinking, enemy, enemy! I do gaze so, though hating myself, obviously. . . .
>
> (p. 17)

Skinner thinks that she should be punished but Ann finds her anger excessive:

SKINNER. . . . We have done such things here and they come back and straddle us, where is the strength if we go up against the wall skirts up and occupied like that? [*Pause*] I do think, I do think, to understand is not to condone, is it? [*Pause*] I do feel so alone, do you feel that? [*Pause*] It always rains here, which we loved once. I love you and I wish we could just love, but no, this is the test, all love is tested, or else it cannot know its power. . . .

CANT. I'm sorry.

(p. 18)

The problem for the women is power; Skinner begins here to insist on the 'power' of love, on 'strength'; crucially, she accepts the challenge posed by the castle, seeing it as a 'test' of their love. On the other hand, she has moments when she wishes things were as before, and when she says here that she feels alone, she indicates a profound doubt about Ann's love. She does, however, see more clearly than anyone else the long-term implications of the castle:

SKINNER. Where there are builders, there are whores, and where there are whores, there are criminals, and after the criminals come the police, the great heap heaving, and what was peace and simple is dirt and struggle, and where there was a field to stand up straight in there is a loud and frantic city. Stucley will make a city of this valley, what does he say to you?
ANN. Nothing.

(p. 18)

Ann's lack of response in this scene is similar to her behaviour with Stucley. Like Stucley, Skinner is persistently attempting to probe and elicit reassurances that are not forthcoming. Like Stucley, she is continually forced to control her emotions:

> Angry? Me? What? Mustn't be angry, no, be good, Skinner, be tolerant. . . .

(p. 18)

Eventually, Skinner confronts Ann directly:

SKINNER. . . . I WOULD RATHER YOU WERE DEAD THAN TOOK A STEP OR SHUFFLE BACK FROM ME. Dead, and I would do it. There I go. WHAT IS IT? YOU LOOK SO DISTANT.
ANN. I think you are – obsessive. [*Pause*]
SKINNER. Obsessive, me? Obsessive? [*Pause. She fights down something.*] I nearly got angry, then and nearly went – no – I will not – and – wait, the anger sinks – [*Pause*] Like tipping water on the sand, the anger goes, the anger vanishes – into what? I've no idea, my entrails, I assume. I do piss anger in the night, my pot is angerfull. [*Pause*] I am obsessive, why aren't you? [*Pause*] Every stone is aimed at us. And things we have not dreamed of yet will come from it. Poems, love and gardening will be – and where you turn your eyes will be – and even the little middle of your heart which you think is your safe and

> actual self will be – transformed by it. I don't know how but even the way you plait your hair will be determined by it, and what we crop and even the colour of the babies, I do think it's odd, so odd, that when you resist you are obsessive but when you succumb you are not WHOSE OBSESSION IS THIS THING or did you mean my love, they are the same thing actually. [*Pause*] They have a corridor of dungeons and somewhere are the occupants, they do not know yet and she fucked in there, not knowing it, of course, not being a witch could not imagine far enough, it is the pain of witches to see to the very end of things. . . .
>
> (p. 19)

Apart from showing the intensity of Skinner's passion for Ann, there are a number of significant points here. First, Skinner is fully aware of the extent to which the castle will transform everything – 'even the little middle of your heart' – in which case their love will not survive in its present form. Second, Skinner assumes initially that Ann is objecting to her obsession with the castle; it only occurs to her later that she could be referring to the quality of her love. What is interesting is that she declares them to be the same thing. Her love for Ann has become indistinguishable from her resistance to the castle. As a seductive personality Ann perceives Skinner's resistance – in other words her commitment to sustaining particular truths in a hostile environment – as being 'obsessive'. The use of this pejorative word serves yet again to underline their characteristic differences. Skinner also connects the dungeons here with sexuality of a brutal and loveless kind – 'fucked in there'; this is a theme which will be developed later.

The crucial issue that separates the women concerns the most effective way of proceeding: Ann believes she must continue to talk to her husband whereas Skinner thinks there can be no talk between man and woman. Seduction, as far as she is concerned, is mere exploitation with the woman as victim:

> . . . No talking. Words, yes, the patter and the eyes on your belt –
>
> (p. 19)

The distinction she makes here is between a full speech, face to face, and an indirect, manipulative and, ultimately, coercive communication. Skinner is also concerned about Ann having contact with her husband or men in general: she shows this again at the end of the scene when

Ann tries to talk to Krak, who appears from the shadows of his creation:

ANN. Have you no children? I somehow think you have not looked in children's eyes –
SKINNER. DO YOU THINK HE LISTENS TO THAT MAWKISHNESS? [*Pause*]
KRAK. Children? Dead or alive?

(p. 20)

This is the beginning of Ann's attempt to seduce Krak, which, as a strategy, proves to be more effective than Skinner's confrontation. The challenge Krak poses Ann is that of re-awakening his humanity, of discovering his 'kindness', just as he, in his extremity, found Batter's. Though Krak's response here is intended to be disparaging, he does at least respond – divulging personal information and emotion – and Skinner's claim that he does not listen is refuted. Both Krak and Skinner establish their destinies in maintaining a contract of resistance to seduction and change; Skinner asserts the permanence of her bond with Ann:

SKINNER. . . . I am in the grip of this eccentric view that sworn love is binding – [*Krak steps out of the shadows.*]
KRAK. Why not? If sworn hatred is.

(p. 20)

Krak's contract, concealed in and by his reason, is with his butchered family – for vengeance on his captors. Ann, on the other hand, can be seen continually to evade this kind of commitment, an evasion that manifests itself in her evasion of language, her avoidance of speech: she tells Skinner to 'trust' her, to 'trust signs'. As Stucley says:

. . . trust me, what does that mean?

(p. 8)

Act I Scene 4 is principally concerned with Stucley's doctrinal reorganisation of religion in the light of his sufferings during the Crusades and the insights we have seen him pluck from the adversities of his homecoming. It will be recalled that he had concluded God was a sadist. Stucley, as a lord, has the power to re-establish his domain, his world, to accord with his own particular sensibilities. Reactions to this scene tend to be extreme – some find it shockingly blasphemous, others grotesquely comical; the scene is not constructed, however, with sensationalism in mind – the action here is a logical growth from what has preceded it. Things begin dramatically enough with Stucley entering to the praying figure of a recanted Nailer:

STUCLEY. Christ's cock.
NAILER. Yes . . . ?
STUCLEY. IS NOWHERE MENTIONED! [*He flings the Bible at him. Nailer ducks.*]
NAILER. No . . .
STUCLEY. Nor the cocks of his disciples.
NAILER. No . . .
STUCLEY. Peculiar.

(p. 20)

Stucley takes up the conventional view of Christ as the deity made flesh, as the link whereby humanity may be reconciled with its creator – Christ as both fully man and God. Through sexuality, Stucley has known pain and ecstasy; he says

STUCLEY. . . . The deity made manifest knows neither pain nor ecstasy, what use is He?

. . .

STUCLEY. . . . this Christ who never suffered for a woman, who never felt the feeling which MAKES NO SENSE. [*Pause*] He can lend no comfort who has not been all the places that we have.

(p. 21)

He is unable to identify with an asexual Christ and at this particular moment he feels the need for religious consolation, sublimating his thwarted desires. He has decided that Christ 'slagged Magdalene' but that all references to his sexuality have been deleted from the Bible by 'neutered bishops'. He orders Nailer to write the true account of Christ and Magdalene according to his dictation:

STUCLEY. Yes, this is the Gospel of the Christ Erect! [*He is inspired again*] And by His gentleness, touches her heart, like any maiden rescued from the dragon gratitude stirs in her womb, she becomes to him the possibility of shared oblivion, she sheds all sin, and He experiences the – IRRATIONAL MANIFESTATIONS OF PITY WHICH IS – [*Pause. He looks at Nailer, scrawling.*] Tumescence . . . [*Pause*] Got that?

NAILER. Yes . . .

STUCLEY. Now, we are closer to a man we understand, for at this moment of desire, Christ knows the common lot. [*Pause*] And she is sterile.

NAILER. Sterile?

STUCLEY. Diseased beyond conception, yes. So that they find, in passion, also tragedy . . . (*Nailer catches up, looks at Stucley.*) What use is a Christ who has not suffered everything? [*He wanders a little*] They say the Jews killed Christ, but that's nonsense, the Almighty did. Why, did you say?

NAILER. Yes . . .

STUCLEY. Because His son discovered comfort. 'Oh, Father, why hast thou forsaken me?' Because in the body of the Magdalene He found the single space in which the madness of his father's world might be subdued. Unforgivable transgression the Lunatic could not forgive . . . [*Pause. Stucley is moved by his own perceptions. He dries his eyes.*] You see how once Christ is restored to cock, all contradictions are resolved . . .

NAILER. The Church of Christ the Lover . . .

(p. 22)

Stucley's version of Christianity naturally insists on a male dominance. Christ's attraction for Magdalene is described as the irrational manifestation of pity – irrational because the seductive relation involves the element of weakness subduing strength; this relation is seen as redeeming the woman – 'she sheds all sin'. His addition of sterility is again relevant to his own case but, notably, he fastens the blame for this on the woman (Ann, though childless with him, has had children while he was away). All of this describes his perception of himself up until his home-coming when the lunatic/Cruel Father jealously murdered his son – Stucley/Christ – for having discovered 'the single place in which the madness of his father's world might be subdued'. Stucley's emphasis on the physicality of sex – 'cock', 'erect', 'tumescence' – serves to underline the conventionally Freudian analogy of this with the 'erection' of the castle. Skinner talks in Scene 3 of the men 'boring into' the (feminine) 'hill'. Both erections – physical and theological – go together to form a system of total psychological and physical domination. Stucley makes this clear when he ordains Nailer bishop by placing a tool bag on his head and tells him to go out and preach:

STUCLEY. . . . No, I mean invoke Christ the lover around the estate. I mean increase the yield of the demesne and plant more acres.

Plough the woods. I want a further hour off them, with Christ's encouragement, say Friday nights –

(p. 23)

This apparent cynicism in no way invalidates Stucley's own religious feelings: the Church of Christ the Lover is not solely intended as an instrument of exploitation though obviously it lends itself to this and as such, he finds it useful.

When Ann enters, significantly, Stucley finds it necessary to flaunt his success with the castle:

STUCLEY. . . . [*Ann enters. He turns on her.*] We have the keep up with your horror! For some reason I can't guess the mortar is not perished by your chanting, nor do the slates fall when you wave the sapling sticks. [*He goes towards her*] As for windows , none, or fingernails in width. Stuff light. Stuff furnishings!

(p. 23)

In so far as the castle connotes male sexuality, it is a sexuality erected in defiance of the female, violent, hard, and comfortless. Krak had stated in Scene 2 that the castle was not a 'house' – meaning not a domestic place where the masculine and the feminine live together in peace and reconciliation. On the other hand, Stucley is exerting his power to insist on the *appearances* of domestic harmony:

. . . YOU DISCUSS THINGS LIKE A PROPER WIFE! [*Pause*] Terrible impertinence.

(pp. 23–4)

Stucley rushes off to hasten the building work leaving Ann with the newly ordained Nailer, who is mumbling prayers in a corner with the tool bag/mitre on his head. When she tries to remonstrate with him, he vents his detestation of the women's endless discussions:

ANN. Reg, there is a tool bag on your head. [*Pause. He regards her with contempt.*]

NAILER. Oh, you literal creature . . . It was a tool bag . . . it is no longer a tool bag, it is a badge . . . IF YOU KNEW HOW I YEARNED FOR GOD!

ANN. Which god? [*Pause, then patiently*]

NAILER. The God which puts a stop to argument. The God who says, 'Thus I ordain it!' The God who puts his finger on the sin.

ANN. Sin . . . ?
NAILER. WHY NOT SIN? [*Pause. He gets up*] And no more Reg. [*He looks at her, goes out. A wind howls over the stage.*]

(p. 25)

We have already seen how Hush desires his own subordination. This also applies to the more educated and superficially liberal Nailer, whose longing for God is a longing for dogma. He seeks a form of certainty – literally, an end to the argument. At the same time, Nailer's ordination means that he takes on a new authoritative identity – 'no more Reg'. The seductive challenge here is for Nailer to carry off his new identity in defiance of Ann insisting on his old one. In terms of seduction, he must be totally taken in by his own illusion. In this respect, the transubstantiation of the tool bag is both symbolic and of the essence. As a man with a tool bag on his head, Nailer is an object of ridicule; as a bishop in a mitre, he is an object of veneration. It is a severe test but he succeeds triumphantly, marking another step in the advance of the castle and the retreat of the women.

In Scene 5, the final scene of Act I, Stucley appears, cavorting childishly in the wind. The castle has even altered the weather; he asks Krak to make it snow and when a flurry drifts across, he wrestles delightedly with the engineer. Suddenly Krak begins to strangle him and, just as suddenly, stops. Both men are shocked at the hatred Krak has revealed. The effect, however, sends both of them scurrying back to the building. After a pause, Skinner enters with Cant; ironically, it appears she has been trying to use her witchcraft to make it snow – presumably to hinder the progress of the castle. The amount, however, is negligible and she feels that she is losing her power: this for her is a moment of deep despair. There is a clear contrast here between the manipulative and coercive power of Krak's rational technology ('the wind is trapped') and the seductive power of Skinner's witchcraft. (Typically, in Barker's dramaturgy there is no objective indication as to who or what has caused the snow.) At her request, Cant leaves her and, in the snow, she sees a nightmare vision of armoured figures swearing an oath of endless warfare and slaughter. This is another of Barker's male covens, bonded by ritual and secrecy. They dedicate themselves to an orgy of violence –

> – until such tyme we have our aims all maken wholehearte and compleate!

(p. 26)

What these aims might be is not mentioned and seems of little real importance; the aims are a means to the means, which clearly amounts to an infatuation with atrocity:

ROLAND. . . . The flaming cow ran with its entrails hanging out –
BALDWIN. I cut the dog in half –
THEOBALD. One blow –
BALDWIN. The dog in two halves went –
THEOBALD. The head this way –
ROLAND. Its entrails caught around the post –
REGINALD. Double-headed axe went –

(p. 27)

As their voices cease, Holiday, the builder, enters –

Yep? [*He looks around*] Somebody ask for me? [*Pause*]

(p. 28)

– in rational terms possibly in response to Stucley's call earlier in the scene – irrationally, Skinner calls him with her 'underneath', just as she accused Ann of calling Stucley.

HOLIDAY. . . . [*He is about to go, then, looking around him.*] I saw your arse . . . [*Pause*] Excuse me, but I saw your arse – you showed your arse and I – they say you don't like men – which is to do surely with – who you 'ad to do with, surely . . . [*Pause*] Anyway, I saw your arse . . . [*He turns, despairingly, to go*]
SKINNER. All right.
HOLIDAY. [*Stops*] What – you –
SKINNER. All right . . .
[*The walls rise to reveal the interior of a keep. Black out.*]

(p. 28)

In spite of its brevity and relatively undramatic nature, this is a seduction of particular importance. Holiday has paradoxically found seduction in Skinner's gesture of contempt. He is well aware of the consciously intended meaning of the gesture but deliberately tries to subvert that by using it to claim a kind of intimacy between them. Skinner realises this but seizes the opportunity to kill the builder: in this world now dominated by reason, sexuality is the only natural magic left. It is significant that the sexuality in question is soulless and instrumental (Skinner claims later that the builder talked of 'mutual pleasure'.) This 'dirty' quality is emphasised by Holiday's secretive approach – 'looking round him'. The seduction also signals, as the final stage directions of the act indicate, a shift into the interior of the castle.

Act II begins with Krak, in a soliloquy, describing the progress of the building. It appears that Stucley is demanding more and more fortifications, which, in a way, are logical extensions of each other. The process has evidently run away with Krak, who has tried to persuade Stucley that he is secure enough already behind three walls:

> . . . A fifth wall I predict will be necessary, and a sixth essential, to protect the fifth, necessitating the erection of twelve flanking towers. The castle is by definition, not definitive. . . .
>
> (p. 29)

This mushrooming of the castle suggests that the original 'definitive' and exact creation has taken on a life of its own, which involves a constant and 'organic' process of reshaping – a process that is both escalatory and vertiginous. And all this is to confront an enemy who has not yet but 'cannot fail to materialize'.

This is immediately followed by a hue and cry over Holiday's death, which, it is quickly established, is a case of 'woman murder'. Stucley's first concern is to complete the castle and he gives the job to Holiday's foreman, Brian.

> STUCLEY. WHO WILL TRANSLATE MY BLUEPRINTS NOW! [*Ann enters. Stucley turns on her.*] Who did this, you? Oh, her mask of kindness goes all scornful at the thought – what, me? [*He swings on Brian*] YOU DO THE JOB! [*And to Ann*] And such a crease of womanly dismay spreads down her jaw, and dignified long nose tips slightly with her arrogance – what, me? IT STOPS NOTHING, THIS.
>
> (pp. 29–30)

It is important to note that Ann's continuing silent and disapproving presence is a significant factor in Stucley's world. He is infuriated by her passive defiance and assumes here that her response to the murder and her 'womanly dismay' are hypocritical. He sees his most effective counterstrike as being the continuation of the castle but with the addition of a new wall:

> Listen, I think morality is also bricks, the fifth wall is the wall of morals, did you think I could leave that untouched?
>
> (p. 30)

Stucley's comments here foreshadow his reinforcing of morality with the trial of Skinner in the following scene. As I suggested earlier, he is retreating into a woman-hating male camaraderie.

Ann is left alone with Krak and seduces him, overwhelming his resistance with an inexorable feminine power:

ANN. Gravity. Parabolas. Equations. The first man's dead. Gravity. Parabolas. Equations. Are you glad? [*Krak does not move.*] Say yes. Because you are. That's why you're here. Grey head. Badger gnawed about the ears and eyes down, bitter old survivor of the slaughter, loosing off your wisdom when you think yourself alone, I know, I do know, grandfather of slain children, aping the advisor, aping the confidant, but actually, but actually, I do know badger-head, you want us dead. And not dead simply, but torn, parted, spiked on the oaks, limbs between the acorns, a real rucking of the favoured landscape, the peace when you came here made your heart knot with anger, I know, the castle is the magnet of extermination, it is not a house, is it, the castle is not a house . . . [*Pause*] I am so drawn to you I feel sick. [*Pause*] The man who suffers. The man who's lost. Success appals me but pain I love. Your grey misery excites me. Can you stand a woman who talks of her cunt? I am all enlarged for you . . . [*He stares at her.*] Now you humiliate me. By silence. I am not humiliated. [*Pause*]

(p. 30)

First, she confronts Krak with his secret purpose and his reasons for that purpose. After the pause – which one could read as an acceptance of her claim – she states her intense attraction very directly. As is frequent in seduction, it is not his strength but his weakness and hopeless misery that draws her. In stating her sexual attraction in this very direct way, she gives him the opportunity of humiliating her: he attempts to shame her by staring silently. By stating his intention, thereby refusing the shame and exposing the tactic, she redoubles the pressure on him. This is a familiar seductive tactic, which I have already discussed with reference to numerous other Barker characters. Krak decides he has no alternative but to confront the issue:

KRAK. They cut off my mother's head. She was senile and complaining. They dismembered my wife, whom I saw little of. And my daughter, with a glancing blow, spilled all her brains, as a clumsy man sends the drink flying off the table. And her I did not give all the attention that I might. I try to be truthful. I hate exaggeration. I hate the cultivated emotion. [*Pause*] And you say, come under my skirt. Under my skirt, oblivion and compensation, shoot your anger in my bowel, CUNT ALSO IS A DUNGEON! [*Pause*]

ANN. Enthralling shout . . . [*Pause, then he suddenly laughs.*] And laugh, for that matter . . . [*Pause, then he turns to leave.*] I mean, don't tell me that it's virgins you want, the unmarked flesh, untrodden map of girlhood, the look of fear and unhinged legs of – [*He returns, slaps her face into silence. Pause*] You have made my nose bleed . . .
(p. 30)

When he describes the various fates of his family, Krak appears to be trying to put his emotions into perspective by distancing himself from them: he is being objective and rational – remaining in control. The seductive ingredient of these qualifications, however, is guilt; this is particularly clear when he talks of his neglected daughter. When he turns savagely on Ann with 'CUNT IS ALSO A DUNGEON', it is because he sees no possibility of salvation for himself in what she is offering: he risks losing his absolute autonomy and opens himself up to new tortures. Instead of addressing his accusation, she rejoices in his emotional release. He tries to counter this by releasing his intensity in laughter, simultaneously signalling contempt: again, this is unprecedented for him (Ann commented earlier that he never smiled). As a rebuff it fails. Finally, he tries to escape by walking out but she taunts him into returning and slapping her – a crucial loss of self-control. In a metaphorical sense, it is almost as if she systematically breaches each of the walls he refers to at the beginning of the scene.

It is worth commenting at this point on Krak's name, which in the historical context of the Crusades, suggests the famous castle, Krak des Chevaliers. *Krak* or *kerak* is the Levantine Arabic word for 'fortress'. Krak too *is* the castle, both by name and by nature, in that he exists behind an elaborate system of defences. Barker is also evoking the English homophone 'crack'; appropriately, the first phrase cited in connection with this word in the *Concise Oxford Dictionary* is 'crack of doom'; even more significant in the context of the play is the slang use of the word to denotate the female sexual organs (see Partridge's *Dictionary of Slang and Unconventional English*). Krak's obsessive drawing of fortifications becomes obsessive drawing of 'cunt' later in the play.

Another significant link connects Krak with Pain in *Crimes in Hot Countries*; T.E. Pain is Barker's version of Lawrence of Arabia. Like Krak, Pain is very consciously the 'genius', the man of massive intellectual inspiration; like Krak, he is located 'in exile' – not merely in the 'hot country' but in the cultural desert of the 'other ranks' of the British Army, casting his perfectly phrased pearls before swinish squaddies; like Krak, he enjoys a privileged if ambiguous relationship with authority which is mesmerised by his seductive charisma; on another level, the violent and thuggish Music's attraction to Pain's intellectual sophistication parallels Batter's fascination with Krak. Both geniuses have a passion for military strategy and classical logic. Barker has reversed the situation of T.E. Lawrence in the case of Krak; instead of an Englishman devising Arab military strategy in Arabia, an Arab devises English military strategy in England. The historical Lawrence was a devotee of medieval castles, travelling in 1905–1910 thousands of miles on foot and by bicycle in Britain, France, Syria, and Palestine to visit notable sites. The fruit of these investigations was the thesis he submitted for his degree at Oxford, later published under the title *Crusader Castles* (1936).[11] In it, he enthuses over Krak des Chevaliers as 'perhaps the best preserved and most wholly admirable castle in the world'.[12] A notable feature of this fortress is its great south wall, known to Arab historians as 'the mountain', which, towards its base, eschews the vertical in favour of a steep slope – a feature described in architectural parlance as a 'batter'. Of this, Lawrence says:

> The reason for making the wall with so great a batter and such thickness – nearly 80 feet – is a little hard to find. Against an earthquake it would be useful perhaps, though no part of Crac has been damaged by one: the castle stands on rock, so mining was not greatly to be feared: and half the thickness would have been secure against any ram that ever was imagined.[13]

Krak des Chevaliers provides not only the name – Batter – but also the enigma of a strength massively in excess of any conceivable demands that might be made on it – bringing to mind Stucley's 'unknown enemy . . . who does not yet exist but who cannot fail to materialize'(p. 29). Lawrence also remarks on the entry to Krak, which is via a vaulted passageway described as 'almost dark', 'dark', 'steeply ascending', and 'most confusing'. When Ann proposes to Krak that they leave the castle, she says:

> It is you that needs to be born. I will be your midwife. Through the darkness, down the black canal –
>
> (p. 35)

thus making yet another symbolic connection between the castle's architecture and the human body. Finally, there is the 'historical'

Lawrence himself: dazzling seducer of establishment luminaries, the enigmatic 'genius' with iron self-control and tortured sexuality – but also a supreme bluffer, poseur, charlatan, and betrayer who serves to remind us that Krak, although he claims to 'hate the cultivated emotion', is certainly not beyond cultivating appearances: the all-rational military 'genius', whom Stucley refers to as 'the Great Amazer', is also a performance.

Act II Scene 2 is a trial scene. Barker has always been particularly adept at satirising the protocols and etiquettes of groups who consider themselves social élites – especially, as is usually the case, when these comprise an all-male preserve. The scene begins with the arrival of the two prosecutors. Nailer puts the case against Skinner in a manner that is erudite, objective, balanced, and apparently motivated by a selfless concern for the general good. The informal chat the two have before formal proceedings begin, however, subverts completely their 'official' performance:

NAILER. Thank you for coming.
POOL. Thank you for asking me.
NAILER. The rigours of travel.
POOL. Not to be undertaken lightly.
NAILER. No, indeed. Indeed, no. His trousers were down.
POOL. So I gather.
NAILER. I do think –
POOL. The absolute limit.
NAILER. And misuse of love.
POOL. Make that your angle.
NAILER. I will do.
POOL. The trust which resides in the moment of –
NAILER. Et cetera –
POOL. Most cruelly abused. Make that your angle.
NAILER. Thank you, I will.
POOL. Fucking bitches when your goolies are out . . .
NAILER. [*To the court*] A man proffers union – albeit . . .

(pp. 30–1)

It can be seen here how formal pleasantries rapidly lead on through a process of hints to expressions of male solidarity in outrage and, finally, deep misogyny. The mask of Nailer's rhetoric is exposed before he begins. What is 'different' about this trial is that Skinner's crime is not simply murder (in the world of the castle, violent death does not *per se* excite moral outrage), but 'woman murder'. Once Nailer starts his peroration, Barker intercuts this with a speech from Skinner that is addressed not to the court but to Ann; in terms of the staging, this needs to be produced in a stylised manner to suggest the two speeches are in fact going on simultaneously (there is no communication whatsoever between defendant and prosecutor – they exist on different planes). Nailer's case is that in offering sexual intercourse, the man lays aside 'all those defences which the male by nature transports in his demeanour'.

> NAILER. A crime therefore, not against an individual – not against a single man most cruelly deceived . . . but against that universal trust, that universally upheld convention lying at the heart of all sexual relations. . . . And thereby threatening not only the security of that intimate love which God endowed man with . . . for peace and relief but . . . the very act of procreation itself . . .
>
> (p. 31)

The siege mentality of the castle serves to generate hysterical fears about any remaining areas of vulnerability or insecurity. The work of the court therefore seeks to establish and encase the sexual relation 'within a secure framework of law'. External law being, as I have argued, fundamental to the control-based world of rationality – as opposed to the immanent rule of seduction.

Dramatically, the most powerful aspect of the scene is contributed by Skinner. She is brought into court having been hideously tortured so that her utterances have the appearance of abjection and at times madness. Her concern is to speak to Ann and to express her anger:

> ANN! . . . ANN! . . . WHERE ARE YOU, YOU BITCH – no, mustn't swear –
>
> (p. 31)

The physical memory of the torture she has suffered causes her to check her outbursts and apologise abjectly: as she says of her tormenters:

> – beg pardon – I have this – tone which – thanks to your expertise is mollified a little –
>
> (p. 32)

She attributes her anger to the unaccustomed exposure to daylight and tries desperately to reassure all that she is genuinely 'reformed':

SKINNER. I am not ill-tempered as a matter of fact, I don't know where that idea's come from that I – and anyway I know you hate it, loudness and shouting, you do, such delicate emotions and I – THEY HAVE DONE AWFUL THINGS TO ME DOWN THERE – do my best to be – to be contained – that way you have, you – THERE IS A ROOM DOWN THERE AND THEY DID TERRIBLE THINGS TO ME – I mean my cunt which had been so – which we had made so – THANKS TO YOU WAS DEAD – so it wasn't the abuse it might have been, the abuse they would have liked it to be had it been a living thing, were it the sacred and beautiful thing we had found it out to be and – am I going on, I do go on – are you – so thank you I hated it and the more they hurt it the better I – I was actually gratified, believe it or not, yes, gratified –

(p. 31)

The words in capitals suggest breaches in Skinner's self-control and should be blurted – almost involuntarily. Barker deliberately seeks to make the words 'DOWN THERE' ambiguous, intending them to signify both dungeon and 'cunt'. This conforms to the symbolic theme of equating the land with the female body. The dungeon is, conventionally, where the edifice of the castle penetrates the land – under ground. The most significant statement, however, is Skinner's assertion that she willed the torture of her sexual organs; she wanted them to suffer because Ann had betrayed their love ('my cunt which . . . THANKS TO YOU WAS DEAD'). This is another example of a crucial seductive reversal, an acceptance and willing of calamity that parallels Stucley's acceptance of the lashes of fate administered to him by a cruel and sadistic deity.

The central thematic of the scene is of a tortured sexuality – in the widest possible sense of that phrase. Skinner's words referring to her own sufferings are clearly relevant to the institutionalised misogyny of patriarchal society:

> They think of everything – they do – imaginations – you should see the – INVENTION DOWN THERE – makes you gasp the length of their hatred – the uncoiled length of hatred –
>
> (p. 32)

Peering round the court, Skinner is unable to see Ann and asks for a stool to sit on. When one is brought, she leaps back from it expecting a trap, then in complete contradiction to her alarm, she sinks wearily onto it – as if she didn't care whether it bit her or not; this sudden change of attitude is typical of her fragmented personality in this scene.

If Skinner here seems remote and disconnected from the court, Stucley is even more so:

STUCLEY. . . . Having hewn away two hills to make us safe, having knifed the landscape to preserve us we find – horror of horrors – THE WORST WITHIN. [*Pause, he looks at all of them.*] I find that a blow, I do, I who have reeled under so many blows find that – a blow. Who can you trust? TRUST? [*He shrieks at them, the word is a thing butted at them.*] I say in friendship, I say in comradeship, I say without malice YOU ARE ALL TRAITORS!

(p. 32)

Stucley's intensifying paranoia in this scene clearly marks another stage in the escalating process of the castle: he goes on to insist on all the repressive measures of a police state. Nailer shows that he understands his role as ideologist:

STUCLEY. . . . I have changed my view of God. I no longer regard Him as an evil deity, that was excessive, evil, no. He's mad. It is only by recognizing God is mad that we can satisfactorily explain the random nature of – you say, you are the theologian.
NAILER. It appears to us He was not always mad –
STUCLEY. Not always, no –
NAILER. But became so, driven to insanity by the failure and contradiction of His works –
STUCLEY. I understand him!

(pp. 32–3)

Stucley requires a deity fabricated in his own image. As a tyrant, giving ear only to what he wants to hear, he presumably surrounds himself with people like Nailer. From this scene on, his presence conveys a sinister remoteness that most of us are familiar with only from witnessing on television the grotesque charades of third-world dictators. Particularly bizarre and embarrassing is his reference in open court to his sexual incontinence:

STUCLEY. . . . I sleep alone in sheets grey with tossing, I cannot keep a white sheet white, do you find this? Grey by the morning. Does anyone find this? The launderers are frantic.
BATTER. Yes.

STUCLEY. You do? What is it?
BATTER. I don't know . . . it could be . . . I don't know . . .
STUCLEY. Why grey, I wonder?

(p. 33)

While it is necessary to express agreement with him, Batter finds it impossible to state the obvious. Like Skinner, Stucley presents another aspect of tortured sexuality. Barker also makes Stucley express himself in a manner similar to Skinner, suddenly blurting out statements that appear involuntarily to voice semi-repressed fears and intuitions:

STUCLEY. THEY ARE BUILDING A CASTLE OVER THE HILL AND IT'S BIGGER THAN THIS. [*Pause*] Given God is now a lunatic, I think, sadly, we are near to the Apocalypse. . . .

(p. 33)

The first of these sentences should sound almost as if spoken by another voice from deeper within Stucley; when he reverts to character to speak the second sentence, it should be performed as if the first had not been uttered. His intuition about the other castle – it is at this stage pure intuition, though confirmed in the following scene – together with his thoughts on the Apocalypse, strongly suggest that he is in the grip of a powerful death wish.

Suddenly, Skinner sees Ann and leaps to her feet:

SKINNER. WHAT HAVE YOU DONE TO YOUR HAIR? [*Pause*] It's plaited in a funny way, what have you – IT'S VILE. [*Pause*] Well, no, it's not, it's pretty, vile and pretty at the same time, DID YOU TAKE HIM IN YOUR MOUTH, I must know.

(p. 33)

It will be recalled that Skinner had said previously that the castle would affect everything – even the way Ann plaited her hair; she is particularly shocked because her former lover's appearance strikes her as being intended to please someone else. A violent spasm of jealousy gives way after a pause to melancholy reflection:

SKINNER. . . . This floor, laid over flowers we once laid on, this cruel floor will become the site of giggling picnics, clots of children wandering with music in their ears and not one will think, not one, A WOMAN WRITHED HERE ONCE. The problem is to divest yourself of temporality, is that what you do? [*She looks at Nailer*] I

> gave up, and longed to die, and yet I did not die. That all life should be bound up in one randomly encountered individual defies the dumb will of the flesh clamouring for continuation, life would not have it! I hate you, do you know why, because you prove to me that nothing is, nothing at all is, THE THING WITHOUT WHICH NOTHING ELSE IS POSSIBLE.
>
> (p. 33)

Skinner said in Act I Scene 3 that it was 'the pain of witches to see to the very end of things'; here, she sees beyond the physical end of the castle to the contemporary world with its indifference to her struggles; the word 'writhed' is deliberately ambiguous implying both sexual love and torture. Her comment about temporality indicates that she recognises this awareness of time or memory is precisely the source of her pain. Nailer, whom she addresses here, seems to have no difficulty in consigning to oblivion all previous commitments and professions of faith in the interests of physical survival – 'the dumb will of the flesh clamouring for continuation'. She sees that her commitment to Ann ('one randomly encountered individual') is opposed by life itself – which is why she wanted to die. Life itself, however, would not let her die. She hates both Ann and life because they have proved to her that 'the thing without which nothing is possible' – love – does not exist. In banal terms, she is disillusioned. Her language indicates that she has succumbed to the world of banality – of rationalism. Ann is referred to as 'one randomly encountered individual' but the concept of the random is essentially rational; in seduction, it does not exist because everything is destiny. In Act I Scene 3, Krak stated:

> . . . The whole of life serves to remind us that we exist among inert banality.
>
> (p. 16)

Skinner, who insisted that there was no separate 'love life', that 'the colour of the love stains everything', that one did not step from one life to the other – 'banality to love, love to banality' (p. 19) – now lives 'amongst inert banality'.

Skinner's performance here is based on the confident assumption that she is about to be executed – which is what she wants; death will at least provide the oblivion she seeks. However, in a fit of bravado, she dismisses the right of the court and challenges Stucley to pass sentence – on the grounds that only those who have suffered like herself should have this prerogative. In so doing, she underestimates his cruelty. What

Stucley had found so irresistibly seductive about his deity was not death, as Skinner states earlier, but 'his grasp of pain and pressure' (p. 9). He takes up Skinner's challenge and sentences her to the embrace of the rotting corpse of her victim:

STUCLEY. Tie her to the body of her victim. [*Pause*]
SKINNER. Tie her to –
STUCLEY. And turn her loose.

(p. 33)

She is horrified.

Scene 3 begins with massive explosions and panic. Krak tells Stucley that there is – in actual fact – another castle in the East:

KRAK. You knew, and I knew, there could not be only this one, but this one would breed others. And there is one. Called the fortress.
STUCLEY. Bigger than this . . .
KRAK. Bigger. Three times the towers and polygonal. With ravelins beyond a double ditch, which I never thought of . . . [*Stucley stares for a moment in disbelief.*]
STUCLEY. Everything I fear, it comes to pass. Everything I imagine is vindicated. Awful talent I possess. DON'T I HAVE AN AWFUL TALENT? TALENT?

(p. 34)

Barker's writing demonstrates very clearly how Stucley's death wish works. It is significant that his line – 'Bigger than this . . .' – is not a question; by positing the other castle in his imagination, ultimately, he conjures it into existence. He is seduced by the power of his capacity to envisage catastrophe, his intuitive comprehension of a cruel fate. He orders massive increases in the fortifications of the castle, increases which confound Krak. After a fourth boom, Stucley demands to know what the noise is:

KRAK. The coming of the English desert . . . [*Pause*]
STUCLEY. Yes . . .
NAILER. Almighty! Almighty!
STUCLEY. Yes . . .
NAILER. Oh, Almighty, Oh, Almighty . . . !
STUCLEY. Extinction of the worthless, the obliteration of the melancholy crawl from the puddle to the puddle, from the puddle of the

maternal belly to the puddle of the old man's involuntary bladder . . . Good . . . and they make such a fuss of murder . . . NOT ME THOUGH.

(p. 34)

Stucley assents to universal destruction, the extinction of a life that is worthless. His final words reassert his rigorous self-control, his stoicism and his sense of superiority. The events of this scene serve to intensify the doom-laden atmosphere and sense of looming catastrophe.

The others all depart leaving Krak, who reflects uneasily on the new castle or perhaps rather on the mind of its designer – an enigma to him. Ann enters, pregnant, and proposes that they leave together:

ANN. We find a rock.

KRAK. Stink of death to English woods. Hips on the fence. Flies a noisy garment on the entrail in the bracken.

ANN. I have your child in here.

KRAK. The trooper boots the bud open and sends my – [*Pause*] said my, then . . . [*Pause. He smiles.*] Error.

(p. 35)

The present situation seems to present the imminent fulfilment of Krak's secret purpose – the total destruction of his captors and their land. Here he attempts to cling to this strategy in the face of Ann insisting that he cannot simply divorce himself from life in the way that Stucley has; he is involved through his child. Because his present life, as birthed by Batter, is in fact dedicated to death, she offers herself as midwife for yet another birth. He tells her (and there is a clear parallel here with nuclear warfare) that there is no refuge or escape from the death-engines of the castle. Ann turns on him with what is her first truly violent outburst:

ANN. ALL RIGHT, WISDOM! ALL RIGHT, LOGIC! [*Pause*] I have a child in here, stone deaf to argument, floats in water, all pessimism filtered, lucky infant spared compelling reasons why it should acquiesce in death. [*She turns to go.*]

KRAK. IS THERE ANY MAN YOU HAVE NOT COPULATED WITH? [*She stops*] I wonder. . . .

(p. 35)

What Ann is roused to anger by is the spiritual and ideological climate of acceptance of death, the malaise and miasma which dominate the castle; also, as I have remarked already, she has always believed in the possibility of passing on – of 'Otherness'; now she finds herself trapped. As she turns to go, Krak attempts to distance himself from her and the child. I think that the stage direction here – 'She stops' – is particularly important, for it suggests that his comment has wounded her deeply. His follow-up – 'I wonder' – indicates that he realises this and is, in a clumsy way, an attempt to retract.

Before she can leave, however, Skinner enters with the corpse of Holiday chained to her front, an object of contempt and abuse. The stage directions say she is 'a grotesque parody of pregnancy' and, as such, she confronts the pregnant Ann. Her first statements all concern the practicalities of coping with her condition, which she ironically compares to pregnancy: 'much morning sickness all times of the day'. Her condition has brought about two horrific discoveries: first, she has gotten used to it and in fact quite accepts it (when Ann suggests she goes elsewhere to 'find peace and rub the thing off you', she refuses: 'Yes to punishment. Yes to blows'). Second, she has discovered she can live without others and seems to take a certain pride in the uniqueness of her state. Ann weeps in despair but Krak stares fixedly at Skinner throughout the scene in much the same way as he stared at the hill in Act I, building a dramatic tension. Ann's distress is, at least in part, because she feels she is responsible for Skinner's plight – a notion Skinner herself derides, mockingly warning Krak:

SKINNER. . . . careful! She's after your suicide! Hanging off the battlements for love! The corpse erect! Through her thin smile the knowledge even in death she got you up! [*Mimicking*] Did I do this? [*She turns to Ann*] This is my place, more stones the better and pisspans, pour on! You and your reproductive satisfactions, your breasts and your lactation, dresses forever soddened at the tit, IT DID GET ON MY WICK A BIT, envy of course, envy, envy, envy of course. I belong here. I am the castle also.

ANN. You do suck your hatreds. You do – suck – so. And he – also sucks his.

(p. 36)

Skinner's attitude to Ann manifests a pattern fairly similar to Stucley's: passionate love followed by violent and anguished hatred, followed by a settled hatred as expressed here; it will be recalled that Stucley similarly mimicked and sneered at his wife's femininity. Skinner sees Ann here as deliberately thirsting for the anguish and suffering she leaves in her wake – even though she pretends that it distresses her.

Skinner also admits her envy of Ann's fertility, an envy that apparently was always there: her final words here indicate that she feels it is because of this envy that she 'belongs' – she too is the castle. Ann's comment points out how Skinner, Krak and Stucley are comparable in the way they feed off negative emotions – a few lines further on she specifies pessimism and fear. Her words are illustrated immediately when a group of hooded prisoners shuffle in; Skinner gleefully directs them to the dungeon and mockingly anticipates what is in store for them. Batter, who is conducting them, confirms her status as an accepted part of castle life by greeting her in a familiar and almost friendly fashion:

BATTER. English summer . . .
SKINNER. Fuckin' 'ell . . .
BATTER. [*As he passes.*] Take care . . .
SKINNER. Will do . . .

(p. 37)

Ann, unable to contemplate this, has already fled, so when Batter and the prisoners file out, the silent and staring Krak is left alone with Skinner who, unconcernedly, starts to eat an apple.

To Skinner's amazement, Krak suddenly kneels at her feet:

KRAK. The Book of Cunt. [*Pause*]
SKINNER. What book is that?
KRAK. The Book of Cunt says all men can be saved.

(p. 37)

Beginning to doubt the value of the science with which he has identified himself, he sees in Skinner an alternative to the beliefs he confidently proclaimed. It will be recalled that she had confronted him in Act I Scene 2 draped in flowers and ordered him to contemplate the 'superior geometry' of a flower; then, he completely ignored her. What draws him to nature, however, is not the flower but 'cunt':

KRAK. Where's cunt's geometry? The thing has no angles! And no measure, neither width nor depth, how can you trust what has no measurements? Don't tell them I came here. . . .

(p. 37)

Skinner seduces Krak intellectually; he sees her essentially as an enigmatic source of female wisdom (the symbolism of the apple-eating strongly suggests this): whereas before her conscious struggle to move him did nothing, he is seduced now by her self-possession and indifference. Krak's 'confession' to Skinner shows that he is in a state of confusion. Ann has sexually seduced him and in that seduction he finds the promise of salvation:

KRAK. . . . She pulled me down. I did not pull her. She pulled me. In the shadow of the turret, in the apex of the angle with the wall, in the slender crack of thirty-nine degrees, she, using the ledge to fix her heels, levered her parts over me. Shoes fell, drawers fell, drowned argument in her spreading underneath . . . [*Pause*] European woman with her passion for old men, wants to drown their history in her bowel . . . ! [*Pause*]

SKINNER. Scares you . . .

(p. 37)

Krak's description of Ann's actions here with the references to his fortifications is intended to suggest the breaching of the castle; she takes him by force. What had attracted Ann to him was his pain, his history; this she absorbs into her body, providing him with oblivion and peace. Krak is compulsively drawn to questioning Skinner here because she had known Ann as a lover. The possibility of salvation, however, lies in 'cunt' – which has no fixed geometrical properties and, as such, cannot be controlled in the way that rational constructs can. Krak is terrified at the possibility of his fate being beyond his control. His repeated plea – 'Don't tell them I came here' – suggests that commerce with Skinner is forbidden in spite of the fact that her presence is tolerated. The arrival of Cant and Hush with food for her indicates that she is becoming a focus of unarticulated dissent within the castle; her previous opposition, together with her apparent martyrdom, will confer an aura of deity upon her. As Harriet Walter, who played Skinner in the first RSC production of the drama in 1985 said:

> . . . the only time she wins back support is when she is considered a figure who is emptied, who has conquered pain and is above and beyond desire and therefore a political totem, the perfect leader. She attracts the villagers with their thought of that personal vacuum. . . .[14]

The realisation nevertheless comes as a shock to Skinner:

SKINNER. Oh, God, Oh, nature, I AM GOING TO BE WORSHIPPED.

(p. 37)

These words suggest she sees this as yet another malicious trick played by a cruel and ironic fate: she has just accommodated herself to total abjection; she is not actually being worshipped yet, but she suddenly intuits the next cards she will be dealt because, like Stucley, she understands and can anticipate the mind of God.

In Scene 4, Stucley confronts Krak with an accusation of treachery, claiming that he has personally witnessed him trading drawings with the engineer of the Fortress. Krak is apparently unimpressed by this; his pride in his creation, which in Act I Scene 2 he claimed could not be destroyed, has been shattered:

KRAK. Gave him all my drawings. And got all his. They are experimenting with a substance that can bring down walls without getting beneath them. Everything before this weapon will be obsolete. This, for example, is entirely redundant as a convincing method of defence –

(p. 39)

In broad historical terms this can be seen to correspond to the redundancy of vertical fortification in the face of massive advances in firepower. In terms of the three classic elements of military strategy – armour, firepower and mobility – the castle represents the zenith of armour. Defence from firepower thereafter was sought by digging down into the earth – as in trench warfare. Krak, however, has lost interest in military architecture and is obsessively drawing 'cunt' – 'in 27 versions'. It is interesting to note the element of unlikely continuity between castle and 'cunt' in this respect. The former had started life as a single sharply and geometrically definitive drawing; gradually, as more walls and towers were added, Krak was forced to admit that the definition was lost – 'The castle is by definition, not definitive. . . .' Now he pours out drawing after drawing in an attempt to define the indefinite. (And here there is a parallel with another 'genius' whose name is linked to military architecture – Leonardo da Vinci.) As was the case with Ann, in spite of his outrage, it is clear that Stucley is prepared to overlook or turn a blind eye to any treachery, provided Krak humours him and they carry on with the game:

STUCLEY. DON'T DRAW CUNT. I'M TALKING! [*Pause*] This is a crisis, isn't it? Is it, or isn't it? You sit there – you always have been so – had this – manner of stillness – most becoming but also sinister – dignity but also malevolence – easy superiority of the captive intellect – IS THAT MY WIFE'S BITS – I wouldn't know

Figure 6 *The Castle* (dir. Nick Hamm). Paul Freeman (Krak). Royal Shakespeare Company, 1985. Photo: Donald Cooper.

them – what man would – I know, you see – I am aware – I do know everything – I do – I think you have done this all to spite me – correct me if I'm wrong –

KRAK. Spite –

STUCLEY. Spite me, yes –

KRAK. Spite? I do not think the word – unless my English fails me – is quite sufficient to contain the volume of the sentiment . . .

(p. 38)

The relationship between Krak and Stucley has also been a seductive duel – a game of challenging each other by constantly escalating the castle: now one has demanded staggering additional defences, now the other. Latterly Krak, who has lost his positive, creative fascination with the castle, has challenged Stucley by his relationship with Ann and by his blatant treachery: he is pushing the limits of Stucley's dependence on the castle and on himself. Stucley, for his part, is prepared to use his weakness and dependence to seduce Krak – 'This is a crisis, isn't it?' Even when the moment of confrontation is forced upon him and he voices the ultimate, unspeakable secret – that Krak had intended the castle to destroy him (which he knows and Krak knows he knows and he knows Krak knows he knows, etc.) – he plays his weakness in the rider 'correct me if I'm wrong'. Ann had accused Krak of 'aping the adviser, aping the confidant'; the problem for Krak is how far he is seduced by his own role-playing – and by Stucley. This moment, for the latter, represents another catastrophe similar to his confrontation with Ann in Act I Scene 1. What amazes him is the magnitude of Krak's anger and the measure of his self-control:

STUCLEY. You blind draughtsman . . . all the madness in the immaculately ordered words . . . in the clean drawings . . . all the temper in the perfect curve . . . [*He pretends to flinch.*] MIND YOUR FACES! DUCK HIS GUTS! INTELLECTUAL BURSTS!

(p. 38)

He attempts to refuse Krak's 'spite' in the same way that Ann refused Krak's attempt to humiliate her:

STUCLEY. . . . But I am not spited. If you do not feel spited no amount of spite can hurt you, Christ was the same, NIGEL! [*Pause*] We burn people like this. Who give away our secrets. Burn them in a chair.

Fry them and the fat goes – human fat goes, spit . . . ! Does – spit!

(p. 39)

As he did with Skinner, Stucley seeks here to turn the tables on Krak by an act of malevolent imagination that takes his opponent's move and caps it – a seductive reversal: he will return Krak's 'spite' by physically transforming him into 'spit(e)'. While a desire to punish Krak might be deemed rational, the particular form it takes here is consonant only with the pure artifice of seduction.

At this point Ann enters and looks at them:

ANN. The ease of making children. The facility of numerousness. Plague, yes, but after the plague, the endless copulation of the immune. All these children, children everywhere and I thought, this one matters, alone of them this one matters because alone it came from love. But I thought wrongly. I thought wrongly. [*Pause. She looks at Krak*] There is nowhere except where you are. Correct. Thank you. If it happens somewhere it will happen everywhere. There is nowhere except where you are. Thank you for truth. [*Pause. She kneels, pulls out a knife.*] Bring it down. All this. [*She threatens her belly. Pause.*]

STUCLEY. You won't. [*Pause*] You won't because you cannot. Your mind wants to but you cannot, and you won't. . . . [*Pause. He holds out his hand for the knife. She plunges it into herself. A scream. The wall flies out. The exterior wall flies in. In a panic,* SOLDIERS. *Things falling.*]

(p. 39)

Ann's speech here should be considered in the light of Krak's sneer in the previous scene when he rejected her: 'IS THERE ANY MAN YOU HAVE NOT COPULATED WITH?' – as well as Skinner's and Stucley's jibes at her fertility. She is shattered by what she sees as her failure in love with Krak, and has decided to kill herself and her child. She has taken the logic of Krak's assertion that there is nowhere else and has intuited from this that 'If it happens somewhere, it will happen everywhere'. Like Skinner and Stucley, she feels she has lost love but understands clearly that love is not possible in the life of the castle and no 'other' life is possible. The will to love can only triumph by willing the end of the life of the castle. There is also a sense here that her threat is a challenge to Krak (the stage directions say she looks at him); she pauses after saying 'I thought wrongly', giving him the opportunity to disagree; she pauses when she kneels, when she threatens her belly, and there are pauses during and after Stucley's lines. Throughout all of this, Krak refuses to intervene. The stage directions at the end of the scene suggest the cosmic repercussions of Ann's individual act. The castle remains but the action is flung outside; this is the necessary prelude to its demolition, in the sense that it no longer encompasses everything but is present now as an object.

In the 'haze of light', we discover that the 'things falling' are the bodies of pregnant women who are throwing themselves in numbers off the walls. Ann's death has proved as seductive as she perhaps intuited it would be and has provided the catalyst to spark off a suicide epidemic among the other women. This spectacular sequence, shifting rapidly from Ann's suicide to the mass suicides outside the castle, parallels the sequence in Act I when Krak seduces Stucley with the plan and suddenly we are presented with its implementation. Nailer vainly threatens the women with judgement in the afterlife but finally orders the imprisonment and shackling of all those who are pregnant. Batter, who has already shown signs of impatience with Stucley as well as amiability towards Skinner, doubtfully asks Cant's opinion:

CANT. We birth 'em, and you kill 'em. Can't be right we deliver for your slaughter. Cow mothers. Not an opinion.

(p. 40)

A dazed Krak wanders among the bodies of the dead women, reflecting on his relationship with Ann:

KRAK. She undressed me . . . [*They look at him.*] I lay there thinking . . . what is she . . . what does she . . . undressed me and . . . [*Pause*] What is the word?

BATTER. Fucked?

KRAK. Fucked! [*He laughs, as never before.*] Fucked! [*Pause*] Went over me . . . the flesh . . . with such . . . inch by inch with such . . . [*Pause*] What is the word?

CANT. Desire. [*He stares at her, then throwing himself at her feet, tears open his shirt, exposing his flesh to her.*]

KRAK. Show me.

(p. 40)

He is still attempting to reduce his experience with Ann to a set of concepts, reproducible technology – an attitude that lies at the basis of much contemporary thinking about sex: the whole notion of a science of sexuality is inimical to desire. Krak insists on Cant attempting to demonstrate and replicate 'desire'; she makes half-hearted efforts to touch him then runs out.

KRAK. Not it . . .
CANT. Trying but I . . .
KRAK. Not it!
CANT. Can't just go –
KRAK. NOT IT! NOT IT!

(p. 40)

When Stucley enters and sees him, he immediately recognises his condition:

STUCLEY. Lost love . . . ! Nothing, nothing like lost love . . . [*He rests a hand on Krak's bent head.*] And she was of such sympathy, such womanly wisdom I could not bring myself to take revenge, any man would, you say, yes, any man would! Not me, though . . . ! [*He draws Krak's head to his side.*] And you, dear brother in lost love, I UNDERSTAND.

(pp. 40–1)

Stucley can reconcile himself to Krak in their common grief. The engineer's desolation is the greater because Ann's final gesture has implicated him in her fate and won the duel for her: he called her bluff in the matter of the suicide. Krak's belated discovery of love parallels Ilona's in *The Power of the Dog*: as with Lvov's in *The Last Supper*, the manner of Ann's death has had the effect of imposing an inescapable obligation on those implicated in it.

Amidst the general atmosphere of catastrophic grief, Stucley announces that the new walls will be built low, thereby preventing such fatalities. They all stare at him and, after a pause, Batter invites him to go for a walk. Stucley demurs but Batter soothes him like a child, reminding him of former triumphs in Jerusalem, eventually picking him up and carrying him out in his arms. Stucley no longer has any power to resist; his very substance seems to have vanished leaving only a thin husk. The only person to protest is Krak:

KRAK. [*to the soldiers*] His last walk. His last walk. [*They ignore him.*] Listen, his last walk . . . !

(p. 41)

His intervention serves to underline the fact that there is a bond between himself and Stucley, who is not merely the hated captor marked down for destruction. As a final gesture, Krak offers the soldiers his own head to be sliced through with an axe:

KRAK. . . . Slice it round the top and SSSSSSS the great stench of dead language SSSSSSS the great stench of dead elegance dead manners SSSSSSS articulation and explanation dead all dead YOU DON'T HOLD WOMEN PROPERLY IN BED.

(p. 41)

At the outset of the play, Krak considers the brain he offers here to be that of a genius, priding himself on his intellectual sophistication; now he considers all that as 'dead' – and not only dead but putrefying. Interestingly, his words here ('language', 'elegance', 'manners', etc.) seem to refer to his seductive charisma rather than his scientific skills. The important thing is 'to hold women properly in bed'. This sentence betrays his persistently rationalist turn of mind; he realises that the whole catastrophe of the castle concerns relations between men and women; however, the notion that there is a 'proper' way of approaching this is perhaps somewhat reductive and a continuation of the thinking he has just shown in his 'experiment' with Cant.

The final scene, again outside the walls, begins with Batter and Nailer approaching Skinner with the offer of a new church. By this time the body of Holiday is reduced to a skeleton.

BATTER. New church. Tell her.
NAILER. The Holy Congregation of the Wise Womb.

(p. 41)

With the removal of Stucley, Batter wishes to set up a new state; as he appears to be wise to Hume's maxim that all government is founded in opinion (we have already seen him fishing for Cant's), he has had Nailer assemble a new thealogy (sic):

NAILER. . . . We acknowledge the uniquely female relationship with the origin of life, the irrational but superior consciousness located in –
SKINNER. Sod wombs –

(p. 42)

This is obviously a reaction against the male, rationalist culture of Stucley's regime. Skinner is disinclined to cooperate because she hates wombs; being barren herself, she envied and resented Ann's easy fertility. Additionally, she sees no reason why she should help Batter:

SKINNER. . . . I won't help you govern your state, bailiff made monarch by the stroke of a knife . . .

(p. 42)

He reflects for a moment and then offers power directly to her. At first, ever-suspicious, she thinks they are joking or playing some cruel trick, but when she realises they are sincere, the effect is dramatic:

SKINNER. . . . Wait a minute, wait, what's your – get me swelling, get me gloating, dangle it before her eyes – she blobs about the eyes, the eyes are vast and breath goes in and out, in-out, in-out, pant, pant, the bitch is hooked, the bitch is netted, running with the water of desire GIVE ME POWER WHAT FOR – [*Pause*] All right yes. . . .

(p. 42)

Skinner's self-description here is of a sexual excitement but what produces this is not the prospect of sex but the prospect of power. When Nailer throws the keys down, she pounces upon them and instantly demands vengeance for all her sufferings:

SKINNER. . . . Reconciliation and oblivion, NO! GREAT UGLY STICK OF TEMPER RATHER [*She turns on her heel*] Nobody say it's all because I'm barren! I have had children; I have done my labour side by side, and felt myself halved by her spasms, my floor fell out with hers and yes, I haemorrhaged. [*Pause. They stare at her. She goes to the wall, runs her hand over the stone*] I can't be kind. How I have wanted to be kind. But lost all feeling for it . . . Why wasn't I killed? The best thing is to perish in the struggle. . . . [*She turns to Batter and Nailer.*] No. [*She tosses the keys down.*] I shall be too cruel. . . .

(p. 43)

What one has to account for here is Skinner's sudden change of heart: how she can renounce the power, the prospect of which excited her so violently. In Act I Scene 1, Skinner reminded Ann of the births she refers to here:

Figure 7 *The Castle* (dir. Nick Hamm). Harriet Walter (Skinner). Royal Shakespeare Company, 1985. Photo: Donald Cooper.

SKINNER. I helped your births. . . . And washed you, and parted your hair. I never knew such intimacy, did you? Tell me, all this unity!

(pp. 6–7)

In recalling the shared births, she touches upon the moment when she was closest to Ann – so close in empathising with her birth-pains that she herself bled. The resurgence of this terrible and painful memory in Skinner, who has apparently succeeded in obliterating love from her life, momentarily counteracts her lust for vengeance, and she turns to the castle wall as if searching for a way through. After a moment, she despairs of the effort, feeling that kindness is now beyond her. Harriet Walter, the actor who played Skinner in the first production of the play, said:

> she knows she still has embers burning inside her which, in the final scene she does not want to have stirred up again. Right at her core is a connection between power and love; if love is killed, what use is power –[15]

When she renounces power a voice is heard from the wall:

KRAK. Got to.
SKINNER. Who says?
KRAK. Got to! [*Pause. She looks around*]
SKINNER. Out of the shadows who thinks the only perfect circle is the cunt in birth . . . [*Krak emerges from a cleft in the wall.*]
KRAK. Demolition needs a drawing too . . . [*Pause*]
SKINNER. Demolition? What's that? [*A roar as jets streak low. Out of the silence, Skinner strains in recollection.*] There was no government . . . does anyone remember . . . there was none . . . there was none . . . there was none . . . – !

(p. 43)

For a moment it seems as if the wall itself is speaking, or Skinner is being exhorted by a disembodied imperative. It is significant, symbolically, that she summons Krak out of the wall – as if the human faculty that created it is now to be used against it. His comment on demolition serves to confirm this. It also implies, however, that the removal of the castle needs to be planned – a matter of organisation – which is why he insists she takes power. Skinner's assertion that there was no government may be seen as countering Krak's reliance on reason and power. But as the jets emphasise the essential contemporaneity of the play, the final impression of them both struggling with the issue is a positive one.

In this examination of *The Castle*, I have attempted to sketch an outline of what may be said to happen in the play. To do this it has been necessary to consider the texture of the symbolism and to set the play within a wider cultural context in order to illuminate some of the thinking which informs it. Having done this, however, I am aware of a range of different possibilities available to performers at any particular moment in the drama.

A character expresses an attitude; who is to say what their intention is? The actor performs the lines but this performance is informed by reacting with sensitivity to a context provided by the other characters' performances. What makes any performance dramatic is the extent to which the action is 'live' and actors are making genuine choices on stage. Barker's plays allow them to do precisely this.

I have taken speeches at face value that could be played as bluff. Take, for example Ann's suicide: does she adhere simply and unswervingly to a course of action determined before she enters – as might perhaps be the impression formed on an initial reading of the script? Could it be the case that she enters without the slightest intention of killing herself, confident in her power to force a response from Krak – as well perhaps as from the other party to the castle 'duet', Stucley; that both men 'see through' the bluff, 'call' it, and force upon her an escalation she had not intended? Do her own words, initiated as a performance intended to seduce others, finally and fatally end by seducing her? To what extent does she take Stucley's words – 'You won't' – as the final and most crushingly humiliating challenge? To what extent are they intended as such? Or does Ann consider them merely impotent bluster, being entirely fixed upon Krak's obdurate silence? To what extent is Krak bluffing indifference?

In the Royal Shakespeare Company's premiere of *The Castle* (The Pit, October 1985), Penny Downie played Ann:

> This is what I learnt more than anything from the play, that the Stanislavski idea of working in a totally logical set of progressions – 'if she eats this for breakfast then obviously she will be like this for lunch' – the questions 'who am I, what is my process' are useless.[16]

She views character as essentially unstable:

> With Ann, you are a walking set of contradictions, which create your character. It's not logical, it's very, very dangerous. Unless you've got danger – which is sexual energy on stage, to me – you're depriving an audience. To me, the most important thing is a character's sexuality, and therefore the way they think, it's extraordinarily dangerous. Your character becomes the sum total of the contradictions within it – you are your contradictions, you're not your logic – because if you always know how you're going to react in any given situation, you might as well just telephone it in![17]

The stress she lays upon 'sexual energy' corresponds with the emphasis I have laid on seduction, which is of course most easily and obviously identified within the context of sexuality. Penny Downie also refers specifically to the element of risk and the possibility of illogical reversal (contradictions) – both of which have been discussed as integral to the processes of seduction. An important factor in the potency of seduction is the sense of an opening up of possibilities:

> It's made me completely reassess how I play a part. It's difficult, because it is a matter of letting go all of your preconceptions and logic and, once you've made some preliminary choices, going on stage every night open and blank to some extent.[18]

Penny Downie does emphasise, however, that this openness is an informed openness where the actor has fully considered all the implications and possibilities available to their character. It is in no sense a plea for the retention of some sort of unsophisticated naivety:

> Harriet Walter's greatness in the role of Skinner was I think something to do with the fact that she'd made a lot of choices, she'd done heaps of work, technically, emotionally, examining possibilities and all of this was 'on tap', but was, on each night, open – that's what makes it wonderfully clean.[19]

This studiedly ontological approach to acting, the eschewing of conscious objectives – particularly the highly structured and prescriptive systems of the Royal Court 'clarity' school of Gaskill and Stafford-Clark – makes possible Grotowski's demand for a performance that is not willed:

> To act – that is to react – not to conduct the process but to refer it to personal experiences and to be conducted. The process must take us.[20]

Seduction is interaction and the energy of seduction arises out of interaction. By clearing the mind in the way suggested here, the performer lays him/herself open to respond with maximum sensitivity to other performers and to the audience.

While it is not inaccurate to say that Barker's characters 'perform' themselves, it needs to be emphasised first that the most important performances are 'duets', not solos; and second, that performances are often undercut or, as Barker puts it 'abolished', by others. In productions of his work the most salient impression has often tended to be of actors performing their own speech acts rather than reacting to those of others; because he endows all his characters with articulacy, this can make it appear as if they are permanently 'in control' – a collection of impenetrable pebbles rattling around within the structure of the play. The essential drama, however, as I have suggested, is where control is relinquished in seduction or lost altogether, and the emotional interactive element needs to be brought out strongly by the actors. Whether one defines this as 'subtext' is a matter of semantics; what is involved, however, is a secret economy, a shifting web of pacts, challenges, betrayals, and complicities. Both *Judith* and *The Castle* demonstrate this clearly. It is interesting that, in the case of the premiere production of *The Castle*, the actors had actively to resist the director's attempts to impose ideological 'messages' upon the theatrical text. Thus Kath Rogers, who played Cant:

> Nick Hamm, the director, was terrified that the play would be thought anti-feminist. He spent weeks . . . trying to soften the women – he kept saying: the audience will go mad, they won't listen to you. He didn't want us to be hard, he didn't want us to be unsympathetic, and we had to insist on our weaknesses, our flaws. . . . He would have liked us to hang up baby clothes, add Greenham incidents. We kept saying no . . . by making too many parallels with Greenham, you trivialise the play. . . .[21]

As directors, actors, academics or audiences, we none of us approach a drama with completely 'open' minds, allowing the work to 'speak' directly to us. We bring expectations, preconceptions, 'knowledge', a mountain of second-hand experience in terms of which Barker is often dismissed as incomprehensible or ideologically unsound. I believe that contemporary requirements and expectations from theatre have become extremely narrow and specialised, the 'function' of drama understood in terms of crude communication theories. In a way, people 'know' too much and all knowledge can serve to conceal. If my study has relied heavily on the philosophical, then this is because a return to first principles helps us to put knowledge in perspective and opens up the possibility of *not knowing* – as Barker says – 'the pain of unknowing', 'the ecstasy of not knowing for once'.[22] This, in turn, makes possible exploration and discovery. Barker uses the interactive format of drama to re-pose the question of what it means to be human; 'freedom and obligation, will and decision', as Szondi put it.[23] I would suggest that the concept of seduction provides an apposite focus for those concerned with staging his work. For seduction is the art of the irrational. Not in order to purvey some doctrine of irrationality; but only the irrational can challenge Reason (the active virtue, not the abstraction) into being. Just as it is only the moral dilemma, the moral abyss, the moral vacuum, that activates serious ethical reflection. Democracy, the political practice of freedom, atrophies not so much when people believe the 'wrong' things but when the capacity to reason falls into desuetude. The irrational is the necessary Other of Reason without which it quickly falls into its proper vice of self-communion.

6 The shape of darkness

In the preceding chapters, having argued for a shift in theoretical perspective, I restricted myself to the detailed analyses of two very different plays. This resulted in a focus on work written and staged in the 1980s and early 1990s. Since then, Barker has been as productive as ever, writing prolifically and directing his own work with the Wrestling School. The chief development, however, has been the huge growth in international interest, particularly in Europe, where Barker seems to be attaining the status of a major European dramatist. At the same time, productions of his work in the UK, other than those of the Wrestling School, remain remarkably few. Among British theatre critics there is probably a consensus which acknowledges Barker's unique talent, which would agree that the failure of our major national dramatic institutions – the National Theatre and the Royal Shakespeare Company – to stage any of his work in any auditorium over the past fifteen years amounts to a scandal, but which would nevertheless accuse him of being the author of his own neglect by deliberately creating work that makes extreme, if not impossible demands on audiences.

In this final chapter, I wish to consider a number of questions and issues arising out of the developments in Barker's work that have taken place during this period. In doing so, I shall refer to a broad sweep of his more recent plays. In spite of Barker's admission in the interview presented in Appendix 1 that he has changed his views, I find that apart from this one significant exception, he has been remarkably consistent in his theoretical position. Within the plays, however, there have been shifts in focus upon thematic concerns, as well as changes in style and stagecraft.

While my perspective to date has been largely that of the practitioner, concerned with the challenge of staging and arriving at a performer's working knowledge of a role, in this chapter I want to reflect on the Barker *oeuvre* more from the viewpoint of the audience.

In his theoretical writings, he has again been very clear as to how he defines their role: the dramatist essentially writes what he or she wants or needs to; the audience are invited to witness the work which 'lends them experience'[1] and which

> is not about life as it is lived at all, but about life as it might be lived, about the thought which is not licensed, and about the abolished unconscious.[2]

In particular, the audience are lent pain and – according to Barker – 'the spectacle of pain, rendered in poetry – is aphrodisiac . . . !'[3] We are 'lent' the pain because we do not experience it directly but it comes to us via the seductive magic of the actor. This is a process which – in spite of the collective nature of the theatre experience – is essentially private and secret. As such, it is consistent with the unique nature of pain, the experience of which, in mind and body, serves to individuate and confine us within ourselves. More than anything else, physical pain is resistant to the collective. It may be seen that Barker's recanting of the forty-sixth aside[4] –

> Because they have bled life out of the word freedom, the word justice attains a new significance. Only tragedy makes justice its preoccupation.[5]

is in accord with the general drift of his case, the concept of justice necessarily involving the social. In fact, in his advocacy of tragedy as an 'invitation to a suicide of conscience within the dark space of privileged time',[6] he is insisting on a suspension of the very social that justice implies. To put it in terms of seduction, the social relation is replaced by solitudes or dual relations and the place of the law is supplied by pacts.

> If you hate the world . . .
> You must invent another . . .[7]

So says Poussin at a moment for him of acute pain in *Ego in Arcadia*. As the invention of worlds is Barker's self-allotted task, it is interesting that a number of his plays reflect – and reflect on – this activity. *Victory* is haunted by the spectre of Bradshaw: regicide and author of 'Harmonia Mundi', a Utopian socialist tract written in Latin and now banned under the Restoration. *Brutopia* concerns the home life of Thomas More, author of the original *Utopia* (1516); the title of the play refers to a putative rival work written by More's unloved daughter, Cecilia, who has been provoked into literature in reaction to her father's rejection of her. Barker clearly views the utopian project as an attempt to postulate the ideal society, a literature of the final solution to the problem of communal life, which extends from Plato's *Republic* and Augustine's *City of God* to Marx and the totalitarian tendencies of contemporary liberal-humanism against which his own aesthetic is directed. The central theme of *The Bite of the Night* is the war between the civilising and the erotic impulse as Troy is undermined by an increasingly maimed Helen. For the Utopianist, therefore, love is a problem. Bradshaw (Mr) adopts the tactic of sanitising it by investing it with an aura of holy innocence:

> And there will be love betwixt man and woman of a sort not known yet, founded on freedom of will and desire, so that she shall not be hampered by false modesty nor him by his cult manliness. . . .[8]

More's answer is a draconian regime of criminalising extra-marital sex, thereby domesticating the erotic, which he further trivialises by reducing to a material transaction. He notoriously advocated that suitors should have the opportunity to inspect each other stark naked:

> When you're buying a horse and there's nothing at stake but a small sum of money, you take every possible precaution. The animal's practically naked already, but you firmly refuse to buy until you've whipped off the saddle and all the rest of the harness, to make sure there aren't any sores underneath.[9]

More himself was reported to have granted Roper (a suitor uncertain which of his two daughters to espouse), such an inspection by sneaking him into their bedroom and suddenly removing the bedclothes. Cecilia alludes bitterly to this incident in the play and it is typical of the experience that leads her to the writing of 'Brutopia'. It can be seen that Barker has continued the exploration of the experience of Bradshaw in *Victory* – a woman linked to a socially progressive hero – in Cecilia More; both of them find their lives loveless and oppressive, and both experience degrees of liberation through accepting violence, chaos and transgression – exposing themselves to pain. Cecilia's book, in so far as we are vouchsafed an impression of it, is a highly perceptive and brutally honest appreciation of her world as it is:

CECILIA. [*Aside*] In Brutopia, nothing is what it seems to be. This is universal and a source of comfort. Where nothing is expected, disappointment is unknown, and hope entirely redundant.[10]

Her father is presented as a domestic tyrant who insists on performing his own myth – genius, wit, enlightened hero and saint, possessing, nevertheless, the common touch. He requires from his educated daughters adoration which Meg provides but Cecilia refuses. One of the most fascinating scenes occurs at the climax of the first half of the play, when More realises that Henry will execute him:

MORE. [*In despair*] *Meg! Oh Meg!* [*Cecilia enters. She watches him.*] *Oh, Meg!* [*He is weeping. Cecilia's face is taut with pain and confusion. She hurries to him. He clasps her in his arms.*] Oh, Meg!
CECILIA. I'm not Meg –
MORE. *Going to die, Meg!*
CECILIA. Die . . . ?
MORE. *Die, die!*
CECILIA. Why die?
MORE. Because I'm honest! [*He buries his head in her hair. The rain runs down.*]
CECILIA. Be dishonest, then . . . [*Pause. His face emerges from her hair.*]
MORE. You're not Meg . . .
CECILIA. No, I'm Cecilia . . . [*He searches her face.*] *Forgive me, I'm Cecilia.* [*She stares at him. His hands grip her by the shoulders. A long pause. She trembles.*]
MORE. Oh, wonderful . . . her womanly nature yields to see my ashen mask for the last time . . . indelibly stamped on memory the visage of her doomed father, Thomas More . . . [*She frowns.*]
CECILIA. Who is Thomas More . . . ? [*He does not relax his grip.*] What are you – [*He stares.*] You are – [*Pause. It dawns on her.*] Are you – instructing me in – sham life? [*He merely stares.*] Are you – for love – teaching me to lie – and lie – even to myself? [*Pause*] You are . . . [*Pause*] You are trying to save me from the world . . .
MORE. [*Booming*] *Meg!*[11]

Meg arrives immediately and More transfers his grief to her. However, there is the stage direction 'As he recites, his eyes meet Cecilia's who is slowly drifting away from them'.[12] Apart from the obvious comedy of More, in his egotism, failing to recognise which daughter he was dealing with, this is a moment rich in subtlety and ambiguity. More's anguish elicits a generous and sympathetic response from his hitherto – according his point of view – unresponsive daughter. When he utters the line 'You're not Meg . . .', given her generous impulse, it must be a particularly wounding rebuff: she is merely perceived, impersonally, as 'not Meg' – a deficiency. When More 'searches her face', he perceives this injury as well as her sympathy for him and is moved by it. In the 'long pause', there arises the possibility of love. More, however, relaunches the performance of his grief, referring not only to Cecilia in the third person – 'her womanly nature yields' – but also, in the Caesarean mode,[13] to himself – 'Thomas More'. At first, she is baffled by this, but quickly comes to the conclusion that her father, 'for love', is instructing her in 'sham life'. She puts this to him but, of course, he cannot reply: to do so would be to ruin his 'instruction' – not to mention undermine his worshipful status. Is the profoundly selfish More – as she thinks – performing a selfless act in repelling her love at this inauspicious moment? The incident perfectly illustrates the generalisations asserted in Cecilia's aside quoted above.

There is an interesting parallel here with a number of other Barker plays that replicate this situation where the author of a world – and More is author not only of *Utopia* but of the domestic island bounded and symbolised by the garden setting of the play – becomes embroiled in contradictions within his own creation. This is the case with Poussin in *Ego in Arcadia*, Chekhov in *Uncle Vanya* and – most explicitly – Benz in *Rome*. In *Brutopia*, More offends his adoring daughter by biting her hand; he tries to jest his way out of the situation but is eventually reduced to insisting he cannot apologise. In *Rome*, Benz who is God, attempts to apologise to Abraham on account of the Isaac affair:

BENZ. Perhaps I owe you an apology.
ABRAHAM. An apology? A God who apologises? A *sorry God?* Please, let a man do his garden, let a man . . .
'. . . Sacrifice the ram instead . . .' Oh, *Deity without imagination*. A graven image knows better than you do how we long for our subordination. 'Sacrifice the ram instead . . .'
God's human![14]

Benz complains that he wanted to be loved, whereas his worshippers only want to fear him.

In the case of *Ego in Arcadia*, we have a Utopia that is diametrically opposed to those of More and Bradshaw. Whereas their projections are functional and utilitarian, 'Arcadia' is essentially aesthetic, the ideal of innocence and the pastoral life – a world of poetry and song. The play's title refers to Poussin's painting *Et in Arcadia Ego*, which depicts a group of classically draped figures poring over the words inscribed on a tomb. The Latin is normally construed as 'I too am in Arcadia', the 'I' here being death. This assertion needs to be seen in the context of an idyllic world where it may be assumed that eternal youth obtained. The discovery of death's presence would then constitute a profoundly dramatic moment. The expression has also been translated as meaning that 'self' is to be found 'even in Arcadia'; one of the attributes of the pastoral world was that it was viewed as an alternative to the ambition and intrigues of the city and the court, as the simple life where emulation restricted itself to affairs of the heart and to song contests. At a particularly fraught moment in Congreve's *The Way of the World*, Lady Wishfort raises the possibility that she will

> retire to Desarts and solitudes; and feed harmless Sheep by Groves and purling Streams. Dear Marwood, let us leave the World, and retire by ourselves and be Shepherdesses.[15]

In Barker's Arcadia, however, the sheep have all been eaten by starving packs of dogs who have abandoned the cities in search of food; this has brought about the demise of the shepherds. While the landscape still boasts the 'detritus of heroic cultures', it is traversed by crowds of refugees harassed by strafing war-planes. The sounds of social disintegration punctuate the action, which is divided into a series of 'eclogues' – a catastrophic Arcadia. Barker retains the essential elements of the classical tradition in that this is a utopia where the individual pursuit of love is placed above all other considerations – including social harmony. As Mosca, an ex-minister of state declares:

> This is Arcadia . . . where nothing lives but love . . . and therefore . . . is a place of infinite suffering. . . .[16]

We also find the traditional prevalence of song, and that mirroring, self-consciously artificial process whereby the genre comprises songs about lovelorn shepherds who attempt to seduce by singing songs about lovelorn shepherds who are attempting to seduce, etc. Appropriately, this is a world where artists (a painter, a novelist, an actor, a dancer, an artist's model) outnumber the politicians (a queen, a courtier, a revolutionary). What is particularly interesting, however, is Barker's treatment of the death implied in the 'Ego'.

In *Brutopia*, Cecilia comes to the conclusion that

> And it was Death that governed Brutopia, His imminence was everywhere proclaimed, so the old men, by their proximity to Him, had most respect, and the young were pitied and their shallowness bewailed.[17]

Barker's Arcadia, on the contrary, appears to be ruled (though 'overseen' is perhaps a better word) by Poussin, who declares:

> No one dies in Arcadia . . . That is the horror of the place. . . .[18]

He adds, however, echoing the famous phrase:

> And Death is here. Certainly, he's here, but so discriminating, you will hate him for his impeccable disdain . . .[19]

A number of the characters do, in fact, kill each other but the corpses merely come back to life.

The first group we meet are the politicals, with Sansom, the revolutionary, about to execute Dover, a Queen; the latter uses her considerable personal charms in order to seduce the former from his purpose. She succeeds but before she has to reward him, her long-term lover intervenes, 'killing' Sansom with a knife. This is Mosca, a sophisticated and urbane courtier, who is strongly reminiscent of Stendhal's Count Mosca from *The Charterhouse of Parma*. When he revives, Sansom persists in his adoration of Dover, for whom Mosca – a fish out of water in Arcadia – has suddenly lost all his attraction. Instead, she conceives an adamantine desire for Poussin:

> Obviously, you are the master here. Obviously you govern. And equally obviously, I am your natural partner . . .
>
> I have to be the queen.[20]

The painter, however, is an utterly self-absorbed solitary – so Dover, like Poussin's mistress, Verdun, suffers.

The other group have very precise literary origins: Sleen, Lilli and Le Vig are based on characters from Louis Ferdinand Céline's 'autobiographical' novels – in particular, his late masterpieces *D'un château l'autre* and *Nord*, where the novelist along with his dancer wife and a movie 'heart-throb' actor, Le Vigan, flee across war-torn Europe as the Nazi power to which he had made his very public commitment crumbles under the Allied onslaught. Céline had written anti-semitic pamphlets and supported the transports of Jews to death camps from occupied France. Even before he conceives a hopeless passion for Dover, he is begging Poussin to let him die. Lilli admits to worshipping Sleen:

> Any man who suffers as he does must be a god surely! I mean, let's not be fussy who we worship as long as we worship somebody! A life without abasement, imagine it![21]

She hates Arcadia, however, on account of the complete absence of mirrors and her faith in Sleen is shaken when she discovers him crying (a 'sorry god'?). At the end of the play, she is the character most fixed on escape. For her fellow refugee, Le Vig, the mirror problem will lead to a crisis:

> I am a narcissist. Sleen says that is why I am unhappy, but he is also unhappy, and he hates himself. The fact is I find myself both more attractive and more interesting than anybody else.[22]

In fact, Le Vig has his philosophy fully worked out – all desire is merely a form of self-love – and Barker allows him to enunciate it in the smug, rhetorical tones of crass egotism:

> When you look into another's eyes, what do you see? *You see yourself reflected.* Admit it! When their pupils dilate the pleasure you feel is nothing but *aggrandizement*. No one wishes to admit this. It spoils the cherished fallacy of love.[23]

Sleen, maliciously, brings this hymn to an abrupt and premature end by faking an air-raid alarm, which sends Le Vig sprawling in the dust. In some ways, he is the clown of the play and his hubris is cruelly punished when he becomes 'addicted' (Poussin's word) to Madame Poussin, the artist's aged but sexually voracious mother. This lady has a particular talent for promiscuity and insinuating herself with men in a state of frustrated desire. She provides gratification to Sansom, Le Vig and – eventually – Mosca. These loves are characterised by hatred, as Cecilia states in *Brutopia*:

> In Brutopia love was impossible, and anger took its place. This anger was, in certain ways, indistinguishable from love.[24]

As Barker continually reminds us, however, the sexual act is always a dangerous locus, which retains a powerful potential for seductive reversal: Madame Poussin is drawn to Mosca anticipating sophistication in the arts of sexual gratification but, as Le Vig senses instantly, a transformation has taken place. His subsequent jealousy feeds his own passion and what began for him as sordid humiliation assumes the possibility of a social triumph:

LE VIG. I want to walk with her in Paris –
SLEEN. You can't –
LE VIG. *And show her body to the world its full and mobile shape* –
SLEEN. Le Vig . . . your juvenile infatuations – [*He stops. Pause. He shakes his head*] are no worse than anybody else's . . .[25]

This uncharacteristic generosity on Sleen's part is because he himself is hopelessly infatuated with Dover. When Sansom revives after being killed by Mosca, Sleen is the first person he sees and consequently becomes for him his master. By advising this acolyte on his hopeless passion for Dover, Sleen is himself 'infected': as he maintained, love is 'a bacillus'.[26] When he declares it, his passion, needless to say, falls on deaf ears.

Barker then sets up a finale to this concatenation of romantic entanglements via the traditional and thoroughly Arcadian device of a song contest. As Sleen is the first to realise, death is in fact present in Arcadia in the shape of the aptly named Tocsin. The discrimination ascribed to him by Poussin, however, is by no means benign; in this landscape of infinite suffering, only annihilation offers an end commensurate with the characters' desire while simultaneously offering to assuage their underlying longing for an escape from their misery. Though the direct purpose of their songs is to move the object of their desire, they recognise the hopelessness of this. The prize for the successful contestant is death and their appetite for victory attests to the strength of their passion. The dramatic presentation of these logical formulations allows Barker to explore the symbolic ambiguities of this territory shared by Eros and Thanatos.

Le Vig's initial reduction of the seductive dual relation to essential narcissism is apparently borne out in his song – according to Sleen 'another advertisement for someone called Le Vig.' The same reduction is attempted by Mosca in order to pulverise his passion for Dover – with his song he claims to have 'thought love to extinction':[27]

Cunt
A corridor of self again
What hangs on womb's wall but mirrors.[28]

Just before this, he dismisses an apparent concern on Dover's part for his dignity as 'self-regard' – '*was that idiot mine . . . ?*' – significantly summing up the perception as 'Ego . . . in . . . Arcadia . . .'.

This hard-won indifference is belied, however, and his philosophy opened to question, when an attempt by Dover to placate him produces an explosion of resentment. His hatred of life is warmly applauded by Poussin, who appears to represent the supreme ego in Arcadia. Indeed one of the key perspectives of the play would appear to be a reflection on the artistic ego, raising questions about the erotic and the aesthetic imagination. Poussin, like Sleen and Le Vig, seems to require worship rather than the unstable dual relation of erotic attraction. He claims to love Verdun, but she is tortured by her apparent inability to dent his composure; it would appear that he basks in this adoration and, to an extent, enjoys her pain; she describes him as absolutely selfish and his mother characterises him as 'an unhappy and inveterate prig'.[29] Similarly, Sleen says he loves Lilli but clearly gets pleasure from humiliating her. Poussin has invented Arcadia – the world the other characters have wandered into – and he captures and uses their agonies to people his landscapes:

POUSSIN. [*To Mosca*] I drew you . . .
I so rarely draw from life . . .
But I drew you . . .
Pure
Pure
Arcadia . . .[30]

Sleen is described in the Dramatis Personae as 'a fugitive novelist'. As I have suggested above, however, the 'real' Céline created a fictional Céline, so it could be argued that Sleen's artistic creation is himself: he performs himself. Although he counsels Le Vig against abjection, for his own part he seems irresistibly drawn to it as he staggers quite wittingly from one humiliation to another, oscillating between arrogant impudence and the grossest sycophancy. In a sense, his infatuation with Dover seems an opportunity for new indignities. Sleen's art is an art of abjection, but remains an art nevertheless and he takes a pride in it. In the song contest, Mosca is desperate to avoid what is for him pure humiliation and when he 'sings', what communicates itself is unvarnished pain. The power of this is attested by the long silence that follows his performance, a silence Sleen breaks because he's challenged:

SLEEN. There . . . [*Pause*] I do have competition . . . and I thought I would romp home. . . .[31]

His own offering is impressive but he breaks any 'spell' he might have built up by an unseemly 'plugging' of his own cause:

Come on, Mr Tocsin, that's the best yet. . . .[32]

In the event, it is Poussin himself whom Tocsin selects – much to the former's dismay. In his desperation, he turns to his devotee, Dover, who urges him not to die and seduces him – the inventor of Arcadia – by begging him to invent *her*. This appears to give Poussin the courage to resist, and he succeeds in turning the tables by executing Tocsin.

One of the most interesting aspects of *Ego in Arcadia* is the idea of a world where death – or rather, death as oblivion – is absent. Existence, therefore, cannot be refused; as Poussin says, '. . . this is the land of uncommitted suicides . . .'. It dramatises the awesome concept of what Kant referred to as 'unconditioned necessity': 'an abyss on the verge of which human reason trembles in dismay'.[33] The interrogation of the signifier 'Arcadia', which has gone on throughout the drama concludes with a vision of hell. A similar argument goes on in *Rome*[34] – an even broader concept – where the final definition characterises Rome as 'wanting'. The subtitle, *On Being Divine*, signals that Barker intends to explore further the complexities of the worship pact, where the urge for self-abasement encounters the appetite for adoration and what sounds as if it should be an ideal complement turns out to be something much more complicated and contradictory.

The play follows the lives of a group of Romans who experience the fall of Rome to Barbarian conquerors. This is familiar Barker catastrophic territory – in this instance, characterised mainly by the exigencies, physical and psychological, of the siege. The structure of the piece is epic in scale, with a dozen major roles as well as a continuous requirement for crowds – soldiers passaging across the stage, parties of Roman socialites, processions of servants saving art objects, assembly members of the French Revolution in full conclave, hordes of looters, choruses of cardinals, 'the leisured' in their deck chairs, and a particularly repulsive group of religious zealots called 'the

Devots'. *Rome* invites comparisons with that other Barker epic – *The Bite of the Night*. The dramas focus on the beginning and end of the classical world – the Homeric epic of the Trojan wars and the final collapse of the Roman imperium. The scope of both works is highly ambitious, not only with regard to their thematic content but also the matching breadth and complexity of their formal architecture. It almost goes without saying, that neither are – in any conventional sense – historical. The meanings of Rome that Barker plays on most are Rome as 'civilisation' (its enemies are 'barbarians'); Rome as supreme imperial power (in a state of wholesale collapse); Rome as repository of 'culture'; but also Rome in the religious sense as supreme spiritual authority.

One aspect of the complex architecture mentioned above consists in the intercutting of the main action with a series of scenes that provide a species of sub-plot or interlude. These usually develop thematic ideas to be found in the main plot; there are, therefore, three Abraham scenes that present two versions of the Isaac sacrifice story plus a coda. The first of these follows the Biblical version most closely but it is clear that, in order to comply with God's will, Abraham has worked himself into a kind of ecstasy of murder:

ABRAHAM. To love is this. To love is to inflict impossible pain. On self, and others. That's love.[35]

whereupon, he erupts into a 'song of madness'. In spite of this, however, there are suggestions that he is experiencing some degree of struggle with himself in maintaining his divinely ordained purpose. Just as he is about to slice Isaac's throat, God enters in the form of Benz and tells him to sacrifice the ram instead. In conventional terms, this should be a moment of relief and rejoicing. Barker's Abraham, however, experiences a profound disappointment. In seductive terms, God has extended Abraham a challenge to prove the extent of his devotion by an action that takes both of them, in a pact, beyond the law. He responds to this only to have the dual/duel aborted in a manner that proclaims God unworthy of his devotion; in particular it is the petty insistence on having 'the ram instead' – as mocked in the quotation cited above – that renders him banal and 'unseductive.'

In the 'Second Abraham', confronted with the same mandate, Abraham takes a different tack:

> *I honour you with deeper truths my son.* [*Pause*] I tell you, rather, the savage and relentless nature of all life. [*Pause*] What other parent

> would? What other parent cast aside the consoling lies of parenthood? *None I promise you . . .*
>
> . . . No, this chain of deception must be snapped. And you – you are the link.[36]

This time, when he is stopped, Benz complains:

> You cheated me. . . . What sacrifice was it, when you convinced yourself that life was vile? It was a liberation you were threatening your loved boy with. . . .
>
> You were to submit, in all clarity, in the fullness of understanding, to the wholly irrational act. You were to kill your son without the benefit of philosophy. You were to make no sense of the deed, but to endure the purest pain. For my sake.[37]

If what has happened up to this point is reminiscent of Kierkegaard's *Fear and Trembling*[38] with its 'teleological suspension of the ethical', what occurs next pitches us straight into Nietzsche. First Abraham, and then Isaac, physically attack Benz – with fatal consequences. God lies dead.

> ABRAHAM. Oh, now things will be hard . . . Now we will have only ourselves to blame. . . .[39]

Isaac has had enough of filiality and escapes from this Biblical enclave into a street in Rome where he joins the main plot.

The setting of *Rome* reflects the progress of the action, Part One taking place in a 'hall of culture' and Part Two in the 'ruins of Rome'. The former implies a range of connotations: in the first instance it is contemporary, suggesting the museum, the cathedral, the castle, the palace, the gallery, etc., wherever, in fact, the tourist might experience 'culture' – perhaps even a theatre. Perhaps, in particular, a theatre. I am thinking here of the 'dying pope' who is slowly 'flown' in; this is a self-consciously theatrical device suggestive of the traditional 'magic box' of the stage. The expiring pontiff is Pius, whose suspended entrance symbolises his ambiguous status *vis-à-vis* life and death. We have already considered the issue of death in respect of its dominance of life in *Brutopia* and its exiguity in 'Arcadia'. Pius, we are informed, has had a lifelong obsession with death, possesses 'total recall' even to the moment of his conception, and is now 'clinically dead'. He is unable, however, to relinquish life because of his passion for his mistress Beatrice's arse:

PIUS. When I first saw your arse, I yielded you my life. One look and I was altered. Its poise, its pride, its plenitude, its pity and its vigour, I saw God in its motion! . . .
. . . *I cannot die no matter that I want to.* [*Pause*] Sickness. Pain. Delirium. Nothing. [*Pause*] And my heart has stopped.[40]

This unusual status sets Pius on the edge of the play's action, whence he continues to haunt Beatrice. The church authorities are concerned and embarrassed at this predicament – not least because of the deteriorating political situation with the barbarians at the gates of the city. This leads to the unceremonious removal of Pius – he is literally disrobed by his successor, Park – and for the remainder of the play is wheeled about in a handcart – a symbol of undignified redundancy. He is not abashed, however, claiming that death has made him coarse, and he is the only character in the play who addresses the audience directly. He is reminiscent of Murgatroyd, the dying soldier in *Pity in History* and Sleen in *Ego in Arcadia*: the former in respect of his 'suspended' status, and both with regard to their whole-hearted espousals of abjection. All flaunt their humiliations and all are cruelly abusive. Pius speculates on his situation:

I'm all absence. Is that death?
I'm nothingness wanting. Is that death?[41]

It is worth noting that the view of death he expresses here comes very close to Park's final definition of Rome, and therefore the essence of its value, as 'wanting' – a coincidence that furthers the exploration of the link between desire, ecstasy and death.

The style of Pius' final speech is very similar to the direct-address format of the prologue from *The Bite of the Night* cited in Chapter 3:

Death's endless. First blow to the optimists. Death's an ante-room, tell the tired old lady who aches for peace. Ante-rooms all the way! *I was the most perfect man of my time* and that's not difficult, the competition was negligible *I boast I boast* the proof however yes the proof exists the proof is that I ceased to please when I ceased pleasing *I flourished I put forth leaves*
True
True
Your scepticism is a passing shower
And I fucked deeply

Deeply yes
Jeer on
Howl on [*Smith enters, immaculately clothed*]
I do not argue with the living
Who are they?
I am in the ante-room.[42]

Here, Pius performs his abjection directly to the audience, his words suggesting they are responses to reactions from them of contempt, scepticism and ridicule. His initial assertions can be interpreted as a discovery that existence is endless: death is not an end and does not entail oblivion; it is merely a door through which we pass into another room, which itself contains another door, and so on. . . . Pius appears to provoke the implied audience responses by his claims to former glory (in contradistinction to his pathetic present), and in particular he insists that he was the most 'perfect' man of his time. Issues of characters seeking or attaining 'perfection' are frequently encountered in Barker's dramas, so the word merits some consideration. It will be recalled that Pius clings to life because he is drawn to the perfection of Beatrice's arse – an experience he describes in terms of 'seeing God in . . .'. Perfection, it would appear, is integrally linked to the thematic of 'being divine'. It could be argued that Pius' real abjection is not that he clings to life but that he clings to a rejected passion: Beatrice refuses his challenge to commit suicide and insists she must look for another man. This seems to be her instinctive response but, at the same time, she feels

I am in need of a change. . . .
This change cannot come from an encounter with a man. I am convinced of it. . . .[43]

In the event, she finds herself the object of Benz's (God's) forceful attentions and is compliant. The domestic ideal that he appears to desire, however, is not one she finds herself capable of accommodating. Finally she asserts her perfection in a public display of nakedness:

Look
I shan't resist a moment longer your determination to adore me
Look I said
Isn't every part immaculate the flaws even the essence of perfection and marks of decline sites of my perfect history

I am incapable of love
A thing I now confess
A thing I hid even from myself
A thing I felt shame for
I am impervious
So worship
I have turned all that caused me pain into
A catalogue of qualities
Worship then.[44]

She claims furthermore that Pius ceased to love God when he encountered her and Benz, when he met her, ceased to be God. Her claims are immediately tested by Benz murdering their baby. When she receives the knowledge of this with apparent equanimity, he is compelled to acknowledge her divinity:

BEATRICE. I am greater than you
Lonelier and greater than you. [*Benz falls at her feet, rocking to and fro on his knees.*][45]

Beatrice achieves her divinity – her 'perfection' – through accepting her own 'inhuman' nature – she is 'incapable of love.' She therefore ceases to attempt to love and refuses to feel guilty about her 'inadequacy' in this respect. It is also noteworthy that she achieves for the first time an articulacy that has hitherto eluded her. (Both Pius and Benz complained about her 'absurd and haggard language'.) This 'shamelessness' is complemented and symbolised by the physical gesture of open nakedness. It can be seen that her ethical position accords with the perfection retrospectively claimed by Pius – specifically that he 'flourished' when he stopped trying to please. Beatrice's alteration from her uncertain and confused state of mind at the start of the play also extends to death: whereas she fled from Pius' challenge to die with him, ashamed and humiliated, she calmly refuses to humour the Devots by reciting the dogma they demand and is killed by them. Benz claims her action was intended to 'spite' him; her daughter Smith is of the opinion that she was tired of 'pretending'. Beatrice herself says nothing, but her decisive exit contrasts with the lingering of her erstwhile lover, Pius. Barker has stated that his tragedy is intimately concerned with death, and specifically with 'the means by which a character arrives at death.'[46] It would appear that the achievement of perfection is an appropriate time to die. As the servant, Nixon, says to the anatomist, Doja, in *He Stumbled*:

> . . . you have for such a long time cultivated a supreme indifference to the panics and pretensions of the governing life . . . I admire it, and yet, the nature of perfection is precisely – its own redundancy. . . .[47]

In *Uncle Vanya*, the beautiful Helena, like Beatrice, comes to terms with herself and achieves a moment of perfection, which she chooses to terminate by successfully engaging Vanya, her lover, to shoot her dead. (This contract with Vanya is a significant variant of a character 'entering Death' – a theme we shall consider in more detail later.) At the very end of *Rome*, the ascetic Park, Pius' successor and another 'perfectionist', submits to being drowned by his beloved, Smith.

When the cardinals became exasperated with Pius' lingering, led by Lascar they decide the time has come to elect a new pope. This process is derailed, however, by the intervention of soldiers engaged in defending the city, one of whom challenges Park – a priest who claims to have led a life confined to the library – as to what he learned there. Park's response is uncompromising:

> Your pain is insignificant.
> I, who never suffered, say.
> Your squalor is not relevant.
> I, who never went without a clean sheet, say.
> Your coldness is contemptible.
> I, who never went without a fire, say.
> *Do not show me your scars unless they came for Christ.*[48]

Gloy, the soldier, after initially taking offence and striking Park, insists that the conclave elect him Pope. The latter seizes the moment and assumes power. Smith is enthralled and immediately becomes a disciple, finding in Park a perfection she thinks she has long been in search of:

> How perfect you are. And you know nothing of the common life. How intolerably and exquisitely ignorant of things we call our needs.[49]

This perfection is something Park himself already recognises and his opinion is no doubt encouraged by Smith's adulation. When he encounters God (Benz), he confesses his excellence:

> Father, I have never sinned. [*Benz looks at him.*]
> And what is more, not sinning I found easy.[50]

He compounds this hubris by suggesting that Benz experiences the shame of God when he contemplates his (Park's) shamelessness. The new pope has been lured via the ecstasy of being God's mouthpiece into an opinion that he is God's equal; as Benz points out, it is likely that he will soon consider himself superior. Thus Park launches into a seductive duel with God – who responds quickly enough by blinding his opponent and letting the barbarians win the war. Park, however, remains defiant:

> I am more myself than previously and I don't crow and I don't posture *but did he think blindness would silence me. . . .*[51]
> . . .
> *I am all that is correct and history it is that's error!*[52]

In the face of complete defeat, he asserts that he has become Rome – just as Judith claims Israel in *Judith*.[53] Smith seizes the opportunity offered by her god's demise to propose sexual union; if Park rejects her, she will blind herself. He hesitates and she attempts to manipulate him by suggesting he is afraid of being lowered in her esteem; she places his hand on her breast and attempts to kiss him. When this fails, she is humiliated and resorts to blinding as a form of self-abnegation and as an escalation of their seductive duel:

> You think I wanted to be gratified. When what I wanted was to be with you. [*She sways one way and another.*]
> If not in ecstasy . . .
> In pain . . . [*She butts her head twice, savagely.*][54]

Nor has God finished with Park: a torturer arrives with instructions to 'make an idiot' of him. After this, he is variously described as 'disastrous', 'crippled' and with a 'mental age of two', the strategy of the barbarians being to render this prime symbol of opposition to their regime ridiculous. There follows a lengthy period when Park is ensconced on top of a pillar – a move presumably instigated by Smith, who now 'interprets' him to a growing army of 'Devots'. An infuriated Benz wreaks his malice on Smith by brutally raping her, an act that sets a precedent for mass imitation. In doing this, however, he cruelly suggests a reversal of agency:

> Perhaps you blinded yourself only in order to be caught more easily by me. [*Pause. They are still.*]
> Have you considered that? [*Pause*]

> Perhaps the reason you thought you blinded yourself was not the real reason at all?

PARK. *Ro-me!*

SMITH. That is a consideration of truly lethal proportions. . . .[55]

The teachings of 'The Blind Pope Also Dumb' – as mediated by Smith – insist on the values of chastity and cleanliness. She neither affirms nor denies Benz's suggestion but her response indicates nevertheless that she is prepared to entertain it. Park's intervention – which represents the entire range of his current vocabulary – is a reminder that he is the third participant in this scene, a helpless witness of Smith's ordeal. When she is left alone with him, she is quick to use her suffering as another escalation in their seductive duel – a development which vies with his martyrdom on the pillar. At the same time, the particular form of her pain lends itself to consideration in the light of his rejection of her sexual advances to him – her mindset suggesting comparison to that of Skinner in *The Castle*, who wills the torture of her sexual organs when she realises Anne no longer loves her. When Smith's request for 'a sign of love' from Park receives no response from the top of the pillar, she admits:

> The fact is we are held by the impossible.
> The impossible it is that keeps me here and were you to capitulate to my nagging desire for affirmation
> I've no doubt I'd scarper
> like a bottled bee
> into the stagnant world.[56]

By this stage, Park the Stylite, like Skinner the witch, has achieved universal adulation – all in the name of Rome and a set of rigid theocratic values that oppose the vaguely liberal-humanist regime of the barbarians. Smith decides that it is time for him to descend, but when he does so he flings himself upon her in a thoroughly unchaste embrace; she is horrified and runs away. Such is his aura of moral authority, however, that even Benz, beset by the problems of his relationship with Beatrice, approaches him in confessional mood. Park, having been granted a temporary voice in order to respond, uses it to plead for himself:

> Put love in her heart. [*Pause*] They transport me like a relic and quote things from another age my words are out of context and

> half the clauses are removed she has no pity for my solitude put love in her heart, father. . . .[57]

In other words, Park's and Smith's situation has undergone a reversal, with him now maintaining that she is Rome. In a final twist of cruelty, Benz agrees to grant Park a voice so that he may plead his case directly to Smith; this voice turns out to be a squeaky falsetto, rendering the 'Great Pontiff' ridiculous to her. This turn of events, however, prompts the final realisation that the Park she desired and worshipped has gone. I have already noted Barker's interest in the passage from absurdity to the reverential, a good example from *The Castle* being Nailer's transformation from a man with a toolbag on his head to ecclesiastical dignitary. Here, Park sings a song that is entitled '*Park's Annihilation of Absurdity*'. It is a final plea to Smith:

> If I am infantile educate me
> If I am impossible to love
> Instruct me in the necessary qualities
> Teach me the words
> You are a modern woman
> But I am now an ancient man
> All I believed has lost significance
> And time has left me
> A rock
> Of
> Screaming
> Birds.[58]

As the title indicates, this is intended to be a powerful appeal – similar to the songs at the end of *Ego in Arcadia*; its impact is enhanced through Park's overcoming the handicap of his risible voice. Smith does not reply immediately but the stage direction suggests she is almost swayed. Instead she issues the instruction to the returning Devots:

> I speak the Blind Pope Also Dumb
> Take me to the water's edge
> Abandon me to the incoming tide
> I fear nothing
> But my own divinity. . . .[59]

This is a rejection of Park's plea but also a final challenge and escalation in that he has the possibility of saving himself by using the despised voice. The moment allows him the opportunity for the supreme seductive gesture. He remains resolutely silent as Benz wheels him out into the depths, leaving Smith 'perfectly alone'. In *Death, The One and the Art of Theatre*,[60] Barker talks of

> Love's infinite requirement for proofs . . . killing the supreme erotic gift . . . in passion, the insatiable appetite for sacrifice. . . .[61]

I recall a number of years ago visiting the then newly opened Theatre Museum in London's Covent Garden and leaving with a sense of disappointment. Later, on thinking about this, I came to the conclusion that my feeling had to do with the fact that most theatre I was in the habit of visiting *was* museum, a designation merited not only by the physical buildings but by the corresponding antiquity of the repertoire enacted and re-enacted therein. The assembling of a museum to museums from peripheral ephemera such as costumes, set designs, playbills, etc. seemed a fragmentary and sterile exercise given the absence of the central historical element of the performance itself. One of the principle fascinations of museum, the essence of its seductive appeal, lies in its effort to conjure the dead. This effort is not openly acknowledged as such because the social function of museums, arguably, is to allay with the 'pearl' of culture the anxieties aroused by the 'grit' of death. Hence the talk is about 'bringing the past to life', a euphemistic mode similar to the ancient Greeks' re-naming of the Furies as Eumenides ('kind ones'), which can be pretty much summed up in the term 'heritage' – a kind of thinking death in terms of life. The crucial factor, however, about all relics and what gives them their particular aura is that they belonged to the dead, and the dead, by virtue of their status as deceased, are a mystery – as Barker states:

> The greatest mystery of the universe is death. Unlike other mysteries, the mystery of death is characterised by terror.[62]

The paradigm of this fascination in terms of museum is the ancient Egyptian funerary cult, the massive appeal of which lies in its direct focus on death itself, and its passion for excess, sacrifice and secrecy. In *Death, The One and the Art of Theatre*, Barker argues strongly for an 'art of theatre' – specifically tragedy – that engages exclusively with death as its proper subject:

> Nothing said about death by the living can possibly relate to death as it will be experienced by the dying. Nothing known about

> death by the dead can be communicated to the living. Over this appalling chasm tragedy throws a frail bridge of imagination.[63]

Barker does not, first and foremost, seek to justify such a project in terms of social hygiene; the anxiety relating to death, he argues, is the ground of beauty and beauty needs no justification. However, there are two social arguments that can be adduced: first, if it is accepted that we live in an age glutted upon knowledge and information, dedicated to universal transparency, the abolition of the unknown, the optimisation of the pleasure principle, and the medicalisation of mortality, then it could be argued that the truth of death is in effect repressed. Consequently, in Barker's words:

> Should we not speak a simple truth? Death is health to a society. And having spoken it, affirm that anxiety is an inextinguishable feature of existence. In its obsession with the elimination of pain, society sickens itself. . . .[64]

Second, the individual who is 'conversant' with death is 'nobody's fool' as far as collectivist political projects are concerned because s/he is 'equipped against lies.'[65]

Plenty of historical evidence may be adduced to bear witness to a direct link between theatre and death, extending from tribal practices involving the use of masks as repositories for the spirits of the dead in All Saints type ceremonies, to the viewing of the entire performance as a re-enactment by ghosts (Noh), the accommodation of ancestral ashes beneath the stage (Noh), the prominence given to ghosts in the Western dramatic tradition such as Dareios in Aeschylus' *Persae* and Hamlet's father, or indeed the whole tradition of tragedy itself. In the twentieth century, Tadeusz Kantor argued the case for a Teatrum mortis:

> Thus I devised two different versions of the significance of the drama. The first went like this: the fictive system is an imaginary system (imagined, that is, and transcribed) which does not exist in the real world.
> This version was, if you like, rationalist in spirit.
> The other version was mystical in the extreme.
> I still find it fascinating: ergo,
> Fictiveness is an impotent concept as far as real life is concerned by virtue of the fact that it is void, and therefore close to the realm of death.

> For this reason I felt justified in thinking of the fictional world of drama as a DEAD WORLD inhabited by the DEAD.[66]

The enduring appeal of the world of Chekhov's plays – especially in England – lends itself to this analysis on a number of counts. First, the dramas present a world that existed with an appearance of an interminable solidity but which was – very shortly – to vanish utterly. Second, Chekhov himself was dying while the plays were prepared for production at the Moscow Art Theatre. And third, the plays have achieved a status within the canon that has tended to endow productions with an aura of religious ritual. Barker's *Uncle Vanya* is fundamentally opposed to this Chekhovian aesthetic: he rejects absolutely the play's apparent endorsement of an ethic of stoical acceptance, of sufferance:

> In its melancholy celebration of paralysis and spiritual vacuity it makes theatre an art of consolation, a funerary chant for unlived life.[67]

In Chekhov, the dramatic climax of the play occurs when Vanya attempts to shoot Serebryakov, his brother-in-law, after the latter proposes selling the estate on which Vanya and his niece, Sonya, have toiled for twenty-five years to provide him (Serebryakov) with an income as befits his professorial status. The brutality of this proposal, compounded with the fact that Vanya is in love with Helena, Serebryakov's young and beautiful wife, drives him beyond restraint. His attempt founders in debacle, however, and the play ends with the status quo restored. There is the usual Chekhovian tangle of desire, with Sonya pining for Astrov, a local doctor, who in turn is drawn to Helena, who loves no-one but is inclined to the doctor out of sheer boredom. None of these experience any fulfilment but the conclusion with characters throwing themselves into 'work' suggests an endorsement of stoical repression. Vanya's passions are absurd and he is heroic to the extent that he represses them.

Barker uses the melodramatic incident with the gun to shatter the Chekhovian structure by having Vanya kill Serebryakov, thereby rendering reconciliation impossible. This is the door to another world. Vanya insists on a new identity – 'Ivan' – thereby repudiating the claims made on him by 'Vanya' and 'Uncle' and leaving him 'cleansed of the detritus of familiarity, domesticity and recognition'.[68] His action is a catalyst for most of the other characters to liberate desires hitherto restrained or repressed beyond conscious recognition. Thus, Helena discovers an appetite for the man who shot four bullets into her husband's face and Sonya strangles Astrov. Barker, having convincingly established an atmosphere of Chekhovian torpor, shows how the seductive effect of the killing lightens and enlivens the characters. Vanya's tragedy, however, lies in his discovery that he is impotent – unable to consummate his passion:

> VANYA. . . . I experienced the beginnings of a profound horror. A howling night which came down on my eyes and she was by no means charitable *thank God Helena is not charitable*
> not
> one
> word
> of
> comfort.
> And in the wilderness I came to myself. I met myself. Between such a wanting and such failing was – [*Pause*] Truth. . . .[69]

His defiant response is to refuse shame and, in this instance, he clearly sees himself as engaged in a duel with Chekhov, the creator and god of the world of the play – much as Beatrice and Park are with Benz in *Rome*. Chekhov's intention is to enforce his particular vision and this dictates that Vanya remains a figure of ridicule: the impotence is Chekhov's response to the murder. Vanya refuses the shame of this humiliation:

> Listen, he who refuses shame becomes a master. *I did not let Chekhov kill my pride, I did not let his fingers throttle my desire.*[70]

Chekhov's attitude is represented initially by the two murdered men, who return more or less immediately to the stage with faces hooded or bandaged, commenting chorus-like on events. They may be seen to symbolise the 'world' of the original play that has now been sidelined; their condition also adumbrates the links postulated above between theatre and death. These are made explicit in Act II:

ASTROV. The theatre is a contract
SEREBRYAKOV. Between the living and the dead
ASTROV. The dead inform the living of their fate
SEREBRYAKOV. A requirement
ASTROV. A necessity.[71]

The disintegration of the Chekhovian world is presented in the cracks and ruptures that afflict the set; another world seems to be symbolised in the sudden and incongruous appearance of the sea – an entity of questionable reality, which releases a playful spirit in most of the characters. The sea is also commonly encountered as a symbol of death and there are a number of indications that this is the case here (a man is seen drowning in it). Part of the jubilation that greets this phenomenon arises from the conviction that it will now prove impossible for Chekhov to come and restore order – a turn of events they had anticipated with varying degrees of apprehension and dread.

There is an argument about the drowning man: Vanya is in favour of letting him drown, perceiving him as a possible threat to their new lives; Mariya, his mother, and Sonya want to save him, the former from moral conviction that she claims is instinctive and the latter because she feels this is a man who will give her a child. The first act ends with Mariya rejoicing at their successful rescue while Vanya, having suddenly intuited who the rescued is, races round looking for the gun. It is, of course, Chekhov – and Act II begins with the characters lined up in silence, heads hanging, while their creator paces up and down before them towelling his hair. Apart from the sycophantic Telyeghin, however, there remains a mood of defiance and a battle develops as the dramatist attempts to reassert control. This revolves in the main around Vanya's rejection of Chekhov's characterisation of him as clownish; he insists on his status as a murderer – in response to which Chekhov replies:

CHEKHOV. Vanya, I have such a withering knowledge of your soul. Its poverty. Its pitiful dimensions. It is smaller than an aspirin which fizzes in a glass . . .
VANYA. I don't give in . . .
CHEKHOV. An innocuous fizz audible only to those who place their ears against the rim . . . [*Pause*]
VANYA. I don't give in . . .
CHEKHOV. *Oh, Ivan, Ivan, your resilience, your adamantine naughtiness!* [*He laughs at his own wit.*][72]

Now just prior to this, Chekhov was insisting that his categorisation of Vanya as comic was entirely innocent:

CHEKHOV. You fill me with laughter
VANYA. Do I.

CHEKHOV. A laughter which is without malice or contempt, a laughter such as the moon might laugh at the homeward journey of a drunken man. . . .[73]

This vaunted detached objectivity in humour, enhanced by the 'beautiful' simile of the moon/drunkard, does not square with the clear contempt explicit in the 'poverty of soul' remarks quoted above with its mischievous 'fizzing aspirin'. And, of course, the more detached ridicule appears to be the more it wounds, because it is harder to ascribe simply to malice or hatred. But hatred – eventually – is what Chekhov owns up to:

CHEKHOV. Will someone sit with me? [*Pause*] Ivan . . . [*Pause*] Preferably . . .
VANYA. Me? But you hate me.
CHEKHOV. Yes. [*Pause*][74]

The significance of the admission is underlined by its monosyllable and the ensuing pause.

Helena realises that Chekhov simply uses his wit to provoke Vanya and that the dramatist's apparent tolerance and humour mask a profound hatred; he is – to use a word from the play's discourse – thoroughly 'toxic'. She insists on her passion for Vanya, knowing that this lies beyond his comprehension and goes to the heart of the argument:

CHEKHOV. . . . It is preposterous you love this man, a woman with such thudding veins should cling to *Ivan* such flooding such pulsing in her belly *Ivan of all people* isn't he a fumbler in women's wardrobes?
HELENA. Yes.
CHEKHOV. There are things even I do not understand *and impotent at that* really it is so unclean I could laugh, I do laugh, I resort to laughter when I am in deepest offence, listen I am dying I have come here to die . . . [*Pause*][75]

It is perhaps in the realisation that his laughter has become a threadbare reflex that Chekhov plays his last and strongest card here. I refer to Baudrillard's dictum cited earlier in Chapter 3 on seduction:

> We seduce with our death, with our vulnerability and with the void that haunts us.[76]

Vanya takes up the challenge of sitting with the dying man against the advice of Helena, who is – rightly as it turns out – thoroughly suspicious of the request. When the others have gone, Chekhov, who is dying of a disease that – according to the chorus of the dead – comprises 'self-murder', 'self-betrayal' and 'self-disgust', confesses to a sense of artistic failure:

> I am talking of a truth so absolute, so ponderous, that even to enunciate its laws would command more energy than we possess. It would, I honestly believe, kill us with the exhaustion of articulating it, and though it is proximate enough, though it is manifest enough – like some meteoric relic protruding from the soil – it is far better left undisturbed. I am tired.[77]

It is hard to escape the conclusion here that Chekhov's repeated appeals for support in this judgement betray a profound uncertainty and even a sense of failure. Anyway, there is a certain absurdity in his so firmly eschewing an action that might prove fatal when he has already admitted that he is dying. The final confession is the most significant: Chekhov tells Vanya of his dream to 'pour' himself into another: in other words, to experience a love such as that Vanya feels for Helena (Vanya talked of how he 'inhabited Helena'). But Chekhov deliberately abandoned this aspiration:

> And in abandoning that dream, I found something like freedom. In discarding all that was, arguably, the best in me, I found a peace of sorts. We are entirely untransferable. So hold my hand . . . Ivan. . . .[78]

Chekhov's insistence here on solitude as destiny – an argument and an aesthetic he had previously illustrated by exposing Mariya's unloved breasts and locating their beauty in that very quality of neglect – seems somewhat at odds with his dying request. In a perceptive and penetrating consideration of impotence/potency themes across a group of Barker plays, David Ian Rabey accuses Chekhov of requesting 'complicity in empty gestures of impossible reconciliation, as he dies'.[79] It seems to me that his sensing of a 'complicity' here is accurate – the request is a challenge – and rationally the gesture is indeed 'empty', but in seduction (both Vanya and Helena now claim to be 'artificial') the empty/meaningful opposition is redundant. The ensuing stage directions read:

[*Vanya extends a hand to Chekhov, who holds it. Chekhov dies. Telyeghin hurries in.*][80]

Vanya enters the gesture passively, while Chekhov is active in taking the hand and then dies – presumably loosening his grip. Yet the hand-holding continues for quite some time while other characters enter and talk, until:

VANYA. *Chekhov's dead!* [*They all look at him. Suddenly in a gesture of profound ugliness, he lets go Chekhov's hand, which falls. Marina turns.*][81]

The final gesture here indicates that Vanya is doing the holding and he therefore substituted his grip for Chekhov's when the latter died – suggesting a complicity and the possibility that something has indeed been transferred. The audience will certainly be prepared, having been emphatically presented with the 'held' image of this, for some significant outcome. And how is the dropping of the hand not simply 'ugly' but 'profoundly' so? Because having as it were announced its significance for some time in the fixity of the preceding gesture (the holding) it fails to 'cap' it? Because Vanya tries to use it to suggest a triumph over Chekhov – a perfection – and fails? In other words, his gesture re-introduces the truth/falsity principle. With his death, Chekhov seems to have re-established something like the status quo: the sea disappears; Telyeghin discovers intact the guitar we saw him destroy; other characters revert to their original roles; only Helena, who now has the gun, remains committed to the escape that Vanya initiated. She realises, however, that something has changed in her lover: that he is deteriorating and that she herself will be forced to become 'coercive' and, consequently, 'not desirable'. At this point a 'monstrous mirror' descends in which Helena sees herself and giggles.

The final scene opens with Helena fixed before her own image in the mirror. Here, like Beatrice in *Rome*, she seems to have arrived at an acceptance of her own perfection:

> . . . it is so very *undemocratic beauty* it is an unforgivable thing *I have it however so* and all things lead to my body what else is there but my body *all things lead to it. . . .*[82]

Vanya, however, frets about his inability to recall the serial number of the gun and this issue seems to have become the focus of his general malaise. Earlier, the lovers both undertook to be cruel with each other and Helena is now savagely cruel with Vanya. Baudrillard asserts:

> Now seduction belongs to cultures of cruelty, and is the only ceremonial form of the latter left to us. It is what draws our attention to death, not in its organic and accidental form, but as something necessary and rigorous, the inevitable consequence of the game's rules. Death remains the ultimate risk in every symbolic pact, be it that supposed by a challenge, a secret, a seduction, or a perversion.[83]

Vanya suddenly remembers the serial number of the gun:

> 7786955797 . . . [*They laugh*]
> He hated the gun
> Oh, how he hated the gun
> It was as if he knew it was the enemy of all his melancholy compromise . . .
> [*Pause. They look at one another. . . . Helena takes the gun from her clothes. . . .*][84]

The look initiates a suicide pact. They sit opposite each other and Helena throws the gun to Vanya. She wants him to shoot her because she is not confident about shooting herself; they agree there would be 'a possibility of ugliness'. The dialogue between the two builds up momentum and a tension that seems to lead naturally to him firing and killing her. As soon as this happens the other characters chant 'Uncle Vanya', apparently goading him with his old Chekhovian identity. He raises the gun to his head but then discharges the sole remaining round into the floor. Summoning 'Nanny' (Marina) to remove the body, Vanya claims that no-one really liked Helena; he weeps; admits he has failed but speculates that some destiny restrained him. Finally, he admits he has no idea where he is and walks out.

What are we to make of Vanya's behaviour here? He appears to engage in the suicide pact whole-heartedly, but it is noteworthy that earlier in the play he tells Sonya that he does not have the courage to commit suicide and intends to use the gun only to coerce others.[85] This, however, is before he transforms into Ivan, though his behaviour after Helena's death – weeping and calling for 'Nanny' – suggests a reversion to the old Vanya. Helena, like Beatrice in *Rome*, seems deliberately to enter death after achieving a sense of perfection and, like Park, she accepts death at the hands of a loved one. By contrast, Vanya, at the end of the play, presents a shambling figure – very close, in fact, to Chekhov's description of him as 'fundamentally inert'. This deterioration seems to have begun after his encounter with Chekhov. However, the dramatist/god's posthumous victory, demonstrated here by the reversion to normality of the other characters, has to be qualified at the very end by Vanya's blind exit and non-return. The Chekhov world is restored – but without desire (Helena) and death (Vanya.)

In *The Love of a Good Man* (1978), Barker engineered his most extensive exploration of the death theme up to that date. The setting of the play is a section of desolate First World War battlefield, which is about to be transformed into a military cemetery. The date is 1920 and Ronald Hacker, undertaker of Peckham and now government contractor, has arrived to supervise the re-burials. Bride, the military officer in overall charge of the work, explains:

BRIDE. This ridge we are standing on is about a thousand yards in length. It changed hands many times during the war. They do not know how often, but it got very bloody, being so exposed you see. And as a consequence, it is very deep in bodies. I do not want to dramatise, but where we are standing is not ground so much as flesh.[86]

One can think of few more direct and dramatic ways of commencing an exploration of death and its related issues. The main action concerns the arrival of an aristocratic Englishwoman who has come to retrieve the mortal remains of her son and, contrary to the law, repatriate them to be interred beneath the ancestral apple tree. There is a concern here not only with the materiality of the corpse, the relation of the corpse to its living form – the person – but with human bonds – desires, commitments and guilts extending beyond the extinction of life – that seek to reach across the Lethe towards the world of the dead.

We have already noted other instances of 'quests' based on a commitment to 'do right by' the remains of a deceased: Gocher in *Fair Slaughter* and Bradshaw in *Victory*. This thematic, of course, has the status of a founding myth for the genre of tragedy and attained its classic exposition in Sophocles' *Antigone*, which concerns itself with the welfare of the dead as bound up in the treatment accorded to their physical remains. Antigone's compulsion is a loyalty that seems to extend beyond her brother, Polynices, to death itself and it is this that brings her into direct conflict with the state.

In *The Love of a Good Man*, Mrs Toynbee, the aristocratic lady, achieves her objective (more or less) through what might be termed a typically English compromise: both she and the state are satisfied, only Hacker, used by both sides, is left in despair. The penultimate scene involves an attempt to make contact with the dead by conducting a séance on the battlefield – a project that descends into chaotic farce. More profoundly affecting by far is the actual exhumation of the decomposed remains of a corpse. Barker creates a powerful suspense by anticipating this moment, with various characters looking into the hole and reacting with horror and disgust. These are the body parts that are later presented to Mrs Toynbee as those of her son. She,

> . . . in an ecstasy of emotion, leans forward and places her lips on the remains.[87]

Again, this is a powerful and disturbing image, both transgressive and challenging, that is repeated elsewhere in Barker's work: there is Nell Gwynne's kissing of Bradshaw's skull in *Victory*; the schoolboy Natley's attempt to eat Fricker's cremated ashes in *The Loud Boy's Life*; Judith's attempt to make love to the murdered Holofernes in *Judith*; the disciples' physical consumption of Lvov's corpse in *The Last Supper*; and Toonelhuis' ritual consumption of the ashes of the war criminals he condemned to death in *Found in the Ground*.

The significance of the remains, however, does not go unquestioned: Mrs Toynbee's supposed son is actually a German. When the Widow Bradshaw (now Mrs Ball) arrives home with her husband's remains, her daughter, Cropper, who is occupied translating her father's book into English, simply dismisses the relics:

> It is not him.[88]

The final play I should like to consider briefly here takes the death thematic and reformulates a range of the issues already described in a new and powerful way. *He Stumbled* (2000) focuses on the last professional engagement of Doja, an anatomist who 'processes' the dead bodies of royalty. This involves the ritual removal of internal organs and their preparation for burial. Doja enjoys a quasi-royal status himself, presiding as he does over a death cult and acknowledged throughout Europe as the master craftsman in his field. For the audience, at the outset, it is Doja himself who is the mystery. We are presented with a high wall, and every so often, via opening windows and doors, events testify to the presence within of a dying potentate.

Amidst sounds of grieving, these manifestations take the form of pans of sickness or blood as well as individuals desperate to breathe uncontaminated air. One of these, a female novice whom we later learn is called Berlin, has drawn her clothes up over her head in disgust. Doja, described in the stage directions as 'a man . . . grey and powerful', enters, picks her up and carries her offstage. When they return it is clear that they have had sex and, as she re-enters the death chamber, she utters the first line of the play: 'You're God . . .'.[89] Another woman, Todd, enters from the same place, recognises Doja, and, characterising him as a wolf, invites his sexual advances; in spite of rushing crowds and chattering priests he obliges and takes her against the wall. It would appear that Doja's sexual attraction hinges on his mastery within the sphere of death, his perfection within a field that is all abjection. A third woman offering herself is interrupted by the death of the monarch, marked by the flying in of his naked body on a surgical table.

At this point, Doja is joined by his assistants Suede and Pin. Under his direction they proceed with the dissection, which is conducted in a ritualistic fashion with all the protocols of a modern surgical operation. They are interrupted, however, by the arrival of Baldwin, the king's son. He appears profoundly upset at the dissection but insists that he must witness it. Immediately, there is a sense of conflict between the prince and the anatomist. When Doja assures Baldwin that 'the flesh is not the man', the latter questions the whole basis of the anatomist's status:

> . . . If the flesh is not the man, why are you here? I am a boy and vastly ignorant but we have spent huge sums on your services, you're not cheap, your fees are thought by some to be exorbitant, why if the flesh is not the man? A cat would do, surely, a goat ripped off a butcher's hook? . . .[90]

Doja responds witheringly to this in a diatribe justifying himself with reference to market forces and in answer to Baldwin's crucial point, he states

> . . . as for the flesh, my own opinion can be stated very briefly. It is everything and nothing.[91]

This effectively reduces Baldwin to silence. Thereafter, the dissection proceeds in professional Latin until the moment arrives when Doja lifts out the excised heart; Baldwin is hypnotised with wonder just as the queen, Turner, makes an entrance. Unlike her son, she is unimpressed by the sight of her husband's organs, claiming all she loved was visible:

Figure 8 *He Stumbled* (dir. Howard Barker). Nixon (Syd Brisbane), William Chubb (Doja), Turner (Victoria Wicks), Baldwin (Ian Pepperell). The Wrestling School, 2000. Photo: Howard Barker.

TURNER. It must be the same with the character. We love what we see. But that is rather little of it. Really, life is solitude. We collide with others. We attach ourselves to surfaces. But what is intimacy, Mr Doja? A fiction, surely. . . .[92]

While, on one level this is simply a statement of opinion, when coupled with her lack of any obvious signs of grief, it takes the form of a challenge to Doja. She departs abruptly, apparently leaving her son embarrassed, and although he professes a keenness to witness the excision of the bowel, he too retreats from what he provocatively terms 'this butchery'. Before going, however, he announces ominously:

BALDWIN. . . . I do so admire you Mr Doja I want us to be friends I think at this moment you have a terrible attraction for me and my mother also finds you likeable which is odd she likes so few people. . . .[93]

After he walks out, the dissection and the Latin continue for a short time, but this gives way to Doja's reflections on their current predicament. In spite of the mystique attaching to his status as a disposer of the dead, Doja himself is of a profoundly rationalist turn of mind, not unlike Krak in *The Castle*, and he sums up their situation:

> No, it's complicated. The boy does not like his mother. The mother does not like her son. Each of them has discovered in me the alleviation of his solitude. It calls on all my resources to satisfy these competing claims.[94]

One of the aspects of this play that differs slightly from Barker's usual practice involves focusing on a central consciousness: from this point on, the audience tend to see events from Doja's perspective, and we are well aware that there are mysteries that give the drama the feel of a thriller. However, a key element in the staging of this section is the ongoing process of the dissection and the physical presence of the corpse: on the one hand, there is an innate revulsion at the opening up of the human cadaver; on the other, the clinical precision, artistry and mechanical fluency of the anatomists' process stimulate fascination and awe. Just as, in the case of *The Love of a Good Man*, the drama is permeated by the presence of death in the physical ground of the setting (the battlefield, which we are told contains more human bodies than earth), so the physical presence of the royal cadaver in its various stages of dissection, dissolution and decomposition dominates the action of *He Stumbled*. Related to these, there are also particular corresponding moments of powerful action, such as the exhumation of the corpse in *The Love of a Good Man* and the comparable gesture of the excision of the heart in *He Stumbled*: both are acts of profound violation, showings of what should remain hidden within nature.

The exhumation is carried out as part of a process of 'recovering' the dead – especially with reference to returning their identities to them – and of converting the chaos and nausea of violent death to ritual order (the cemetery). In *He Stumbled*, the ritual dissection process that serves to protect the participants against the horror begins to break down as Doja's authority is pressurised and weakened through his entanglements with individuals whose claims upon him are irreconcilable. One of his assistants, Suede, quarrels with and eventually kills the other; later, he usurps Doja's authority, firmly of the opinion that the 'curse' that seems to have descended upon them is a result of Doja's violation of their 'contract' with the dead by his fornications with the dead man's wife. This disintegration is mirrored in the disorder of the anatomy room and the putrefaction of the royal remains – 'In the pans old offal stinking'.[95] Doja's central preoccupation is his affair with the queen, Turner, whose powerful repellent, a strong smell of death, has seductively metamorphosed into an equally magnetic attraction. Their relationship is an ongoing seductive duel, which pivots principally on Turner's secrets and her admission that she lies – a feature which, like Judith and Holofernes in *Judith*, situates their encounter within the register of artifice. Doja's discovery – from Baldwin – that the queen has had 'many, many men', all of whom her husband executed, plunges him into a profound disgust for the body on which he has been employed to work. This, he describes as the 'nightmare of anatomy',[96] and as his status and sense of self hinges on his professional standing, he has no authority to resist Suede's usurpation or indeed Baldwin's sexual advances.

In *The Love of a Good Man*, a similar revulsion occurs with Hacker, the hard-boiled undertaker/contractor employed to bury the fallen, when it occurs to him that the remains in front of him issued from the thighs of the woman to whom he is passionately attracted; in a lifetime of stewarding the dead, this was the first time that death had impacted directly on him. Doja says:

> Murderers, torturers, cannibals who put whole cities to the sword and stewed the infants in the ponds, nothing to me . . . ! Revered archbishops, fratricidal usurpers, guts in the pan and – [*He stops . . . his eyes close . . . pause . . .*]

> In this case however . . . a profound loathing for this degenerate flesh makes me recoil from the most mundane professional activity. . . .[97]

During his engagement, Doja has been repeatedly urged in hinting terms by Todd and the servant, Nixon, to assassinate the current monarchy. He is puzzled by this because the king is dead and he assumes they are referring to Baldwin and his mother. As far as the latter is concerned his love for her prevents him entertaining the thought of murdering her and, in a confrontation with Baldwin, he fails to seize the opportunity he has to kill him. Baldwin indicates that he intends Doja to submit himself to a vivisection conducted by Nixon; fascinated by the previously witnessed excision of the heart, he now wants Doja's heart. As he is about to submit himself to this Doja is deflected by stumbling on a canister of entrails and pauses to look to where Turner is crying out in ecstasy; he sees that she is with another man and divines that this is the king. The cadaver he has worked on, neglected and finally loathed, is a substitute.

This issue of the substitute body is also one that the action in *The Love of a Good Man* hinges upon. Mrs Toynbee resolves that her son who has fallen at Passchendaele will – contrary to military regulations – be retrieved and buried in England. To do this, she enlists the support of the aforementioned Hacker by seducing him. Having put out an offer of reward for the finding of the desired remains, a sceptical Hacker is immediately presented with a body by the group of soldiers working with him. Although he knows that this is a fraud, that the body is actually that of a German soldier, he colludes in deceiving Mrs Toynbee, partly because he is desperate to enjoy his reward and partly because he knows that locating the actual remains would prove well-nigh impossible. Mrs Toynbee accepts the remains as genuine – confirmed by the sensation in her womb – whereupon, by a piece of fraudulence on a breathtaking scale, the body is returned to be buried in the Tomb of the Unknown Warrior in Westminster Abbey. The body is therefore the locus of a web of deception.

I have already referred to Leary and Gocher's challenge of finding Tovarish's body in *Fair Slaughter* so that the excised hand might be laid to rest with it. The solution there appeared in the form of a sheep's bone. In the final play of *The Possibilities, Not Him* (referred to in Chapter 3), the piece turns on the flickering identity of the returning and soon-to-be-dead husband: Him or Not Him?

Tortmann, the king, approaches and Doja bows – only to notice that none of the assembled court show a similar deference:

Why don't they . . . ! [*Pause . . . Then he rises swiftly . . .*]
Obviously, you don't exist . . . outside the bedroom . . .
I'm recruited to a game.[98]

Tortmann seems to belong to an order of reality somewhat similar to that of Pius in *Rome* and like Pius he seems to be chained to life by an obsessive passion for an object that it is impossible for him to own. If Doja has been recruited to a game, the author of this world, like Benz and Chekhov in *Rome* and *Uncle Vanya* respectively, is Tortmann. He describes his passion:

TORTMANN. [*At last*] An obsession . . . what's an obsession, Mr Doja . . . but a privilege . . . ? And because I was a king . . . my privilege was itself privileged . . . because I was a king my ecstasy has been . . . extraordinary . . . an ecstasy akin to God's. . . .[99]

This god-like ecstasy is born of pain:

TORTMANN. . . . I hoarded pain as some hoard money . . . and through hoarding it . . . I found in pain whole realms of pity and excess that butchering cuckolds know nothing of. . . .[100]

For Doja, this is a deeply humiliating and agonising moment. He is aware, however, of Turner's silent presence, and claims to be impatient to become 'another remnant of your passion':

It is not pleasure, is it . . . you two share . . . [*Pause*]
But terror . . . ? [*She remains motionless . . .*]
What's common love alongside that . . . ? [*Pause*]
Answer me . . . [*Pause*]
Oh, *answer . . . !*
No
No
They all say that
They all
They all
They all say that
Don't answer
No
I'll cut
I'll do the cutting
I

I cut
The master me.[101]

There is a parallel, here, between the Tortmann/Turner relationship and that of Vanya and Helena in *Uncle Vanya*. Vanya finally admits that he was always afraid of Helena:

> *Always*
> *Always*
> *Afraid of you*
> Which was correct. Which is the way it should have been. Which is the perfect condition of pure love. *Of course I am afraid of you* this fear made me a murderer. . . .[102]

Doja's decision here to dissect himself, however, represents a stunning seductive reversal by seizing back the possession of his own death. What follows is

> . . . a spectacle of will, dexterity, endurance . . . of magic, therefore. . . .[103]

After the spectacle is over, we hear that Tortmann has drowned himself. Baldwin, Berlin and Turner remain fixed before his corpse. Doja's gesture here suggests comparison with that of Lvov at the end of *The Last Supper* where his disciples are enjoined to kill him and eat his body. Before he is able to accept death, however, Doja struggles to overcome himself. He unthinks his position as dupe and victim by considering every event of life as someone's game (God's?) – as destiny therefore. Barker then presents his effort to abandon hope and master terror in a very striking and powerful way:

> No don't rush me I'm half-way to understanding –
> [*He drags his shirt over his head, stopping half-in, half-out . . . sobs come from within . . . he staggers . . . he wails, fighting his horror in the dark . . . the court observes, unmoving . . . at last the writhing ceases. Doja completes his disrobing. . . .*][104]

He enters death, then, not as a hero attempting to impress others but in search of knowledge ('half-way to understanding'), which is, according to Barker, the motive of the tragic protagonist:

> I did it to be revealed to myself.[105]

Appendix

Interview with Howard Barker

CL One of the most frequently encountered adjectives applied to your early work – apart from 'political', was 'angry'. Critics and audiences experienced a sense of indignation; some described it as hatred. This was interpreted as outrage at injustice – particularly as regards the behaviour of political figures. I'm thinking not simply about your very early satirical work but plays like *No End of Blame*, where you have Bela, the politically committed cartoonist opposed to Grigor who believes in a more traditional notion of high art. Bela says: 'When the cartoon lies it shows at once. When the painting lies it can deceive for centuries. The cartoon is celebrated in a million homes. The painting is worshipped in a gallery. The cartoon changes the world. The painting changes the artist. I long to change the world. I hate the world . . .'. Would you say that anger has disappeared now – like Skinner says in *The Castle*, she waits and the anger goes?

HB I'm not sure the plays are characterised by anger. There is anger in them, but I believe they are more significantly marked by a rudimentary tragic consciousness, which must eliminate anger as an ethical redundancy. Although these plays appear to possess a socialist outlook, they never went down well with the socialist critics here. They never earned me friends on the left, or the right for that matter. I suspect these critics detected a missing element in them, something which committed art must have, if it is not to become simply testament, and that is optimism, because it is not possible to make effective propaganda – which is what the political play is – without optimism. If you are recommending to an audience a certain course, a certain attitude, there has to be a clear implication that it will possess utilitarian value, i.e. it will increase their happiness. No play of mine has ever aimed for, or achieved that. If my life at that time made me political, it didn't make me want to enlighten anyone. The quotation you gave from Bela never did speak for me. Perhaps people have assumed it did.

CL The character was based on the cartoonist, Vicky?

HB No, it was a greater cartoonist in my estimation, Illingworth, whose work was characterised by a Goya-esque darkness, it was less functional than Vicky. But to revert to your question, my work was certainly fuelled by class anger, but not dominated by it. I could not impose a political doctrine on it, for all that I felt myself to be political. . . .

CL Do you still feel angry about things?

HB Not in my artistic life. Which is not to say I do not have opinions. I have many opinions, but I no longer think them worth anything in the wider world, certainly not in my own theatre. I trust my imagination, I don't value my opinions.

CL So you feel that the anger would be a useless emotion?

HB Not useless, but I never derogate instincts. It is the same with violence.

CL You said to me a few years back: 'I'm afraid I'm going to have to write increasingly about sex . . .'. Well, you've done that. I was interested in the way that you put it – the note of regret – as if writing about sex were problematic. However, we seem to live in an age which is saturated with sex; it's ubiquitous and normal. On the other hand, the regulation of sexual activity still provokes anxiety and hysteria. Why did you feel that your work had to take that particular direction?

HB It was always in my work, and slowly it acquired its own profound metaphorical value, it became a way of life and not a marginal expression of needs, a theatricality as such. Because of its complexity, and its threat, it is not simple to address it without some apprehension. I think that is what I might have meant by my suggestion that it caused me anxiety. But after all I value anxiety in theatre above all else, so it was inevitable I would expose myself to it, as well as the public for my work. For me, the sexual is the ungovernable. In tragedy I esteem it for that. In society, it is perhaps very governable, it can become a social soporific, a commodity. Certainly the social obsession with sex has not enhanced its mutinous potential. But the potential is there. . . .

CL Do you think, perhaps, that the concept of sexuality is not a very useful one – because in your plays, sex is intermeshed with desire?

HB Yes, it is more useful to talk of desire than sex as far as my theatre is concerned. Sex is essentially the biological, crucial but unreflective. All the sexual transactions in my plays are self-conscious, and therefore characterised by desire, a desire which is accumulative, a willed extremity which separates the participants from the cultural milieu in which they live. In all my work I reassert the catastrophic potential of the sexual encounter.

CL I was thinking – in this connection – of Dreux-Breze, in *Rome* . . .

HB Oh yes, the last scene . . .

CL Where he feels that love has been tainted by the enlightenment project. . . .

HB Yes, he does say that and whereas he appears to hold these bourgeois women in contempt, he enjoys his possession of something which however unenlightened (perhaps especially because it is unenlightened) makes him irresistible to them. . . . There's a necromancy about him in the end. He's walled up in a tower, ignored by the authorities, presumably for his mild eccentricity, but a source of fascination to the 'knowing' new class. He is in possession of the secret, of course, which revolution reviles.

CL But what about the end of the scene where, after dismissing them, he collapses quite spectacularly?

HB He cries out for love . . . which he senses the new system has abolished, as each generation senses the loss of love in each new political order.

CL He does say to the women that their touches are bargains.

HB Yes, it is the pursuit, isn't it – there is a pursuit in these plays of something immaculate which is not beyond reach, it is just that it oscillates at such a high frequency that it doesn't endure. I suppose that the endurance of sexual desires is one of the most fascinating aspects of them: is it, for example, possible to create a permanent sexual desire between individuals?

CL It would be socially useful, I dare say.

HB In ensuring the triumph of the domestic arrangement, you mean? But it militates against that. However, that said, desire degenerates unless it is perpetually invented. Marriage is an institution which announces itself in the erotic and then proceeds to suffocate the erotic, to substitute property and children for that eroticism. Desire, on the contrary, lives only by the secret – unlike marriage it abhors the public place (except to desecrate it . . .). It values nothing above the sexual encounter with the loved one, but it is simultaneously permeated with a despair – that the encounter cannot be repeated. . . . These are the secrets that I make my subjects now.

CL So, in a sense, you are enlightening? You are pursuing an enlightenment project?

HB No, because they are never explained, they intensify their own mystery. There is no therapy in my theatre, no exposure. The more closely one looks into the ecstasy of the sexual moment in desire the more threatening it becomes.

CL I wanted to ask you about that word 'ecstasy', because you make considerable use of it in your plays. People not only talk about it but they devote their lives to the pursuit of it – to the detriment of everything else. But there is a range of different ideas of ecstasy: in *Crimes in Hot Countries* for instance, there's Erica who rejects happiness and commits to her lover with an heroic crime; then there's Porcelain whose idea of ecstasy is taking tea with his mother.

HB Every individual would want to define it for himself. I was thinking of it in the sense offered by Erica, as a contradiction to happiness, long ago seized by utilitarianism for its anaemic collectivist programme of contentment. I'd go on to say that ecstasy is also beyond pleasure – the obsession of contemporary society, which when it isn't talking about pleasure is usually talking about medicine, only another aspect of the perceived pleasure in living forever. Those who pursue the difficult category of ecstasy – with all its risks – are effectively denying society.

CL It's more individual.

HB Yes, and this mutually created individualism is antagonistic to the collective.

CL And it has a shattering effect. The notion of pursuing ecstasy seems to contain of necessity the idea of things being destroyed.

HB Yes, it is fatal. But that is also its intimate bond with the tragic, which invites death to participate in its transactions.

CL This vertiginous dual relation dedicated to the pursuit of ecstasy – to what extent would you say that its structure is essentially narcissistic? I was thinking of Placida's analysis of marriage when she says that the matrimonial condition is sustained only by vanity – the mirroring of self in self – 'and that forlorn hope that in another's flesh might be discovered that refuge from solitude which in reality pertains only to God'.

HB I think it's not narcissistic at all, but an attempt to break out of the solitude of the self – not into marriage, which institutionalises and destroys the erotic, and creates a different solitude of a particularly toxic kind, but through the dislocation of desire. Placida's judgement is of course conditional on her not yet having encountered the erotic herself.

CL As auteur, are you aware of scripting non-verbal text more than you used to? I have an impression that your more recent work contains more stage directions and more prompts for physically expressive performance. (For example, the page of stage directions at the beginning of *He Stumbled* and the detailed stage directions for *Found in the Ground*.)

HB It's possible. An earlier work like *Victory* has barely any stage direction, I wanted to give ground to the director, thinking the dialogue my principal concern, and the stage picture his. I admit I have, since directing, taken the disposition of actors in the space more to myself. In my own productions the staging has acquired huge importance from the entire anti-realist inclination of them. I permit very little deviation from a structured arrangement.

CL When you talk about an anti-realist inclination – that suggests the evolution of a particular production style with formal conventions. Do you feel that you have arrived at where you want to be with this or is it a continuous process of development and experimentation?

HB There is a very strong aesthetic system at work in my own productions. I don't demand that these values be applied in other circumstances, they are the outcome of my own relation with my texts, but of course they haven't appeared arbitrarily but through long practice, a sense of what is possible, given that neither entertainment nor commercial success, nor political effect, is part of my programme. In eradicating these aspects of common theatre practice, I feel liberated to think of methods peculiar to the needs of the work, strictly imaginative resources come into play that defy the expectations of realist theatre. But the style here – and what is style but the moral authority of an aesthetic – must change to accommodate more ambitious texts.

CL In your work with The Wrestling School, have you found economic restrictions a problem?

HB Certainly, but it isn't a simple equation of resources/achievement. The Wrestling School is a very poor theatre, but you would not guess that from watching the productions, for two reasons: the first is the powerful acting talent we have attracted and retained (and it is virtually an ensemble) and the second is a strong sense of design throughout, at every level, from costume to sound, all governed by a single imagination – one couldn't call it collaboration . . . but we are driven into smaller theatres by management economies, our audience remains stable and therefore we rarely gain access to those big stages where the scale of these plays can breathe, as we did for example with *Ursula* in Birmingham. The illusions, the choreography of scene change, all go to nothing in studios.

CL You have said that you're writing a non-dramatic work on the subject of theatre and death. Could you say a little about what this entails?

HB It may seem obvious to some, but as someone dedicated to the writing of modern tragedy I am persuaded that tragedy is essentially – even simply – about death, the means by which a character arrives at death, admits it to himself. By this I also imply that all disciplines in tragedy – such as social value, ascribed to it by Aristotle – are irrelevant to its purpose – and I do not say function, I think it has no function. I have always sensed the supremely spiritual quality in tragedy marked it out from all dramatic forms, and this arises from its abolition of all values in favour of this profoundly healthy engagement with death.

CL When people talk about death they tend to think in terms of a finality – a nothingness. But in *Rome*, there's Pius who continues in an ambiguous state of suspended life.

HB It is perfectly permissible to think of death as nothingness, and that is as valueless as thinking of it as something-ness. The compelling attraction of death lies in its domination of life, it is not only the Other, it has a secret domination of most, if not all, lived action. Of course the political play can't and dare not admit this. We concede to death – I think even when death is said to be 'instantaneous', we have to admit it. That's evident in my play *Gertrude*, where Claudius is helped willingly into death by Gertrude's terrible narrative, a vastly more moving exegesis than Hamlet's own gesture in drinking publicly what he knows is poison. (Hamlet in my play, of course. . . .)

CL And you still see death as a finality because Pius talks about death as endless – a series of antechambers.

HB How can we know if it is a finality? The fact is we know nothing whatsoever about it, except surely, the single fact that it can't be yet more life. . . .

CL Pius' position interested me because whereas Heidegger sees the subject as defined by its being towards death conceived as a nothingness, Levinas sees the subject as confronted by a being that cannot be refused. That the ultimate horror is that it goes on and on.

HB Yes, there may be no finality. And worse, what is the quality of that non-finality?

CL He uses the expression '*es gibt*' – meaning 'it gives' – emphasising the 'it' quality of utter impersonality which is in many ways more appalling than – say – a cruel God.

HB I talk in the book about the gesture of suicide and what a gamble it is. The suicide wants to leave the world but he doesn't know what he's going into. It might be even noisier, or cruder; there might be as many different versions of death as there were of life. And that's why I think the river Styx remains a powerful image. We keep talking about the other side; we have to talk about the other side because we don't have another metaphor for it. Those on the other side are those who might want to impart something to you but can't; it's very beautifully described in Homer where Odysseus seeks his mother on the other side and she has something to tell him. He goes to grasp her and of course he can't – she's not there. That infinite negotiation with the nothingness seems to me to fill life, to inform it profoundly.

CL One of the things that struck me about *He Stumbled*, was that Doja appeared to be a central consciousness and that the audience perceive the world of the play through him. This is particularly evident in the reversal that occurs at the end where he realises that they've duped him.

HB It's essentially a thriller, the last case of a brilliant specialist. But he becomes the case himself. His status – based on evidence, proof, logic, and so on – is eroded by the desperate power of the erotic, a relation he also thinks himself expert in but which is supremely exercised by the 'deceased' king and his wife. The protagonist only redeems himself – and his own claim on eros, it must be said – by the supreme gesture of dissecting himself beneath the gaze of his mistress – and, as in *Gertrude*, she applauds him.

CL Presumably he cuts very skilfully around everything . . .

HB He excises his own heart, which may be possible for all I know.

CL I assumed he would leave cutting the vital vein or artery until the very end.

HB Who knows . . . it is perfectly possible to stage it without so much detail.

CL It seemed to me there that his professional armour for protecting himself from the horror and natural revulsion of corruption – the ritual, the instruments, the Latin – all of this serves to support his ego. Finally after all his catastrophes, he falls back on and asserts himself through an ideal of his work.

HB The work ethic as a final dignity? That is a possible interpretation, certainly it is a flourish of recovered pride. But, as I suggested, the challenge is again to sexual status. He recovers this by the sheer scale of the gesture. She has not ceased to love him, even if he was in the last analysis, an instrument of her own sexual passion for another. . . .

CL She states that.

HB Yes, and her way is to permit him to die, almost, but not quite, to accompany him.

CL That gesture – of allowing someone to die – figures in *Rome*. Smith, who carries sway with the Devots, allows her mother to commit suicide by defying them. She says 'Everybody understands that in the severest test of love . . . to love is to allow'.

HB Which again emphasises the superior importance of death over sheer survival. How you die – how you make your entrance into death – is so important in tragedy, I think – not the idea that life is everlasting – and should be everlasting, and that I will save you and I must save you. Those gestures are weaker.

CL In *Rome*, one of the main themes – and indeed the subtitle – is *On Being Divine*. Benz obviously is the character who is supposed to be God.

HB But he is the least divine of them, if we think of divine as an expression of perfection. *On Being Divine* means to overcome the meanness of man. Again, so much social propaganda asserts the common ordinariness of human beings, the solidarity of the frail, as if we were destined to love one another. Park's assumption of divinity is in his overcoming of common humanity – in the scene about the war hospital, for example. His divinity is repudiation

CL Well, he encounters God, doesn't he? God is angry with him because he's . . .

HB Proud . . .

CL Because he's proud, yes . . . and what these characters seem to *require* to be divine are people to worship them. Smith worships Park. I think there is a point where she is kissing his feet and he says 'I should not let you do that . . .' but he doesn't stop her. This relationship between the worshippers and the worshipped seemed quite an important aspect of the process we're discussing.

HB Yes, but it has always been possible to improve on God, the more he reveals, the more this becomes obvious. Park's assumption makes him vastly more moral than Benz, whose tempers are those of an Old Testament Yahweh.

CL Benz says to Park 'I am not moral . . . I am devoid of all morality . . . I am will. Will only.'

HB Yes. Well that's what makes him a god.

CL As Heraclitus says: 'For the gods all things are just; for men, some things are just, some unjust . . .'.

HB Yes, and that returns us to tragedy. I once wrote in *49 Asides* that tragedy makes justice its purpose, but I now think it is categorically the opposite, it has no truck with justice, such things as equity seem beneath its gaze, there are no unjust acts in tragedy – to put it another way, you would be wasting your time protesting the immorality of actions in a tragedy – the characters are only what they are, or indeed, precisely what they are, immune from ethical protest. The play is on another ground.

CL It seems to me, however, there's no escape from the ethical which is there in the relationships between the human beings.

HB The ethical is there to be disposed of.

CL Oh yes, I think the characters often over-rule it or violate its demands. They are acutely conscious of it, however. Doja, for instance, at the beginning of *He Stumbled* when he finds he has to sexually disappoint the fourth woman, he immediately complains about remaining susceptible to a sense of 'obligation'. He says: 'My infamy, whilst making me an object of desire, must not create in me some nagging and reciprocal responsibility to those who suffer that desire surely . . .'. Now surely by saying all this, he's trying to divest himself of the unspoken ethical requirement?

HB Yes, Doja has to struggle to disembarrass himself of his (or society's) ethical education. If that tension did not exist there could be no tragedy, only a torrent of atrocities.

CL With the character Park in *Rome*, there is a stage where the torturer says to him that he has to think of his torture as the finishing of one life and the starting of another.

HB Yes, the torturer is conceived as rather social. . . .

CL You mean the happy family man with the child and the lunch box, etc? Isn't that again an example of somebody – like Doja – fortifying himself with professionalism against the chaos and madness – abjection, perhaps – of what he actually has to engage with?

HB That would be a humanist reading of it, as if in some part of his consciousness the torturer was appalled at what he did. But I see no sign of that in very cruel people. What he succeeds in doing is normalising chaos.

CL Yes. He does say, however, that he's been upset on occasions when he admits his victims have 'broken' him.

HB Yes, but that is his professionalism outraged, isn't it?

CL And he also says he was disconcerted by Park's running commentary on his own decline.

HB Indeed, the amoral can always be thrown off course, I dare say.

CL And when he is indignant about the status accorded to thieves being denied to his profession, doesn't this suggest a vestigial ethical sense in him which has been outraged? Or is he merely cynically appealing to a morality in his auditors which he himself does not possess?

HB I resist the idea that these statements are ethical, if only because within the society we inhabit (that of the play also . . .) the ethical can so often be discerned as borrowed, hired, and significantly *performed*, part of the individual's claim on the attention of others.

CL To return to Park, he does actually seem to experience a re-birth, which is emphasised with the suckling.

HB I'm not sure. He's infantilised by torture (by Benz, by God, through the torturer, to be precise) and makes a recovery of some kind. . . .

CL He goes back to a kind of abjection, doesn't he? His world – his ego – is destroyed in that process. The decision as to him going on the pillar – is that more Smith's? Beatrice says that he's going on a pillar but then she says '. . . he is wanted. So it hardly matters what he wants'.

HB Yes, all such celebrity eventually loses control of its own identity – this is a very material example of that. He is his own relic. Relics have uses, they are fetishised.

CL Well, she 'interprets' him, doesn't she?

HB Yes, she interprets him to the Devots, so she's critical in all this. He merely is symbolic, though he sings a song at one point – at a vital moment.

CL Yes, the song at the end but that is where he has experienced this change – a bit like Old Gocher at the end of *Fair Slaughter*, he discovers a humanity . . .

HB What do we mean by humanity here? It's a longing for love. . . . He knows he is human, I suppose, and perhaps he had doubted that.

CL He says Rome is 'wanting'. And presumably he consents in his death at the end, where Benz comes and wheels him out into the sea. Smith orders that – she tells the Devots to abandon him to the incoming tide.

HB And she is left by herself. A totem of true significance and not a negativity. This solitude – in her case a blind solitude (I think she's still rather immaculately dressed) – doesn't seem to me to be loss but a triumph – the ability to exist alone. That these people suffer to the extent they do, gives an audience a sense of human potential beyond the norm. And I do think that's why tragedy is a necessary art form. It doesn't make you feel life is good – or anything like that, or we can do it better, or wouldn't it be good if collectively we sorted something out . . . it is purely the fact that its extremity, however painful, lends the audience power.

CL Individually.

HB I think of the audience as individual.

CL A point I've had made to me quite frequently, mainly by admirers of your work, concerns the sheer quantity of incident that you incorporate in your plays. I've heard people say that – with a show like *Gertrude* – they would have preferred to watch the first half on one night – presumably gone away and thought about it – then returned to see the second half the following night. They find the work immensely stimulating but can only digest so much at a time.

HB I aim to be profuse. It is profusive. It is excessive – and the excess is part of the experience – I don't apologise for that at all. The fact that people find it an overload could be merely a reflection of their ability to concentrate at this given moment in culture. I suspect they can't take *Hamlet* either, frankly. So it's probably that I haven't geared myself to the diminishing concentration levels – but that would be a purely technical fact. What I'm most interested in is loading the emotions. I've no belief at all that most people can follow all of it or even hear all of it, and that's why I think the directorial aspects are pretty critical in being able to provide a sort of magnetism between the performer and the audience which overcomes the alienation created by loss, because the audience is forever getting lost – I know it is. It listens to a long speech and I know it gets lost. But somehow there has to be an adhesion.

CL It happens in Shakespeare all the time. You listen to a speech; something is said that causes you to reflect. . . .

HB Yes, and consequently you miss the next five lines. Is that necessarily a bad thing? The principle that shapes productions around the audience's mastery of the stage is a wrong one and limited to *meanings*, which interest me less than the compulsion of the experience. The compulsion must come from different angles.

CL And this is principally the task of directors, performers and designers?

HB No, in the first instance it is the responsibility of the dramatist – the quality of the ideas, or if not ideas, the imaginative world described – that dictates the outcome. The director has to present physical form for this – not to clean it up, to make it 'accessible', to civilise it, but to increase its anxiety by stimulating the ear and eye of the public, to maintain the tension that exists in the text. As I said earlier, it is a profusion of body and image that overwhelms tolerance, eliminating any pretence that we are being 'entertained.'

CL You have for some years been interpreting your own work as director. Economic restrictions aside, should we regard these productions as definitive? Or are you happy with the potential of your work to be interpreted by others in radically different ways?

HB It is never possible to talk of the definitive in play-production, the idea of the definitive must be provisional. All I have sought to do in developing a clear aesthetic for these texts is to satisfy myself that on this occasion at least, I the author got the kind of presentation I am most nearly satisfied by. I have seen these plays performed in wildly different ways, sometimes beyond recognition. That's all right, because the text is public property in the last analysis. I have even seen some of these texts played better than I myself did them, but interestingly, on these occasions the directors shared my analysis of the theatre – they were not reduced, simplified to single messages, or ironised. . . .

Interview conducted by Charles Lamb, 24 August 2003.

Notes

1 Barker and the British theatre

1 Howard Davies. 'Stock-take at the Warehouse', in *Platform 2*, Summer 1980, p. 16.
2 Ronald Hayman. Review of *Hang of the Gaol*, in *Plays and Players*, February 1979.
3 W. Stephen Gilbert. Review of *Fair Slaughter*, in *Plays and Players*, July 1977.
4 James Fenton. Review of *The Loud Boy's Life*, in *The Sunday Times*, 2 March 1980.
5 Howard Barker. Interview with Simon Trussler and Malcolm Hay, in *New Theatre Voices of the Seventies*, London: Eyre Methuen 1981, p. 187.
6 *Claw* in *Stripwell and Claw* by Howard Barker, London: John Calder 1977, p. 136.
7 Ibid., p. 137.
8 Ibid., pp. 142–3.
9 *New Theatre Voices of the Seventies*, ibid., pp. 189–90.
10 *Claw*, p. 217.
11 Ibid., pp. 226–7.
12 Ibid., pp. 227–8.
13 Ibid., p. 230.
14 Howard Barker. Unpublished interview with Charles Lamb, 23 April 1987. Appendix to doctoral thesis *Irrational Theatre* by Charles Lamb, Warwick University Library 1993.
15 Howard Barker. '49 Asides for a Tragic Theatre', *Guardian*, 10 February 1986. (Later published in *Arguments for a Theatre* by Howard Barker, London: John Calder 1989.)
16 Howard Barker. Unpublished interview with Charles Lamb, 23 April 1987. (See Note 14 above.)
17 Ibid.
18 For example, 'No Consistent Viewpoint' by Jonathan Hammond, *Plays and Players*, November 1975.
19 Robert Shaughnessy. 'Howard Barker, the Wrestling School, and the Cult of the Author', *New Theatre Quarterly*, Vol. V, No. 19, August 1989.
20 Ibid., p. 266.
21 *A Sense of Direction* by William Gaskill, London: Faber 1988, p. 49.

22 See Margaret Eddershaw's essay 'Acting Methods: Brecht and Stanislavsky', in *Brecht in Perspective*, ed. Bartrum, G. and Waine, A., London: Longman 1982.
23 Stanislavsky's opening address to the assembled company of the first Moscow Art Theatre, 14 July 1898. Quoted in *Stanislavski: A Biography* by Jean Benedetti, London: Methuen 1988, p. 68.
24 *Stanislavski: A Biography*, Jean Benedetti, p. 46.
25 Brecht. 'Short Organum for the Theatre', in *Avante Garde Drama. A Casebook*, ed. Dukore, B. and Gerould, D., London: Crowell 1976, p. 507.
26 Ibid., pp. 508–9.
27 Introduction to *The Fool and We Come to the River* by Edward Bond, London: Methuen 1976, p. xiii.
28 Howard Davies. 'Stock-take at the Warehouse' in *Platform 2*, Summer 1980, p. 14.
29 Interview in *Plays and Players*, February 1979.
30 Danny Boyle. Talk at a day school on Howard Barker at Birbeck College, London, 10 December 1988.
31 *Arguments for a Theatre* by Howard Barker, second edition, Manchester: Manchester University Press 1993, pp. 67–70.
32 Ibid., p. 38.

2 Postmodernism and the theatre

1 *The Worlds* with *The Activists Papers* by Edward Bond, London: Methuen 1980, p. 160.
2 'The New Citröen', in *Mythologies* by Roland Barthes, London: Paladin 1976, p. 88.
3 *The Age of Enlightenment* by Isaiah Berlin, Oxford: Oxford University Press, 1979, p. 28.
4 *Phenomenology of the Spirit* by G.W.F. Hegel, tr. A.V. Miller, Oxford: Oxford University Press, 1977, p. 140.
5 *The Woman* by Edward Bond, from 'A Short Essay', London: Methuen 1979, p. 136.
6 *The Worlds* with *The Activists Papers*, Edward Bond, London: Methuen, p. 91.
7 Jean Baudrillard. 'Symbolic Exchange and Death', in *Jean Baudrillard: Selected Writings, Cambridge*: Polity Press 1988, pp. 145–6.
8 Ibid., 'The Political Economy of the Sign', p. 87.
9 J.K.Galbraith. *The New Industrial State*, Harmondsworth: Pelican 1969, p. 41.
10 *Jean Baudrillard: Selected Writings*, p. 73.
11 Jean-Francois Lyotard. From an interview 'On Theory' with Brigitte Devismes, printed in *Driftworks*, New York: Semiotext(e) 1984, p. 29.
12 *Paraesthetics* by David Carroll, London: Methuen 1987, p. 188.
13 *The Postmodern Condition* by Jean-Francois Lyotard, Manchester: Manchester University Press 1986, p. 74.
14 Ibid., p. 27.
15 David Edgar. 'Ten Years of Political Theatre 1968–78', in *Theatre Quarterly*, No. 32, 1979, p. 27.
16 Ibid., p. 27.

17 See *Theatre at Work: The Story of the National Theatre's Production of Brecht's Galileo* by Jim Hiley, London: Routledge 1981.
18 See *Bertolt Brecht: Chaos According to Plan* by John Fuegi, Cambridge: Cambridge University Press 1987, p. 84.
19 *The Life of Galileo* by Bertolt Brecht, tr. Willett, London: Methuen 1980, p. 129.
20 Ibid., p. 101.
21 *The Sleepwalkers* by Arthur Koestler, Harmondsworth: Pelican 1968, p. 484.
22 Cited in *The Sleepwalkers*, Arthur Koestler, p. 484.
23 Ibid., p. 487.
24 See *Galileo: Heretic* by Pietro Redondi, tr. Rosenthal, Harmondsworth: Allen Lane 1988.
25 *The Theatre of Bertolt Brecht* by John Willett, London: Eyre Methuen 1959, p. 170.
26 *The Theory of the Modern Drama* by Peter Szondi, Cambridge: Polity Press 1987, p. 7.
27 Ibid., p. 7.
28 Ibid., p. 7.
29 Ibid., p. 8.
30 *Formalism and Marxism* by Tony Bennett, London: Methuen: New Accents 1979, p. 54.
31 'Bond Unbound' by Martin Esslin, review of *Saved* in *Plays and Players*, April 1969.
32 Howard Barker. Unpublished interview with Charles Lamb, 23 April 1987. (See Chapter 1, Note 14 above.)
33 *At the Royal Court – 25 Years of the English Stage Company*, ed. Richard Findlater, Amber Lane 1981, p. 109.
34 Aristotle. *Poetics* 3.
35 As defined in Liddell and Scott's *Greek–English Lexicon*, Oxford: Oxford University Press.
36 Aristotle. *Poetics* 6.
37 Ibid., 26.
38 Ibid., 26.
39 *The Post Card* by Jacques Derrida, tr. Alan Bass, Chicago: University of Chicago Press 1987, p. 123.
40 *The Dehumanisation of Art* by Ortega y Gasset, New Jersey: Princeton University Press 1969, p. 21.

3 Seduction

1 *Anti-Oedipus* by Deleuze and Guattari, tr. Hurley, Seem and Lane, London: Athlone 1984.
2 *Selected Writings*, Jean Baudrillard, p. 149.
3 *Being and Time* by Martin Heidegger, tr. Macquarrie and Robinson, Oxford: Basil Blackwell 1980, §29, p. 52.
4 *Selected Writings*, Jean Baudrillard, p. 149.
5 Ibid., p. 162.
6 *Totality and Infinity* by Emmanuel Levinas, tr. Alphonso Lingis, Pittsburgh: Duquesne University Press, Pittsburgh 1969.

7 Emmanuel Levinas. 'Difficile Liberté', cited by Derrida in *Writing and Difference*, tr. Alan Bass, London: Routledge 1978, p. 91.
8 Ibid., p. 93.
9 *Collected Philosophical Papers* by Emmanuel Levinas, tr. Lingis, Dordrecht: Martinus Nijhoff 1987, p. 41.
10 *The Possibilities* by Howard Barker, London: John Calder 1987, p. 56.
11 *Selected Writings* by Jean Baudrillard, p. 159.
12 Ibid., p. 158.
13 Ibid., p. 159.
14 Ibid., p. 161.
15 *Seduction* by Jean Baudrillard, tr. Brian Singer, London: Macmillan 1990, p. 69.
16 Ibid., pp. 69–70.
17 *Selected Writings*, Jean Baudrillard, p. 162.
18 Ibid., p. 163.
19 Howard Barker. From an unpublished interview with Charles Lamb, 23 April 1987. (See Chapter 1, Note 14.)
20 Ibid.
21 See *Arguments for a Theatre* by Howard Barker, London: John Calder 1989.
22 *Fatal Strategies* by Jean Baudrillard, New York: Semiotext(e)/Pluto 1990, p. 156.
23 *The Bite of the Night* by Howard Barker, London: John Calder 1988, p. 4.
24 *The Last Supper* by Howard Barker, London: Calder 1988, p. 2.
25 Ibid., p. 2.
26 Ibid., p. 2.
27 *Seduction*, Jean Baudrillard, p. 85.
28 *The Bite of the Night*, p. 3.
29 Ibid., pp. 3–4.
30 See for example '49 Asides for a Tragic Theatre' by Howard Barker, published in the *Guardian*, 10 February 1986. Also in *Arguments for a Theatre*.
31 'The Street Scene: A Basic Model for an Epic Theatre' by Bertolt Brecht, tr. Willett in *The Theory of the Modern Stage*, ed. Bentley, Harmondsworth: Pelican 1968.
32 Barker: '49 Asides for a Tragic Theatre' in *Arguments for a Theatre*.
33 *Collected Philosophical Papers*, Emmanuel Levinas, p. 43.
34 *Fair Slaughter* by Howard Barker, London: Calder 1984, p. 56.
35 Ibid., p. 104.
36 *Crimes in Hot Countries* by Howard Barker, London: Calder 1984, p. 56.
37 *Selected Writings*, Jean Baudrillard, p. 161.
38 Ibid., p. 161.
39 *The Last Supper*, p. 56.
40 *Selected Writings*, Jean Baudrillard, p. 158.
41 *The Bite of the Night*, Act III Scene 2. From an unpublished pre-production text. Not included in the published version.
42 *The Power of the Dog* by Howard Barker, London: Calder 1985, p. 10.
43 Ibid., p. 17.
44 Ibid., p. 5.
45 *The Possibilities*, p. 70.
46 Ibid., p. 71.

47 *Seduction*, Jean Baudrillard, p. 69.
48 *The Bite of the Night*, p. 59.
49 *The Europeans* by Howard Barker, London: John Calder 1990, pp. 4–5.
50 From 'Psychoanalysis and the Polis' by Julie Kristeva, in *The Kristeva Reader*, ed. Toril Moi, Oxford: Basil Blackwell 1986, p. 315.
51 Ibid., pp. 315–16.
52 *North* by Louis Ferdinand Céline, tr. Ralph Manheim, Oxford: The Bodley Head 1972, p. 1.
53 *The Kristeva Reader*, p. 317.
54 Howard Barker. From an unpublished interview with Charles Lamb, 23 April 1987. (See Chapter 1, Note 14.)
55 From 'La Parole Soufflée', in *Writing and Difference*, Jacques Derrida, p. 183.
56 *The Hang of the Gaol* by Howard Barker, London: Calder 1982, p. 19.
57 Ibid., pp. 12–13.
58 Ibid., p. 31.
59 Ibid., p. 80.
60 Ibid., p. 82.

4 *Judith* – a seduction

1 *The Possibilities*, Howard Barker, p. 57.
2 *Judith* by Howard Barker, London: John Calder 1990 (with *The Europeans*), p. 49. All further quotations in this chapter from *Judith* will indicate directly the page numbers of this edition.
3 *Selected Writings*, Jean Baudrillard, p. 159
4 *The Possibilities*, Howard Barker, p. 57
5 *Seduction*, Jean Baudrillard, p. 74.
6 Ibid., p. 76.

5 *The Castle*

1 *The Castle* by Howard Barker, London: John Calder 1985, p. 19. All further quotations in this chapter from *The Castle* will indicate directly the page numbers of this edition.
2 'Oppression, Resistance, and the Writer's Testament', Howard Barker interviewed by Finlay Donesky in *New Theatre Quarterly*, Vol. II, No. 8, November 1986, p. 338.
3 *Fatal Strategies*, Jean Baudrillard, p. 119.
4 Ibid., pp. 159–60.
5 Ibid. pp. 160–1.
6 *The Architecture of Castles* by R. Allen Brown, London: Batsford 1984, p. 12.
7 Ibid., p. 9.
8 *The Anglo-Saxon Chronicle*, tr. and ed. G.N. Garmonsway, London: Everyman 1953, p. 264.
9 *Fatal Strategies*, Jean Baudrillard, p. 160.
10 Ibid., p. 160.
11 Republished in 1992 under the same title by Immel Publishing Ltd.
12 Ibid., p. 93.

13 Ibid., p. 97.
14 From *Howard Barker – Politics and Desire* by David Ian Rabey, London: Macmillan 1989. 'Appendix: Conversations', p. 277.
15 Ibid., p. 277.
16 Ibid., p. 258.
17 Ibid., p. 258.
18 Ibid., p. 258.
19 Ibid., pp. 258–9.
20 *Towards a Poor Theatre* by Jerzy Grotowski, London: Methuen 1969, p. 205.
21 *Women's Review* No. 2, 'The Castle': Interviews with Helen Carr, p. 33.
22 *The Bite of the Night*, p. 2.
23 *Theory of the Modern Drama* by Peter Szondi, p. 7.

6 The shape of darkness

1 *Arguments for a Theatre* by Howard Barker, third edition, Manchester: Manchester University Press 1997.
2 Ibid., p. 52.
3 Ibid., p. 187.
4 See Interview with Howard Barker in the Appendix.
5 *Arguments for a Theatre*, p. 19.
6 Ibid., p. 189.
7 *Victory* in *Howard Barker: Collected Plays Volume 1*, p. 177.
8 *Utopia* by Thomas More. Translated by Paul Turner. Harmondsworth: Penguin Classics 1969, p. 103.
9 *Brutopia* in *Howard Barker: Collected Plays Volume 2*, p. 152.
10 Ibid., p. 162.
11 Ibid., p. 163.
12 Julius Caesar, in his *De Bello Gallico*, writes of himself entirely in the third person.
13 *Rome* in *Howard Barker: Collected Plays Volume 2*, p. 257.
14 *The Way of the World* in *Comedies by William Congreve*, Oxford: Oxford University Press, 1959, p. 425.
15 *Ego in Arcadia* in *Howard Barker: Collected Plays Volume 3*, p. 271.
16. *Brutopia*, p. 175.
17 *Ego in Arcadia*, p. 274
18 Ibid., p. 274.
19 Ibid., p. 290.
20 Ibid., pp. 274–5.
21 Ibid., pp. 275–6.
22 Ibid., p. 276.
23 *Brutopia*, p. 131.
24 *Ego in Arcadia*, p. 304.
25 Ibid., p. 275
26 Ibid., p. 314.
27 Ibid., p. 312.
28 Ibid., p. 287.
29 Ibid., p. 313.
30 Ibid., p. 312.

31 Ibid., p. 318.
32 *Critique of Pure Reason*, ed. Polites, Vasilis. London: Everyman 1993.
33 *Rome* in *Howard Barker: Collected Plays Volume 2*, published in 1993. Currently unstaged.
34 *Rome*, p. 205.
35 Ibid., p. 229.
36 Ibid., p. 229.
37 *Fear and Trembling* by S. Kierkegaard, tr. Hannay, Alastair, Harmondsworth: Penguin 1985.
38 *Rome*, p. 230.
39 Ibid., p. 204.
40 Ibid., p. 253.
41 Ibid., p. 277.
42 Ibid., p. 208.
43 Ibid., p. 268.
44 Ibid., p. 269.
45 See Interview with Howard Barker in the Appendix.
46 *He Stumbled* in *Howard Barker: Collected Plays Volume 2*, p. 306.
47 *Rome*, p. 215.
48 Ibid., p. 216.
49 Ibid., p. 233.
50 Ibid., p. 240.
51 Ibid., p. 240.
52 *Judith*, p. 67.
53 Ibid., p. 242.
54 Ibid., p. 261.
55 Ibid., p. 263.
56 Ibid., p. 280.
57 Ibid., p. 289.
58 Ibid., pp. 289–90.
59 *Death, The One and the Art of Theatre* by Howard Barker, London: Routledge 2005.
60 *Death, The One and the Art of Theatre*: §39.3.
61 Ibid., §22.8
62 Ibid., §1.5.
63 Ibid., §25.3.
64 *Arguments for a Theatre*, p. 19. 'You emerge from tragedy equipped against lies.'
65 'The Fictive World of the Play is the World of the Dead', in *Wielopole/Wielopole* by Tadeusz Kantor, tr. Tchorek, M. and Hyde, G., London and New York: Marion Boyars, 1990.
66 'Notes on the Necessity for a version of Chekhov's *Uncle Vanya*', in *Howard Barker: Collected Plays Volume 2*, p. 292.
67 *Death, The One and the Art of Theatre*, §3.12.
68 *Uncle Vanya*, p. 316.
69 Ibid., p. 316.
70 Ibid., p. 329.
71 Ibid., p. 330.
72 Ibid., p. 328.
73 Ibid., p. 332.

74 Ibid., p. 331.
75 *Selected Writings*, Jean Baudrillard, p. 162.
76 *Uncle Vanya*, p. 333.
77 Ibid., p. 334.
78 Rabey, D.I. (November 1991) 'For the Absent Truth Erect: Impotence and Potency in Howard Barker's Recent Drama', *Essays in Theatre/Etudes Theatrales*, Vol. X, No. 1, p. 35.
79 *Uncle Vanya*, p. 334.
80 Ibid., p. 334.
81 Ibid., p. 336.
82 *Seduction*, p. 124.
83 *Uncle Vanya*, p. 338.
84 Ibid., p. 302.
85 *The Love of a Good Man* in *Howard Barker: Collected Plays Volume 2*, p. 12.
86 Ibid., p. 36.
87 *Victory* in *Howard Barker: Collected Plays Volume 1*, p. 195.
88 *He Stumbled* in *Howard Barker: Collected Plays Volume 4*, p. 252.
89 Ibid., p. 257.
90 Ibid., p. 258.
91 Ibid., p. 260.
92 Ibid., p. 261.
93 Ibid., p. 262.
94 Ibid., p. 286.
95 Ibid., p. 297.
96 Ibid., p. 292.
97 Ibid., p. 312.
98 Ibid., p. 314.
99 Ibid., p. 314.
100 Ibid., p. 315.
101 *Uncle Vanya*, p. 338.
102 Ibid., p. 315.
103 Ibid., p. 312.
104 *Death, The One and the Art of Theatre*, §47.

Chronology of Barker productions

Dates are of first nights; brackets indicate touring productions opening at particular theatres.

* Indicates the text is unpublished. All others are published by John Calder, with the sole exception of *Cheek*, published by Eyre Methuen.

Date	Play	Venue/company	Director
11.9.1970	*Cheek*	Theatre Upstairs Royal Court	William Gaskill
19.11.1970	*No One Was Saved**	Theatre Upstairs Royal Court	Pam Brighton
15.2.1972	*Edward: The Final Days**	Open Space (Lunch-time show)	
15.2.1972	*Faceache**	Recreation Ground	
17.9.1972	*Alpha Alpha**	Open Space	Peter Watson
9.1.1973	*Rule Britannia**	Open Space	
12.3.1973	*Skipper, and My Sister and I**	Bush Theatre	
23.5.1973	*Bang**	Open Space	
30.1.1975	*Claw*	Open Space	Chris Parr
14.10.1975	*Stripwell*	Royal Court	Chris Parr
13.6.1977	*Fair Slaughter*	Royal Court	Stuart Burge
28.7.1977	*That Good Between Us*	RSC Warehouse	Barry Kyle
19.10.1978	*The Love of a Good Man*	Sheffield Crucible	David Leland

15.12.1978	*The Hang of the Gaol*	RSC Warehouse	Bill Alexander
13.11.1979	*The Love of a Good Man*	Oxford Playhouse UK Tour	Nicholas Kent
26.2.1980	*The Loud Boy's Life*	RSC Warehouse	Howard Davies
8.11.1980	*Birth on a Hard Shoulder*	Royal Dramatic Theatre, Stockholm	Barbro Larsson
11.2.1981	*No End of Blame*	Royal Court Oxford Playhouse	Nicholas Kent
1.12.1981	*The Poor Man's Friend**	Colway Theatre Trust, Bridport	Ann Jellicoe
17.2.1983	*Victory*	Joint Stock/ Royal Court UK Tour	Danny Boyle
15.3.1983	*Crimes in Hot Countries*	Theatre Underground Essex University	Charles Lamb
7.10.1983	*A Passion in Six Days*	Sheffield Crucible	Michael Boyd
14.11.1984	*The Power of the Dog*	Joint Stock/UK Tour Hampstead Theatre	Kenny Ireland
3.4.1985	*Victory*	Rough Magic Theatre Dublin	
7.10.1985	*Crimes in Hot Countries*	RSC Barbican Pit	Bill Alexander
14.10.1985	*The Castle*	RSC Barbican Pit	Nick Hamm
21.10.1985	*Downchild*	RSC Barbican Pit	Bill Alexander
1.2.1986	*Women Beware Women*	Royal Court Theatre	William Gaskill
23.2.1988	*The Possibilities*	Almeida Theatre	Ian McDiarmid
8.3.1988	*The Last Supper*	Wrestling School Leicester, Haymarket Royal Court UK Tour	Kenny Ireland
31.8.1988	*The Bite of the Night*	RSC Barbican Pit	Danny Boyle

4.11.1989	*Seven Lears*	Wrestling School Leicester Haymarket Royal Court/UK Tour	Kenny Ireland
24.11.1989	*Golgo*	Wrestling School Leicester Haymarket Royal Court/UK Tour	Nick Le Prevost
11.1.1990	*Scenes from an Execution*	Almeida Theatre	Ian McDiarmid
21.5.1990	*The Castle*	Moving Being Theatre St Stephen's, Cardiff	Geoff Moore
15.2.1991	*Victory*	Wrestling School/ UK Tour Leicester Haymarket Théâtre de Gennevilliers, Paris	Kenny Ireland
3.3.1992	*A Hard Heart*	Almeida Theatre	Ian McDiarmid
25.3.1992	*Scenes from an Execution*	Mark Taper Forum Los Angeles	Allan Ackermann
10.6.1992	*Ego in Arcadia*	Sienna, Italy	Howard Barker
14.2.1993	*The Europeans*	Wrestling School/ UK Tour Leicester Haymarket Greenwich, London	Kenny Ireland
2.11.1993	*Scenes from an Execution*	Centre Dramatique de Bourgogne, Dijon	Solange Oswald
8.3.1994	*Hated Nightfall*	Wrestling School/ UK Tour Dancehouse, Manchester Royal Court European Tour:	Howard Barker
(18.1.1995)		Hebbel Theater, Berlin	
(7.2.1995)		Théâtre de l'Odéon, Paris	
(29.3.1995)		Kanonhallen, Copenhagen	
(11.4.1995)		Théâtre de la Metaphore, Lille	

1.6.1994	*Scenes from an Execution*	Würtembergische Landesbuhne, Esslingen	Beverly Blankenship
18.11.1994	*Seven Lears*	Théâtre de la Chamaille, Nantes	Catherine Hunault
11.1.1995	*The Castle*	Wrestling School Riverside Studios UK Tour	Kenny Ireland
(18.1.1995)		Hebbel Theater, Berlin	
(1.2.1995)		Théâtre de l'Odéon, Paris	
28.2.1995	*Judith*	Leicester Haymarket	Howard Barker
(22.5.95)		Lisbon Festival	
20.10.1995	*The Europeans*	Escher Theater, Luxemburg	Eric Schneider
18.4.1996	*(Uncle) Vanya*	Wrestling School UK Tour Leicester Haymarket Revival for Copenhagen, Limoges, Riga and Berlin	Howard Barker
9.11.1996	*Scenes from an Execution*	Khan Theatre, Jerusalem	Ofira Henig
6.5.1997	*Wounds to the Face*	Leicester Haymarket Wrestling School	Stephen Wrentmore
17.1.1998	*Judith*	Théâtre de Songes Paris	Jerzy Kleszyk
17.3.1998	*Ten Dilemmas*	Drama Studio Sheffield University	
20.4.1998	*Ursula*	Wrestling School Birmingham Repertory Riverside Studios	Howard Barker
10.11.1998	*Seven Lears*	Théâtre de la Chamaille, Nantes	Claudine Hunault
17.6.1999	*Und*	Wrestling School Riverside Studios	Howard Barker
22.9.1999	*Scenes from an Execution*	Wrestling School Barbican Pit/Tour	Howard Barker

6.3.2000	*The Twelfth Battle of Isonzo*	Théâtre de Folle Pensée, Saint-Brieuc	Annie Lucas Tr. Mike Sens
8.3.2000	*The Ecstatic Bible*	Wrestling School Brink Productions, Adelaide	Howard Barker
1.11.2000	*He Stumbled*	Wrestling School/ UK Tour Riverside Studios	Howard Barker
28.9.2001	*A House of Correction*	Wrestling School/ UK Tour Riverside Studios	Howard Barker
19.2.2002	*Brutopia*	Nouveau Théâtre de Besançon	Guillaume Dujardin
10.4.2002	*Wounds to the Face*	CDN de Montluçon	Jean-Paul Wenzel
10.4.2002	*Judith*	Theatre in Action Glasgow Citizens	David O'Neill
30.4.2002	*Victory*	Edinburgh Royal Lyceum	Kenny Ireland
7.11.2002	*The Europeans*	Colchester Mercury	Janice Dunn
6.11.2002	*Claw*	Comédie de Genève	Anne Bisang
15.10.2002	*Gertrude*	Wrestling School Plymouth/Tour Riverside Studios	Howard Barker
18.3.2003	*The Last Supper*	Théâtre Mains d'Oeuvres, Saint-Ouen	Nathalie Garraud Tr. Mike Sens
18.4.2003	*Claw*	Kazida Productions Greenwich Playhouse	Jonathan Loe
3.10.2003	*13 Objects**	Wrestling School The Door, Birmingham Tour, Riverside Studios	Howard Barker
31.1.2004	*Und*	Théâtre de la Source Bègles	Marie Pourroy Tr. Mike Sens

Bibliography

1 Barker

Almost all of the plays by Barker referred to in this study are published by John Calder. The exceptions are a number of unpublished early plays (see the Chronology of Productions) and *Cheek*, published by Eyre Methuen (*New Short Plays 3*, 1972). Calder has also issued a book of criticism, *Arguments for a Theatre* (1989) as well as six books of poetry: *Don't Exaggerate* (1985), *The Breath of the Crowd* (1986), *Gary the Thief* (1987), *Lullabies for the Impatient* (1988), *The Ascent of Monte Grappa* (1991), and *The Tortmann Diaries* (1996).

Since 1990, Calder has issued five volumes of Collected Plays:

Vol. 1 (1990) *Claw, No End of Blame, Victory, The Castle, Scenes from an Execution.*
Vol. 2 (1993) *The Love of a Good Man, The Possibilities, Brutopia, Rome, Uncle Vanya, Ten Dilemmas.*
Vol. 3 (1996) *The Power of the Dog, The Europeans, Women Beware Women, Minna, Judith, Ego in Arcadia.*
Vol. 4 (1998) *The Bite of the Night, Seven Lears, The Gaoler's Ache, He Stumbled, A House of Correction.*
Vol. 5 (2001) *Ursula, The Brilliance of the Servant, 12 Encounters with a Prodigy, Und, The Twelfth Battle of Isonzo, Found in the Ground.*

Published volumes containing *plays not included in the Collected Plays volumes*:

Heroes of Labour, in *Gambit* 29 (1976).
Stripwell and *Claw*, *Playscript* 79 (1977).
That Good Between Us and *Credentials of a Sympathiser*, *Playscript* 92 (1980).
The Love of a Good Man and *All Bleeding*, *Playscript* 93 (1980).
The Hang of the Gaol and *Heaven*, *Playscript* 94 (1982).
The Loud Boy's Life and *Birth on a Hard Shoulder*, in 'Two Plays for the Right', *Playscript* 101 (1982).
Pity in History, in *Gambit 41* (1984).

Crimes in Hot Countries and *Fair Slaughter*, *Playscript* 107 (1984).
A Passion in Six Days and *Downchild*, *Playscript* 108 (1985).
The Last Supper, *Playscript* 114 (1988).
Seven Lears and *Golgo*, *Playscript* 117 (1990).
A Hard Heart and *The Early Hours of a Reviled Man*, *Playscript* 119 (1992).
Hated Nightfall and *Wounds to the Face*, *Playscript* 120 (1994).

Calder has also published texts of two plays for marionettes, *All He Fears* (1993) and *The Swing at Night* (2001) and one opera libretto, *Terrible Mouth* (1992).

Arguments for a Theatre is now published by Manchester University Press (1993).

Death, The One and the Art of Theatre, Routledge (2005).

2 Critical and other writings on Barker

Other published materials about Barker, or which refer to Barker are:

Ansorge, P. (1975) *Disrupting the Spectacle*, London: Pitman.
Alexander, B. (February 1979) 'Patriotic and Contentiously Left Wing' – Interview with Colin Chambers, *Plays and Players*.
Bannerman, G. (Winter 1990) 'Hitting the Wall: Richard Rose, Howard Barker and "The Europeans" ', *Canadian Theatre Review*: 52, York University.
Barnett, D. (2001) 'Howard Barker: Polemic Theory and Dramatic Practice. Nietzsche, Metatheatre and the Play *The Europeans*', *Modern Drama*, Vol. XLIV, No. 4.
Bull, J. (1984) *New Political Dramatists*, London: Macmillan.
Carr, H. (1986) *The Castle* – Discussion with Harriet Walter, Penny Downie and Kath Rogers, *Women's Review*, No 2.
Chambers, C. (1980) *Other Spaces. New Theatre and the RSC*, London: Methuen.
Cornforth, A. and Rabey, D.I. (1999) 'Kissing Holes for the Bullets: Consciousness in Directing and Playing Barker's *Uncle Vanya*', *Performing Arts International*, Vol. I, Part 4, Amsterdam: Harwood Academic Publishers.
Davies, H. (Summer 1980) Interview, *Platform*.
Donesky, F. (November 1986) 'Oppression, Resistance and the Writer's Testament' – Interview with Howard Barker, *New Theatre Quarterly*, Vol. II, No. 8.
Dromgoole, D. (May 2002) *The Full Room: An A–Z of Contemporary Playwriting*, London: Methuen.
Dunn, T. (1984) *Editorial and Interview with Howard Barker, Howard Barker Special Issue*, *Gambit* 41, London: John Calder.
Dunn, T. (June 1984) 'Writers of the Seventies', *Plays and Players*.
Dunn, T. (Spring 1985) 'The Play of Politics', *Theatre International*.

Dunn, T. (October 1985) 'Howard Barker in the Pit', *Plays and Players*.

Edgar, D. (1979) 'Ten Years of Political Theatre 1968–1978', *Theatre Quarterly*, Vol. 8, No. 32.

Gallant, D. (1997) 'Brechtian Sexuality in the Plays of Howard Barker', *Modern Drama*, Vol. 40, No. 4.

Gottlieb, V. (May 1988) 'Thatcher's Theatre – or after Equus', *New Theatre Quarterly*, Vol. IV, No. 14.

Grant, S. (December 1975) 'Barker's Bite', *Plays and Players*.

Grant, S. (1980) 'Voicing the Protest: The New Writers', in Craig, S. (ed.) *Dreams and Deconstructions*, London: Amber Lane.

Hay, M. and Trussler, S. (1981) 'Energy – and the Small Discovery of Dignity', Interview with Howard Barker, *New Theatre Quarterly*, Vol. II, No. 8.

Hiley, J. (October 1984) 'Language You Can Taste' (article on *Scenes From an Execution*), *Radio Times*.

Hiley, J. (June/July 1985) 'Barker's Bite' (article on *Pity in History*), *Radio Times*.

Itzin, C. (1980) *Stages in the Revolution*, London: Eyre Methuen.

Klotz, Günther (1991) 'Howard Barker: Paradigm of Postmodernism', *New Theatre Quarterly*, Vol. VII, No. 25.

Lamb, C. (1984) 'Howard Barker's *Crimes in Hot Countries*: A Director's Approach', in Bell, L. (ed.) *Contradictory Theatres*, London: Theatre Action Press.

Marks, L. (21 February 1988) 'Off-beat Track' (article based on interview), *Observer*.

Price, A. (1993) 'Introduction to the Second Edition', in Barker, H. *Arguments for a Theatre*, Manchester: Manchester University Press.

Rabey, D.I. (1986) *British and Irish Political Drama in the Twentieth Century*, London: Macmillan.

Rabey, D.I. (1989) *Howard Barker – Politics and Desire*, London: Macmillan.

Rabey, D.I. (November 1991) 'For the Absent Truth Erect: Impotence and Potency in Howard Barker's Recent Drama', *Essays in Theatre/Etudes Théâtrales*, Vol. X, No. 1.

Rabey, D.I. (December 1992) 'What do you see? Howard Barker's *The Europeans*: A Director's Perspective', *Studies in Theatre Production 6*.

Rabey, D.I. (1996) 'Howard Barker' in Demastes, W.W. (ed.) *British Playwrights, 1956–1995: A Research and Production Sourcebook*, Westport, Conn.: Greenwood.

Sens, M. (ed.) (1998) *Alternatives Théâtrales 57: Howard Barker* (Contains writings, paintings/drawings by Howard Barker, a production history, interviews with Barker and Ian McDiarmid, essays by Safaa Fathy, Jérôme Hankins, Ofira Henig, Charles Lamb, David Ian Rabey, Bernard Reitz, Corinne Rigaud, Elisabeth Sakellaridou, Mike Sens, Heiner Zimmermann.) Louvain-la-Neuve, Belgium: Université catholique de Louvain.

Shaughnessy, R. (August 1989) 'Howard Barker, the Wrestling School, and the Cult of the Author', *New Theatre Quarterly*, Vol. 5, No. 19.

Thomas, A. (September 1992) 'Howard Barker: Modern Allegorist', *Modern Drama*, Vol: XXXV, No. 3.
Tomlin, L. (June 1997) 'Building a Barker Character', *Studies in Theatre Production*, No. 15, Exeter: Exeter University Press.
Trussler, S. (1981) *New Theatre Voices of the Seventies*, London: Eyre Methuen.
Wilcher, R. (1993) 'Honouring the Audience: the Theatre of Howard Barker', in Acheson, J. (ed.) *British and Irish Drama Since 1960*, Basingstoke: Macmillan

3 Theatrical/performance theory

Bartrum, G. and Waine, A. (eds) (1982) *Brecht in Perspective*, London and New York: Longman.
Benedetti, J. (1988) *Stanislavsky. A Biography*, London: Methuen.
Bentley, E. (ed.) (1968) *The Theory of the Modern Stage*, Harmondsworth: Pelican.
Brecht, B. (1976) 'A Short Organum for the Theatre, (1948)', in *Avante Garde Drama. A Casebook*, eds. Dukore, B. and Gerould, D., New York: Crowell Casebooks.
Findlater, R. (ed.) (1981) *At the Royal Court: 25 Years of the English Stage Company*, London: Amber Lane.
Fuegi, J. (1987) *Bertolt Brecht: Chaos According to Plan*, London and New York: Cambridge University Press.
Gaskill, W. (1988) *A Sense of Direction*, London: Faber.
Grotowski, J. (1969) *Towards a Poor Theatre*, London: Eyre Methuen.
Kantor, T. (1990) 'The Fictive World of the Play is the World of the Dead' in *Wielopole/Wielopole*, tr. Tchorek, M. and Hyde, G., London and New York: Marion Boyars.
Stanislavsky, K. (1980) *My Life in Art*, London: Methuen.
Szondi, P. (1987) *Theory of the Modern Drama*, tr. and ed. Hays, M., Cambridge: Polity Press.

4 General theory/philosophy

Barthes, R. (1976) *Mythologies*, London: Paladin.
Baudrillard, J. (1988) *Jean Baudrillard: Selected Writings*, ed. Poster, Cambridge: Polity Press.
Baudrillard, J. (1990) *Seduction*, tr. Singer, B., London: Macmillan.
Baudrillard, J. (1990) *Fatal Strategies*, ed. Fleming, J., London and New York: Semiotext(e)/Pluto.
Bennett, T. (1979) *Formalism and Marxism*, London and New York: Methuen: New Accents.
Berlin, I. (1979) *The Age of Enlightenment, Oxford:* Oxford University Press.
Carroll, D. (1987) *Paraesthetics*, New York and London: Methuen.
Deleuze, G. and Guattari, F. (1984) *Anti-Oedipus*, tr. Hurley, R., Seem, M., and Lane, H., London: Athlone.

Derrida, J. (1978) *Writing and Difference*, tr. Bass, A., London: Routledge.
Derrida, J. (1987) *The Post Card*, tr. Bass, A., Chicago and London: University of Chicago Press.
Hegel, G.W.F. (1977) *The Phenomenology of the Spirit*, tr. Miller, A.V., Oxford: Oxford University Press.
Heidegger, M. (1980) *Being and Time*, tr. Macquarrie, J. and Robinson, E., Oxford: Blackwell.
Kant, E. (1993) *Critique of Pure Reason*, London: Everyman.
Kierkegaard, S. (1985) *Fear and Trembling*, tr. Hannay, A., Harmondsworth: Penguin.
Koestler, A. (1968) *The Sleepwalkers*, Harmondsworth: Pelican.
Kristeva, J. (1982) *Powers of Horror: An Essay on Abjection*, tr. Roudiez, L., New York: Columbia University Press.
Kristeva, J. (1986) *The Kristeva Reader*, ed. Moi, T., Oxford: Blackwell.
Levinas, E. (1969) *Totality and Infinity*, tr. Lingis, A., Pittsburgh: Duquesne University Press.
Levinas, E. (1987) *Collected Philosophical Papers*, tr. Lingis, A., Dordrecht, The Netherlands: Martinus Nijhoff Publishers.
Lyotard, J.F. (1984) *Driftworks*, New York: Semiotext(e).
Lyotard, J.F. (1986) *The Postmodern Condition: a Report on Knowledge*, tr. Bennington, G. and Massumi, B., Manchester: Manchester University Press.
More, T. (1969) *Utopia*, tr. Turner, P., Harmondsworth: Penguin Classics.
Ortega Y Gasset, J. (1968) *The Dehumanization of Art*, New Jersey: Princeton University Press.
Scarry, E. (1985) *The Body in Pain*, Oxford and New York: Oxford University Press.

Index